NELSON Criminology DICTIONARY

Robert Drislane
British Columbia Open University
Gary Parkinson
British Columbia Open University

Australia Canada Mexico Singapore Spain United Kingdom United States

Nelson Criminology Dictionary

by Robert Drislane and Gary Parkinson

Associate Vice-President and Editorial Director:
Evelyn Veitch

Publisher:
Joanna Cotton

Marketing Manager:
Lenore Taylor

Senior Developmental Editor:
Edward Ikeda

Production Editor:
Wendy Yano

Proofreader:
Jennifer Goyder

Senior Production Coordinator:
Hedy Sellers

Creative Director:
Angela Cluer

Interior Design:
Roxanna Bennett

Cover Design:
Angela Cluer

Cover Image:
Photonica

Senior Compositor:
Zenaida Diores

Printer:
Webcom

Printed and bound in Canada
1 2 3 4 07 06 05 04

For more information contact Nelson, 1120 Birchmount Road, Toronto, Ontario, M1K 5G4. Or you can visit our Internet site at http://www.nelson.com

Library and Archives Canada Cataloguing in Publication

Drislane, Robert
Nelson criminology dictionary / Robert Drislane, Gary Parkinson.

ISBN 0-17-640608-5

1. Criminology—Dictionaries.
I. Parkinson, Gary, 1940- II. Title.

HV6017.D75 2004 364'.03
C2004-904786-8

Preface

Welcome to the *Nelson Criminology Dictionary*. We hope that you will enjoy using it and that it will enhance your studies.

Our 1400-entry dictionary is designed for undergraduate students and covers the main concepts and events that you will need to be familiar with as you study criminology and criminal justice. An important component of your learning is the acquisition of the somewhat specialized language of the social sciences. Each entry is designed to provide you with sufficient information to grasp the basic content of a concept, how the term is used, and its connection to other concepts. Developing a solid grasp of the meaning of key terms will speed and deepen your learning and will lead to greater success.

We believe that setting a broad context for criminology and criminal justice studies is important since both of these fields of study have important historical, political, sociological, and legal dimensions. This is why we have included some terms that may not at first glance appear relevant, but which will become important as you gain a broader perspective on issues, theories, and debates as your studies progress.

There are several ways to use this dictionary. The first and most obvious is to use it to investigate puzzling words you encounter in your textbooks or readings. When using the dictionary to locate definitions and explanations, be sure to note the way the word was used in the reading; check whether it is used as a noun, verb, or adjective. Also notice if the term is typically used to modify something else or is related specifically to some other concept. Always investigate the words it may be contrasted with or related to. You can also use the dictionary as a general resource and simply spend time reading it to see how clusters of concepts or issues are linked together: for example, the entry on **aboriginal peoples** will lead you to an entry on **overrepresentation** and this will lead you to an entry on the **Gladue case**. Always explore the connections. Another informative approach is to seek out opposing concepts or theoretical perspectives and then investigate how the contrast between them is reflected in many other terms and concepts within the text. For example, taking the entry **positivism** as one side and **postmodernism** as the other, you will find many other entries that are connected to these two. Or investigate **consensus perspective** and **critical perspective** and determine what concepts would be connected to this contrast. Or look for entries related to **positivism** and **symbolic interactionism**. You will find more examples of the inter-connectedness of terms and concepts as you read.

Another feature of this dictionary is the inclusion of brief descriptions of key events and prominent figures that are important for deepening your analysis of Canadian society. For example, you will find descriptions of the **persons case**; **Meech Lake Accord**; **confederation**; **Calder case**; and **Morgentaler, Henry**.

We have also selected events that illustrate the relevance of concepts or theories. As with other entries you can just look these up as you come across them in your reading, or read the dictionary to look for some of these interesting events and then search out additional readings to deepen your understanding. We have provided references for many entries to give you the opportunity to explore ideas more fully.

We wish to acknowledge the support of Nelson in developing this dictionary and to thank Colin Goff, University of Winnipeg; Rick Linden, University of Manitoba; and Julian Roberts, University of Ottawa for reviewing the draft manuscript and providing encouragement and many suggestions. We also thank Matthew Drislane for his assistance in locating terms to include and searching for materials. The final responsibility for what has been included and what has been left out is, of course, ours.

Robert Drislane
Gary Parkinson

A

aboriginal justice inquiry of Manitoba Established in 1988 to inquire into the events surrounding the shooting death of J.J. Harper and the unrelated death of Betty Helen Osborne, as well as the declining relationship between aboriginal people and the justice system. The inquiry reported in 1991, recommending a series of structural changes to the justice system and over the long term recommending the government move towards a separate justice system for the Métis and native peoples of Manitoba. *See also* **Harper, John Joseph**; **Osborne, Helen Betty**.

aboriginal peoples In the Americas, aboriginal peoples have descended from the first inhabitants of the continents, before European contact, and include the peoples broadly classified as Indian and Inuit. The synonymous term *native peoples* is also widely used. Section 35(2) of the Constitution Act, 1982, declares that "aboriginal peoples" includes "Indian, Inuit and Métis peoples of Canada." *See also* **Gladue case**; **overrepresentation**.

aboriginal peoples, state violence against *See* **Oka**; **George, Dudley**; **Harper, John Joseph**.

abortion Abortion was regulated by criminal law in Canada until January 1988 when the Supreme Court ruled the law unconstitutional on the grounds that it was applied in an arbitrary and discriminatory manner. No new law has been enacted, so abortion continues to be legal. The invalidated law was an amendment to the Criminal Code made in 1969, allowing a hospital committee to authorize a therapeutic abortion if it was deemed the life or health of the mother was at considerable risk. In the United States, abortion was legalized in 1973 by the Supreme Court case known as *Roe vs. Wade*. The struggle between pro-life and pro-choice groups over abortion has now shifted to the financing of abortions, hospital policy, and protests outside clinics providing abortions. Conflict over the abortion issue is less intense in Canada, where there is overwhelmingly pro-choice public opinion, than in the United States, where there is a strong pro-life movement linked to fundamentalist religious groups. *See also* **Morgentaler, Henry**. Reference: *Morgentaler v. R.* [1988] 1 S.C.R. 30.

absolute discharge Since 1969, Canadian courts have been able to use absolute or conditional discharges to deal with certain offences. In an absolute discharge the court decides not to convict the accused and to discharge them completely from the jurisdiction of the court. In this instance, the person has no criminal record. This is the least severe sentence available to the courts. *See also* **conditional discharge**.

absolute liability Where an individual may be held liable for a breach of the law without the requirement that criminal intent (*mens rea*) be proven by the prosecution. Usually the illegal action will be one that is manifestly damaging to the public interest. These offences are most likely found in regulatory law. For example, if you are caught speeding while driving, there is no requirement to prove intent.

accelerated parole review The Corrections and Conditional Release Act instructs the parole board to speed up the parole process if it is satisfied that the offender is very unlikely to commit an offence involving violence if released. The board is given criteria to determine eligibility of an inmate.

accounts As used in the sociology of deviance, accounts refers to the rationalizations that people provide for their actions. Two large groups of accounts are distinguished: justifications and excuses. A justification accepts responsibility for an action but denies the wrongfulness of that action. An excuse, on the other hand, denies responsibility while accepting the wrongfulness of the action. These ideas go back to C.W. Mills (1940), Edwin Sutherland (1939), and Donald Cressey (1953). *See also* **neutralization techniques**. Reference: Sutherland, E.H. (1924). *Principles of Criminology*. Philadelphia: Lippincott [1939].

acculturation A process of cultural transformation initiated by contacts between different cultures. At a global level, acculturation takes place as societies experience the transforming impact of international cultural contact. The global trend toward modern economic organization and developed market economies has been accompanied by a process of cultural transformation. A key change is towards a transformation of economic organization: the great majority of individuals come to generate their income through employment or running businesses, rather than from economic bonds with family and community. In the modern world, there is great ease of international communication and interaction between cultures, but sociologists have generally focused attention on the global impact of the capitalist western world on other societies. While each society experiences a unique process of cultural and economic transformation, there are some common trends that appear to be linked to the development of complex market economies, a wage employment system, and urbanization. Individuals experience acculturation when their social roles and socialization are shaped by norms and values that are largely foreign to their native culture. Educational and occupational experiences are the primary agents of the individual's acculturation process. Some sociologists use the term to refer simply to the process of learning and absorbing a culture, making it synonymous with socialization, but *enculturation* is a more appropriate word for that meaning. *See also* **socialization**.

acephalous society Literally "headless," meaning that the society is without any formalized or institutionalized system of power and authority. Collective decisions are made in a variety of ways, including informal community gatherings.

action theory A sociological perspective that focuses on the individual as a subject and views social action as something purposively shaped by individuals within a context to which they have given meaning. This approach has its foundations in Max Weber's (1864–1920) "interpretive sociology," which claims that it is necessary to know the subjective purpose and intent of the actor before an observer can understand the meaning of social action. Those sociologists who focus on "action" tend to treat the individual as an autonomous subject, rather than as constrained by social structure and culture. As a subject, the individual is seen as exercising agency, voluntarism, giving meaning to objects and events and acting with intent. While Weber insisted on the power of society and historical context in giving shape to human action, some sociologists adopting action theory have been accused of neglecting the influence of social structure and culture on people's behaviour.

actus reus One of two components of a crime, the other being *mens rea*. *Actus reus* refers to the physical component of a crime, the act of committing the crime (e.g., actually taking the stereo from someone's house). *Mens rea*, in contrast, is the mental component of crime, the existence of a criminal intent, and this requires the offender to have intended to carry out the physical act. Both components are required for conviction under criminal law, although for some other laws, called laws of absolute liability, only the physical component is required.

Addiction Research Foundations Organizations dedicated to research and education on addiction. These agencies are found in most provinces of Canada. While many tend to associate addiction with drugs, it is possible to be addicted to any number of things, including gambling, love, and sex. It is not against the law to be addicted.

AD/HD *See* **Attention Deficit/Hyperactivity Disorder**.

adjudication The process of judging in a competition, a court case, or a hearing of any case that requires the pronouncement of a decision in a contest over facts, rights, or contesting views. From the Latin, *judicare*, to judge.

administrative segregation *See* **solitary confinement**.

adversary system The criminal justice system used in North America was inherited from England and is based on cases being decided in a contest of evidence between the prosecution and defence before a judge and sometimes also a jury. In this contest, the state charges an individual and it is then incumbent upon the state to prove the charges and the accused defends him or herself from these charges. The truth is decided by the outcome of this public debate, conducted according to very rigid rules. The judge or jury remains neutral and is the decider of the facts, thus ideally establishing the truth. Much of continental Europe uses a quite different system, called the inquisitorial system, in which judges actively interrogate witnesses and lawyers representing both sides in the trial. *See also* **inquisitorial system**.

affect disorder A form of mental disorder in which the individual experiences mood swings greater than normal. This disorder is usually associated with depression and in more severe cases with mania, or periods of excitement and over-confidence.

affidavit Usually a written statement, which the writer declares to be true, used in court as evidence.

affirmative action Policies of governments and other institutions that are designed to actively promote and advance the status and the social and occupational participation of groups of people designated by sex, ethnicity, or another shared characteristic. The intent of such policies is to counteract perceived disadvantagement of such groups. The Canadian Charter of Rights and Freedoms (section 15[2]) allows for the possibility of such policy without it being subject to challenge on grounds of discrimination against non-designated groups. Affirmative action programs are designed to provide greater equality of opportunity since it is known that inequality of opportunity can be linked to crime and deviance. *See also* **Merton, Robert**.

ageism The assumption that a person's age should determine his or her social status and roles in society. This term usually refers to stereotyping and devaluation of seniors. *See also* **stereotype**.

agency This term is linked to sociologies that focus on the individual as a subject and view social action as something purposively shaped by individuals within a context to which they have given meaning. This view is usually contrasted with those sociologies that focus on social structure and imply the individual is shaped and constrained by the structural environment in which they are located. *See also* **action theory**.

aggravating factor Those factors in a criminal case that may lead a judge to impose a harsher sentence than might normally be given in a similar case. For example, a sentence may be increased if the offender abused a position of trust; the offence was committed for the benefit of a criminal organization; or there is evidence that the offender was motivated by bias, prejudice, or hate based on race, ethnic origin, language, colour, religion, sex, age, disability, or sexual orientation.

agoraphobia A form of anxiety disorder in which a person experiences intense fear of open spaces or being in public.

Air India disaster On June 22, 1985, an Air India airplane left Toronto airport with 329 people on board. The majority of the passengers were Canadian women and children of Indian origin. The plane exploded off the coast of Ireland, killing all on board. It was determined that a bomb had been planted on the plane. Authorities investigated a potential link between this terrorist action and some radical groups seeking establishment of an independent Sikh nation separate from India. In October 2000, people were finally charged with this terrible crime; a protracted and difficult trial is expected. On June 23, 1985, a second bomb exploded in Tokyo's airport while baggage was being handled, killing two people. It was bound for a plane connecting to an Air India flight travelling to Bangkok. It is thought that this bomb was also planted by Sikh terrorists and had exploded earlier than planned. A member of the Sikh community was charged with the crime when parts of the device were traced to a store in British Columbia and the customer identified. A new trial of two additional accused, Ripudaman S. Mailk and Ajaib Singh Bagri, was launched in 2003. This trial may be the most complex criminal trial in Canadian history. Reference: Mulgrew, Ian. (1988). *Unholy Terror*. Toronto: Porter Books.

Albion's fatal tree Albion, referring to England, was England's hanging tree located in the centre of London. It was here that criminals were hanged and the community gathered around in festival-like conditions to observe (and to engage in petty crimes such as pickpocketing). Reference: Hay, Douglas, et al. (1975). *Albion's Fatal Tree: Crime and Society in Eighteenth Century England*. New York: Pantheon Books.

Algerians, crimes against Until 1962, Algeria was a colony of France; its independence was preceded by a series of terrorist acts in Algeria and France itself. The revolutionary writer Franz Fanon (1925–61), an Algerian by birth, comes out of this time period. While many French citizens were injured or killed in bombings and attacks, Algerians in France also suffered. In a not very well documented event, for example, approximately 200 Algerian demonstrators were killed in Paris in 1961 during a march in support of Algerian nationalism. Fanon, among others, has argued that colonization results in moral and psychological damage to the colonized. *See also* **colonialism**. Reference: Fanon, Franz. (1961). *The Wretched of the Earth*. New York: Grove Press [1963].

alienation A separation of individuals from control and direction of their social life. The term was used widely in German philosophy in the 18th and 19th centuries, but it has become important for sociology through the ideas of Karl Marx (1818–83). Marx claimed that human alienation was created by a socially structured separation between humans and their work. This separation reached its highest intensity in capitalist society where the great mass of the population depended for subsistence on working under the direction of others. In the capitalist workplace, individuals were separated from ownership, control, and direction of their work, and were unable to achieve personal creative expression. The competitive nature of the workplace also alienated, or separated, workers from each other. Alienation is of interest to those studying workplace crime since it is known that it may result not only in low productivity but in theft of employer property or intentional damage to equipment or products.

alterity From the word *alter*—to make a thing different. A term central to postmodern discussions of identity in which the self is given meaning in terms of an "other." This other is posed or imagined in terms of difference. Alterity then is a state or condition of otherness. The term is useful for thinking about how many peoples throughout history have been cast in the role of inferior and as the opposite of those who look down upon them. Negative qualities are projected onto these "others" and the imagined contrast with them strengthens the sense of one's own rightness and confirms one's sense of identity. For Euro-Canadians, for example, the "Indian" has been a significant expression of the other and hence central to the Euro-Canadian sense of self. "Indian" then is the "other" and has the quality of alterity. *See also* **postmodernism**.

altruism Social behaviour and value orientation in which individuals give primary consideration to the interests and welfare of other individuals, members of groups, or the community as a whole. The term was used by Émile Durkheim (1858–1917) to describe a suicide committed for the benefit of others or for the community; this would include self-sacrifice for military objectives in wartime. Sociobiologists argue that altruistic behaviour has its roots in self-interest, the unconscious desire to protect one's genetic heritage. Critics of sociobiology respond that altruism is evident between individuals and in social situations where people are completely unrelated genetically and claim that human conduct and motivations cannot be explained without reference to the values and norms of culture.

Amazon In Greek legend, the Amazon was a female hunter, unusual for occupying a male role. The Amazon river was named after this legendary hunter when early European explorers encountered women who were hunters and in many ways acted like men. Many cultures have acknowledged a masculine role for women. In Hinduism, this role is an aspect of the female *hijras*. The Kaska Indians of the Subarctic may have selected a daughter when it appeared the family was going to have no sons and perform a transformation ceremony to symbolically turn the daughter into a son. The dried ovaries of a bear were tied to her belt that she always wore; she dressed like a male and engaged in hunting. The counterpart of this role among men is called berdache. Societies with little outlet for non-conventional sexual or gender identities are more likely to have individuals with psychological problems. *See also* **berdache**. Reference: Roscoe, Will. (1998). *Changing Ones: Third and Fourth Genders in Native North America*. New York: St. Martin's Press.

Amish A religious sect related to the 16th-century Mennonites, but emerged under the leadership of Bishop Jacob Ammon. They arrived in Canada in 1825 and settled in Waterloo county, Ontario. This group is more traditional than many present Mennonites and has kept religious beliefs alive as well as the customary forms of living, dress, and work. *See also* **sect**.

Amnesty International Formed in 1961, this organization has become a widely supported and successful defender of human rights. They have given special attention to individuals wrongfully imprisoned.

amplification of deviance Developed by Leslie Wilkens (1915–2000). Deviance amplification refers to the unintended outcome of moral panics or social policies designed to prevent or reduce deviance. Typically, the attention given to deviance by the media and moral entrepreneurs serves to attract new recruits and provides them with a definition of what the public expects, thus amplifying the amount of deviance in society. *See also* **moral entrepreneur**; **moral panic**. Reference: Wilkins, L.T. (1964). *Social Deviance, Social Policy, Action and Research*. London: Tavistock.

androgyny A personality that holds a balance of feminine and masculine characteristics. An androgynous person would be one comfortable with displaying both characteristics and able to move back and forth between the two. Some feminists have advocated gender androgyny as a source of liberation from polarized cultural ideas of masculine and feminine. This is of interest to those studying male violence since there appears to be a relationship between societies that place high value on male characteristics (the military, for example) and high rates of crime against women.

anomia Distinguished from Émile Durkheim's *anomie* as a social psychological condition, rather than a societal condition, which *anomie* refers to. Here, the individual experiences a loss of moral direction and a sense of disconnection from society. This concept has proved much easier to investigate empirically than has Durkheim's. *See also* **anomie.**

anomic division of labour Where the division of labour in the workplace is based on power and social and economic status, rather than on differentiations of individual ability or effort. In such circumstances, according to Émile Durkheim (1858–1917), the division of labour cannot command normative consensus and may become a source of anomie and breakdown of social solidarity. *See also* **inequality of opportunity.**

anomie A concept developed by Émile Durkheim (1858–1917) to describe an absence of clear societal norms and values. Individuals lack a sense of social regulation: people feel unguided in the choices they have to make. Anomie can occur in several different situations. For example, the undermining of traditional values may result from cultural contact. The concept can be helpful in partially understanding the experience of colonized aboriginal peoples as their traditional values are disrupted, yet they do not identify with the new cultural values imposed upon them: they lose a sense of authoritative normative regulation. Durkheim was also concerned that anomie might arise from a lack of consensus over social regulation of the workplace. American sociologist Robert Merton (1910–2003) used the term more narrowly to refer to a situation in which people's goals—what they wanted to achieve—were beyond their means. Their commitment to the goal was so strong that they would adopt deviant means to achieve it. He argued that American society—perhaps more strongly than other capitalist societies—held out the goal of personal wealth and success to all its citizens. It placed extremely high value on the attainment of wealth and high social status. Materialistic goals were so stressed in society, Merton argued, that those groups in society who did not believe in their chance of success through conventional avenues (a good education, good job, good income, etc.), because they were poor or otherwise lacked opportunity, were induced toward unconventional routes to attain wealth—including crime. The social norms against crime were sometimes too weakly implanted in individuals to restrain them from seeking to fulfill the value of economic success through criminal means. They wanted to win the game without regard to the rules. More recently, anomie has been used in a more individually focused way to talk about problems of immigrant youth when faced with a new culture or about the identity crises which often erupt during the age transition from youth to adult. Durkheim's use of the term "lack of social regulation" remains the standard definition. Reference: Durkheim, Émile. (1951). *Suicide: A Study in Sociology.* Glencoe, IL: The Free Press.

anorexia A form of mental disorder in which people are overly concerned about their weight or their image and starve themselves, since regardless of how thin they become they still consider themselves overweight.

anthropology, forensic An area of criminal investigation that applies the knowledge of physical anthropology to the examination of crimes. Methods including DNA analysis and skeletal measurement can be used to determine the sex or race of bodily remains, the age of bones, and characteristics of injuries.

anthropology, physical A specialization within the discipline of anthropology centred on the scientific study of the origins and development of human beings through analysis of fossil and skeletal remains. Many students of physical anthropology were employed during the search for evidence in the missing women case in Vancouver, British Columbia.

anthropology, social Also referred to as cultural anthropology, this discipline is conceptually and theoretically similar to sociology. Anthropology originally developed as the study of non-western cultures, but since many anthropologists now study western societies, the disciplines of sociology and anthropology have been tending to converge. Social or cultural anthropologists are interested in understanding how crime and deviance are responded to in various cultures and in how notions of justice are institutionalized.

anti-Asian riots In 1907, an anti-Asian riot in Vancouver swept through Chinatown, damaging Chinese and Japanese property. The government, after an inquiry, agreed to pay some compensation. The Asiatic Exclusion League had been formed by members of the Vancouver Trades and Labor Council in this year, an indication of increasing racial tensions in the city. It has been argued that one result of this inquiry was a new law prohibiting the use and sale of opium. Reference: Comack,

Elizabeth. (1985). "The Origins of Canadian Drug Legislation: Labelling versus Class Analysis." In T. Fleming (ed.), *The New Criminologies in Canada.* Toronto: Oxford University Press.

anti-combines law In order to protect the principle of competition, valued by all liberal, capitalistic societies, laws have been created to prevent and punish the undermining of free markets by corporate combination. Competition law was first introduced in 1889, but there have been few successful prosecutions in Canada even though Canada has an unusually high degree of corporate concentration, suggesting at least the potential for abuse of the market. Reference: Goff, C., and C. Reasons. (1978). *Corporate Crime in Canada: A Critical Analysis of Anti-Combines Legislation.* Scarborough: Prentice-Hall; Stanbury, W.T. (1991). "Chapter 6: Legislation to Control Agreements in Restraint of Trade in Canada: Review of the Historical Record and Proposals for Reform." In R.S. Khemani and W.T. Stanbury (eds.), *Canadian Competition Law and Policy at the Centenary.* Halifax: Institute for Research on Public Policy.

anti-Semitism A negative and hostile attitude toward Jews and the Jewish religion. As a migrant people, the Jews have experienced anti-Semitism within many societies and throughout much of recorded history. The most extreme expression of anti-Semitism was the Holocaust, when six million Jews were murdered in German concentration camps during World War II. This mass killing, carried out in an advanced and intellectually sophisticated society, traumatized western societies and called into question the then dominant idea that historical development was marked by an increasingly rational commitment to the creation of an enlightened, progressive, and humane society. During recent years there appears to be a rise of anti-Semitism in many western societies partly associated with continuing political conflict in the Middle East. *See also* **hate crime.**

antisocial personality disorder Since 1968, the term used in the Diagnostic Manual of the American Psychological Association to refer to both sociopaths and psychopaths. It is a personality disorder that involves complete disregard for the rights of others and impulsive, irresponsible, and aggressive behaviour. There is a distinction between sociopaths and psychopaths, however. Sociopaths are fully aware that they are breaking laws or normative standards and just disregard any moral regulation. Psychopaths are more likely to have an identifiable mental disturbance or illness which has contributed to compulsive criminal and aggressive behaviour.

Anti-Terrorism Act Passed in 2001, the Anti-Terrorism Act created new criminal offences linked to terrorism. Among other things, the new law gives police forces greater search powers and creates new criminal offences, including knowingly providing funds to terrorist groups, whether committed in Canada or not; contributing to or facilitating terrorist activity; instructing a person to carry out terrorist acts or activities; and harbouring or concealing a terrorist. It also provides that any indictable offence committed in pursuit of terrorist objectives is punishable with up to life imprisonment with no eligibility for parole. Reference: Daniels, R.J., P. Macklin, and K. Roach (eds.). (2001). *The Security of Freedom: Essays on Canada's Anti-Terrorism Bill.* Toronto: University of Toronto Press.

apartheid A policy of racial segregation maintained in South Africa from 1948 to 1994. The policy established the doctrine of "separate development" whereby South African Blacks were segregated into reserves known as "homelands" and subjected to residential and occupational restrictions. Apartheid was maintained by a wide range of laws that included the prohibition of inter-racial sexual intercourse or marriage and outlawed racially integrated political and social organizations. A white-minority government, faced with international pressures and internal conflict, began the process of dismantling apartheid in the late 1980s and eventually extended the right to vote on equal terms to all South African adults. A subsequent election in 1994 installed South Africa's first Black majority government led by Nelson Mandela.

APEC "riot" The Asia Pacific Economic Cooperation conference met in Vancouver in 1997, hosted by the federal government. To highlight the "Cooperation" aspect of the organization, efforts were made to have president Suharto of Indonesia attend. Suharto was responsible for the invasion of East Timor and a policy of genocide. While the details are not known, it is thought that Suharto attended the conference with a guarantee that he would not be embarrassed by protestors. The protestors did of course turn out, and when it looked like they would get too close to the street Suharto's car was travelling on, the crowd was order to disband and then quickly sprayed with tear gas by members of the RCMP. The prime minister of Canada was not called to the subsequent inquiry but there was strong evidence that orders to disrupt the protestors came from his office. Reference: Pue, W. Wesley (ed.). (2000). *Pepper in Our Eyes: The APEC Affair.* Vancouver: University of British Columbia.

appeal court That court which hears an appeal from the participants in a lower court. Also called an appellate court. Each province has an appeal court and the Supreme Court of Canada is the highest court to which one can appeal. An appeal is a mechanism for having a body independent of the first court review the case to ensure appropriate application of principles of law and legal procedure.

Arbour Commission of Inquiry A 1996 report, Report of the Commission of Inquiry into Certain Events at the Prison for Women in Kingston, was commissioned as a result of disturbing events at the Prison For Women involving male guards stripping women inmates and generally treating them in a manner that shocked Canadians. The Arbour Commission resulted in the closure of the Prison For Women (P4W) in Kingston. Louise Arbour later became a judge on the Supreme Court of Canada and in 2004 resigned to become the Human Rights Commissioner of the United Nations.

Archambault report The 1938 Report of the Royal Commission on Prison Reform in Canada led by Mr. Justice Joseph Archambault. The report gave priority to the reformation and rehabilitation of criminals, in fact arguing that while these had been the goals of punishment for almost 100 years they had not been fully implemented. The report then attempted to outline a set of programs that might lead to the rehabilitation of more offenders. An important assumption behind the report is a consensus about the value of rehabilitation and a recommendation that this should be a purpose of imprisonment.

Armenian genocide From 1915 to 1922, approximately 1.5 million Armenians lost their lives as a result of a Turkish government policy of genocide. Many Armenians tried to escape the genocide by emigrating to Canada, only to find they were classified as "Asians" under Canadian immigration policy, making it difficult for them to enter. In 2004, the Canadian House of Commons passed a private member's bill acknowledging the Armenian genocide, to much criticism from the Turkish community. *See also* **genocide.**

arraignment A hearing before a criminal court, usually the first or second appearance, during which the identity of the accused is determined, the accused is informed of the charges and his or her rights, and is asked to enter a plea.

arrest Whenever a person's freedom to leave a situation is curtailed by a law enforcement officer. Usually this means being taken into physical custody for the purpose of charging the person with a criminal offence. Arrests are regulated by a body of due process requirements, including such matters as reasonable grounds for search or seizure, right to maintain silence, and right of access to a lawyer.

arrest warrant A writ issued by an official of the court instructing the police to arrest an specific individual on specific charges.

assimilation Where an ethnic group loses distinctiveness and becomes absorbed into a majority culture. Some sociologists suggest that the process can create a new culture resulting from the fusion of the cultures of different ethnic groups into a new blend, but the term integration is usually chosen by sociologists to suggest this blending of divergent cultures. The concept of assimilation is useful when discussing the persistence of minority cultures within host societies. In Canada, for example, visible minorities have experienced slower and less comprehensive assimilation than many European ethnic minorities. Canada's official government policy of multiculturalism implies resistance to assimilation and support for a society where people preserve their cultural distinctiveness, yet join together for common pursuits and agree on fundamental values. *See also* **acculturation; integration, social; multiculturalism.**

assisted suicide Assisting a person to take their own life. While suicide itself is no longer a criminal offence, it is an offence to assist or encourage someone to take their own life. In the case of Sue Rodriguez the Supreme Court of Canada did not accept arguments supporting assisted suicide thus forcing her and an accomplice to break the law in order to terminate her life. *See also* **Rodriguez, Sue.**

Association in Defence of the Wrongfully Convicted A Canadian association formed in 1993 to provide assistance to those whom the executive of the

Association believe to have been wrongfully convicted. The association has been successful in having some prisoners' cases reopened—resulting in acquittals—and this has brought a great deal of public attention to the problem. Many names have been added to the list of those known to be wrongfully convicted or those probably wrongfully convicted. Among the first group are David Milgaard and Guy Paul Morin, and among the second are people like Stephen Truscott, Romeo Phillion, James Driskel, and Thomas Sophonow. Rubin Carter, himself wrongfully convicted in the United States, is Executive Director of the association. *See also* **Carter, Rubin**; **Milgaard, David**; **Truscott, Steven**; **Morin, Guy Paul**. Reference: Anderson, Barrie, and Dawn Anderson. (1998). *Manufacturing Guilt: Wrongful Conviction in Canada*. Halifax: Fernwood Publishers; Campbell, Kathryn, and Myrian Denow (eds.). (January 2004). "Wrongful Conviction." *Canadian Journal of Criminology* (special issue). Vol 46(2).

assumption of discriminating traits The view that offenders are distinguished from non-offenders by, for example, their high levels of impulsivity and aggression.

assumption of offender deficit The view that offenders against the law have some psychological deficit that distinguishes them from normal law-abiding citizens.

atavism A tendency to reproduce ancestral type in plants and in animals; to resemble one's grandparents or great-grandparents more than parents. In popular speech, a "throw back." This concept was used by Cesare Lombroso (1835–1909) to describe a type of criminal he called the *born criminal*. The atavistic criminal was one representing an earlier stage of human evolution (thus representing the ancestral type more than the parental type). This ancestral type was identified by Lombroso through several stigmatized physical characteristics—including the length of ear lobes and fingers and the bone structure of the head. This supposed physical degeneracy was associated with moral degeneracy and thus more frequent criminal behaviour. These physical stigmata were not found to be especially associated with criminals and this particular theory of criminality was rejected. Lombroso also studied female criminals, and while not finding the stigmata with the same frequency as among men, he did not abandon his theory. Rather he argued that females were less evolved than men and thus had less far to degenerate: this would explain the infrequency of their criminal behaviour and the nature of the criminal behaviour they do commit.

attachment The degree to which an individual has affective ties to other persons. In Travis Hirschi's 1969 work, aspects of the *social bond*.

Attention Deficit/Hyperactivity Disorder (AD/HD) This is the most common reason why children are referred to mental health professionals, since it is believed that about 3 percent of children, most often boys, suffer from this disorder. The symptoms involve lack of attention, impulsivity, and hyperactivity. There has been a long-standing debate about whether this is a really a medical condition or simply the result of a school system and domestic situations that are unable to handle the physicality of boys and their needs. This condition was first recognized as a medical disorder in 1957 with the publication of an article identifying the "hyperkinetic impulse disorder." Although the nature of the link is not thoroughly understood, it has been found that those with this disorder have a higher incidence of delinquency. The major treatment is drugs, such as Ritalin and Dexedrine.

attorney general A cabinet minister in a provincial government with responsibility for the law and its enforcement. Typically an attorney general will oversee the police, the courts, and the corrections system. In the federal government, the minister of justice is also attorney general for Canada.

Auburn system A prison system developed around 1820 in the United States. This system used solitary cells to confine inmates at night but during the day they worked together in what is known as a congregate system. While working together, strict silence was imposed, and efforts were made to prevent inmates from looking at each other. Strict discipline was also enforced. On visiting America's prisons, Canadian officials were impressed with this model and this formed the basis for the Kingston Penitentiary opened in 1835. Most European nations chose to develop the rival American system, the Pennsylvania system, which completely isolates inmates. Critics at the time said the Pennsylvania system produced a deeper effect on the soul of the convict, but the Auburn system is more comfortable to the habits of men in society. *See also* **Pennsylvania system**; **Walnut Street Jail**.

audience A group of individuals attending to a common media. They receive communication from the same source, but are not active participants and do not communicate with each other. In sociology, the term is used to draw attention to the way that media corporations develop audiences of readers, listeners, and viewers with the business objective of selling access to this audience to advertisers. In this perspective, the creation and maintenance of an audience (rather than the activity of communication) is the prime goal of media enterprises. *See also* **consumer culture**.

authority The capacity of an individual or institution to secure compliance from others based on the possession of a recognized right to legitimately claim obedience. Authority is obeyed because the individual or institution issuing commands is believed to have the right to do so. Max Weber (1864–1920) defined three ideal types of authority: traditional, which rests on history, myth, and ritual; charismatic, founded on a belief in a leader's exceptional qualities and inspirational mission; and rational-legal, founded on democratic principles and a framework of law to which all individuals and institutions are subject.

autocracy The concentration of power and authority in the hands of one person. Usually, autocracy refers to a situation where state power is controlled by a monarch, religious leader, or political dictator. The term can also be applied to particular social institutions in which one individual has dominant power and authority. *See also* **democracy**; **meritocracy**; **plutocracy**.

autonomic reactivity A measurement of the extent to which an individual's physical organism reacts to external stimuli.

B

baby boom The substantial increase in the birth rate following World War II (from 1947 to approximately 1966), creating a population bulge slowly working its way through the age structure of society, which affects everything from classroom space to chances of promotion to pension funds. The baby boom was most apparent in Canada, the United States of America, Australia, and New Zealand. In 1996, the baby boom generation made up 33 percent of the Canadian population. This large "bulge" may partially explain the labour market problems and high unemployment Canada has had for the past decade or more. *See also* **birth rate**; **cult of domesticity**; **echo generation**. The baby boom generation has been of interest to criminologists since it is known that crime is strongly correlated with age. It could have been predicted that crime would go up as this generation went through their teenage years and into early adulthood and then declined as they matured. Reference: Foot, David. (2001). *Boom, Bust & Echo: Profiting from the Demographic Shift in the 21st Century*. Toronto: Stoddart.

baby bust The rapid decline in Canada's birth rate following the baby boom years of 1947 to 1966. The baby bust generation followed from 1967 to 1979 as the fertility rate of Canadian women declined to less than half of the rate during the boom years. After 1979, women born in the boom years began to have children, leading to an echo boom or echo generation.

background knowledge As used by ethnomethodologists, it refers to commonsense reasoning and to the way that members of society, and sociologists as well, use background knowledge of culture and social structure as an unstated source of guidance in their reasoning.

Badgley report A 1984 report of the Committee on Sexual Offences Against Children and Youth commissioned by the federal government of Canada and chaired by Robin Badgley. Research found that one-half of girls were victims of unwanted sexual acts and one-third of boys were victimized. The commissioner also examined juvenile prostitution and child pornography. The report's findings were shocking to Canadians, but it took several years for changes to the law to occur.

bail Also known as judicial interim release, it is the money or property pledged to the court or actually deposited, in return for release from custody prior to trial. In deciding if bail is to be accepted and thus the accused released, courts look primarily to the likelihood of the accused returning to court and to issues of public safety.

band A designated group of First Nations individuals, identified in the Indian Act, and usually historically related to each other by kinship and area of residence for whom land and moneys are administered in common.

Banks, Hal It is hard to know where to begin this Canadian tale, but the elements become clear on June 29, 1954, when a one-man inquiry into the status of Mr. Hal Banks finds that he should be deported to the United States. The report is sent to the minister of immigration with this recommendation, but it comes back with the word "rejected" removed and "approved" put in its place. Banks, by an Order-in-Council of the Governor General on the advice of the Cabinet, is now given landed immigrant status in Canada. How did we get to here? Hal Banks entered Canada on a temporary permit in early 1949 at the request of the Liberal government, steamship owners, and unions. He was brought in to "clean up" the Canadian Seamen's Union, which controlled much of the shipping on the Great Lakes and has recently led many strikes and is involved in organizing an international strike. The Union was accused of being run by communists and used for communist purposes. Somehow the union must lose its grip on shipping and this was Bank's job. Banks had been a local tough on the San Francisco waterfront with a criminal record. Using violence, Banks was able to reduce the CSU to an ineffective group and help a breakaway union, the SIU (Seafarers International Union), to get contracts for manning ships on the Great Lakes. Banks quickly took over this union and used gangster tactics to live well while keeping countless union members who did not support him from finding work. Many opponents were seriously assaulted. The Canadian Labour Congress finally tried to assist the union members hurt and intimidated by Banks by organizing a boycott of goods coming and going to the ports. This brought the St. Lawrence Seaway to a standstill. The tactic got the attention of the federal government, who agreed to establish a commission of inquiry into Bank's activities in Canadian ports. The Norris inquiry began August 7, 1962, and after 100 days of investigation concluded that Banks really was a crook, and it placed his union under trusteeship. In the meantime, Banks appeared before a criminal court on a serious assault charge. While out on bail, he skipped town and was found in the United States by a reporter (the RCMP and politicians claimed they had no idea where he was). In a precedent-setting case, the US Secretary of State Dean Rusk decided not to extradite Banks to Canada. Interestingly, it is reported that a $100 000 donation from the SIU appeared in the campaign coffers of the Democratic Party ten days after Rusk made his decision. Case closed. However, many questions about the relation of government officials to Banks remain unanswered. Banks claimed that he had photos taken in his house, which was frequented by prostitutes, of politicians in compromising positions. Banks died in the United States in September 1985. Reference: Edwards, Peter. (1987). *Waterfront Warlord.* Toronto: Key Porter Books.

Barbie, Klaus Known as the "Butcher of Lyon," Barbie (1913–91) was head of the Gestapo in the French city of Lyon, a city also known as the head of the resistance movement in wartime France. In 1987, Barbie, who had fled to Bolivia in 1951, was found guilty of "crimes against humanity" for his war crimes and sentenced to life imprisonment. *See also* **war crimes.**

barrister and solicitor In Britain, the legal profession is divided into these two distinct roles played by lawyers; in Canada, the terms are rarely used since all lawyers are both barristers and solicitors. In Britain, a barrister is one who argues cases in court (and has thus technically been called to the bar) and this court presentation is based upon written summaries of the facts and the evidence, called *briefs*, prepared by solicitors. Solicitors also handle matters such as property transfers, estates, and corporate and taxation law, but may argue cases only in junior courts.

base (or infrastructure) A concept from Marxism that refers to the mode of production of a society: the social and technical organization of its economy. Karl Marx argued that it is upon this base that the superstructure of the society—its institutions and culture—are built. While the social institutions and culture of society are shaped by this base, at the same time, they help to maintain and reproduce the mode of production and may, in certain conditions, contribute to its transformation. *See also* **mode of production**.

battered woman syndrome Although a controversial concept, these psychological ideas provide an explanation for why some women remain in abusive relationships and why some murder their intimate partners when one might assume they could seek an alternative resolution to violence. This syndrome was accepted by the Supreme Court as a version of self-defence and the criteria for allowing this defence were articulated in a 1990 judgment (*see also* **Lavallée case**). A 1998 Supreme Court decision decided that battered woman syndrome was not a defence it itself, but rather a psychiatric explanation that might help understand a women's state of mind (*R. v. Malott*). Reference: Vallee, B. (1986). *Life With Billy*. Toronto: Seal Books; *R. v. Malott* [1998] 1 S.C.R. 123.

bawdy house According to the Criminal Code of Canada, a place "kept, occupied or resorted to by one or more persons for the purpose of prostitution or acts of indecency."

Beaver decision In this case, regarding an alleged crime of drug trafficking, the Supreme Court of Canada decided that the test of *mens rea* (criminal intent) could be, to some extent, subjective. It did not have to depend on what a reasonable citizen might have thought or intended in the situation, but could take into account whether the particular defendant had a mistaken, but reasonable and honest, belief that they were not committing a crime. Reference: *Beaver v. The Queen* [1957] S.C.R. 531.

Beccaria, Cesare (1738–94) An Italian aristocrat who initiated what has come to be called the Classical school of criminology. Beccaria published *On Crimes and Punishments* in 1764, under a false name for fear of the repercussions, outlining what we now see as a rational and utilitarian philosophy of criminal justice administration. Beccaria was arguing against the procedures of a very arbitrary, brutal, and traditional justice system built on patronage, torture, and harsh penalties. *See also* **classical criminology**; **Bentham, Jeremy**. Reference: Beccaria, Cesare. (1764). *On Crime and Punishment*. Indianapolis: Bobbs-Merril [1963].

Becker, Howard, S. (1928–) Professor of sociology at Northwestern University and famed for his labelling theory developed in his 1963 book, *Outsiders: Studies in the Sociology of Deviance*. Becker combined elements of symbolic interactionism with structural perspectives to develop his argument that deviance is a social construction created by the responses of others to the acts of individuals. He linked this argument to structural perspectives by demonstrating that the power to label and the chance of being labelled is linked to the socio-economic status of the individuals or groups involved. Reference: Becker, Howard, S. (1963). *Outsiders: Studies in the Sociology of Deviance*. New York: The Free Press of Glencoe.

bedlam In general, this refers to a great deal of noise and confusion. The term is a shortening of the name of an "insane asylum" in medieval London, St. Mary of Bethlehem.

belief The degree to which an individual believes in conventional values, morality, and the legitimacy of law. In Travis Hirschi's work, aspects of the *social bond*.

bell curve Discovered by Abraham de Moivre (1667–1754) when he noticed that many phenomena cluster around an average value and in so doing form a bell-shaped curve. The heights of Canadians, for example, cluster around the average height and if all heights were graphed a bell-shaped curve would appear. The normal curve is a similar idea, and has a similar shape, but is a theoretical curve (or one derived from mathematical manipulation rather than observation) and was developed by Friedrich Gauss (1777–1855) to depict the effects of random variation. For example, if you collect 100 samples from a population in which you know the average value of a phenomenon (e.g., support for a political party), the means of the 100 samples will cluster around the true mean (the population mean) according to the characteristics of the normal curve. The normal curve is symmetrical so that if we draw a line from the highest point of the curve to the base, half of the curve will lie on one side and half on the other. Further, approximately 68 percent of the area of the entire curve is located between lines drawn at plus and minus one standard deviation (a standardized amount of deviation from the mean), and 95 percent of the area of the curve lies between lines drawn at plus and minus 2 standard deviations. In the example of drawing 100 samples from a population, it can now be said that 95 of the means obtained from these samples will fall within plus or minus 2 standard deviations of the true mean. Once the calculation of standard deviation is learned, one can then calculate the sampling error when doing sampling and estimate the value of a phenomenon in a population based on one sample. This is what is implied when an opinion poll in the newspaper reports that "a sample of this size is accurate to within plus or minus x percent, 19 times out of 20" (i.e., 95 percent of the time).

Bentham, Jeremy (1748–1833) A English philosopher and founder of the Classical school of criminology. Bentham was a utilitarian who believed that the pain or pleasure of all actions could be mathematically determined. This was displayed in his book, *Moral Calculus* (1789). Bentham argued that if his philosophy was followed, every punishment could be rationally determined in order to accomplish the utility desired. Bentham also spent time designing a new prison, the Panopticon. *See also* **Panopticon.**

berdache A male who takes on the roles of women and who may also dress as a woman and engage in sexual intimacy with men. More recently, the term "Two Spirits," which has traditional roots, has been preferred. This status was found in several North American First Nations cultures and is interpreted as a way of integrating deviant members into cohesive, small societies. While the term is sometimes used to refer to women who take on male roles, there does not appear to have been female berdache in North America and authors tend to prefer the term "Amazon" to describe these women. Both of these terms are important parts of the anthropology of gender and sexuality and reveal the social or cultural construction of gender. *See also* **Amazon.** Reference: Roscoe, Will. (1998). *Changing Ones: Third and Fourth Genders in Native North America.* New York: St. Martin's Press.

Berlin Wall A barrier of barbed wire and, later, of concrete and minefields built in 1961 between the eastern (communist-controlled) sector of the city of Berlin and the western sector. The wall was built at the direction of the Soviet Union to prevent migration from east to west and to minimize cultural contact between East and West Berlin. With the uprising against communism in East Germany in 1989, the East German government was forced to declare free rights of emigration for all citizens, and in December of 1989 the wall was opened for free passage. Soon after, Germany was reunited and the eastern part integrated into the Federal Republic of Germany. The divided Germany became a site for criminologists to test theories about the criminogenic character of capitalism and of socialism. It was often argued that East Germany (socialism) produced lower crime rates. *See also* **Cold War.**

Bernardo, Paul Convicted in 1995 of the first-degree murder of teenagers Leslie Mahaffy and Kristen French. It was revealed that Bernardo and his wife Karla Homolka had abducted, raped, tortured, and murdered the two teenagers in separate incidents. The two had also raped Homolka's sister, who subsequently died, perhaps of the drug used to render her unconscious. The couple had videotaped their murders and while these were not found in time to be used as evidence and Bernardo's lawyer did not immediately turn them over to the police, a great controversy ensued about the right to show these tapes. Bernardo was also charged with 18 other rapes over a period of six years. Bernardo received a sentence of life imprisonment. Homolka received a 10-year sentence because she gave evidence of Bernardo's involvement in the murders and she was portrayed as being forced into the activities by her husband. When the evidence of the videotapes became available, it was less clear whether she had been the unwilling accomplice she claimed to be. Reference: Williams, S. (1997). *Invisible Darkness: The Strange Case of Paul Bernardo and Karla Homolka.* Toronto: Little Brown.

beyond reasonable doubt The standard of evidence used in a criminal case requiring the judge or jury to have no reasonable doubt about the guilt or innocence of the accused. *See also* **standard of proof.**

Bhopal The site of a methyl isocyanate gas plant in India, operated by Union Carbide. In 1984, gas from this plant was accidentally released, killing 3000 people and injuring approximately 200 000.

bill In parliamentary procedure, all proposals submitted to Parliament to be passed into law are called bills. Once a bill is passed by both the House of Commons and the Senate and has received royal assent, it becomes a statutory act of Parliament.

Bill of Rights The Canadian Bill of Rights was adopted by the Conservative government of John Diefenbaker in 1960 and was a significant, but not extremely useful, step in the evolution of human rights legislation in Canada. The bill was not part of the nation's highest law (the Constitution), so it could be amended like any other piece of legislation and covered only federal legislation. *See also* **Charter of Rights and Freedoms.**

bin Laden, Osama Born in Saudi Arabia in 1957, bin Laden became known as the most wanted man in the western world due to his direction of and financing of terrorist attacks primarily on the United States. When the Soviet Union invaded Afghanistan in 1979, bin Laden went to Afghanistan to respond to what he saw as an attack on Islam. The resistance movement he was part of eventually gained sufficient support from the United States to drive out the Soviet Union. The resistance movement then began to struggle to create an Islamic state within Afghanistan and to export this revolution to other Islamic nations. Osama bin Laden was in Saudi Arabia during the

Persian Gulf War, a war in which Saudi Arabia surrendered a great deal of sovereignty for United States protection. Again, bin Laden was outraged at this treatment of Muslims and was placed under house arrest. He subsequently returned to Afghanistan and used his wealth to organize the dispossessed and disenfranchised of the Muslim world. *See also* **World Trade Center, New York**; **terrorism**. Reference: Anonymous. 2003. *Through Our Enemies' Eyes: Osama Bin Laden, Radical Islam and the Future of America.* Dulles, VA: Brassey's Inc.

birth rate Calculated as the number of births in a given population during a particular year divided by the actual population and then multiplied by 1000 to give a birth rate per 1000 of the population. The resulting figure is known as the crude birth rate. Generally, to observe trends and predict population growth, demographers (statistical analysts of population) use "fertility rates," which relate the number of births not to total population but to the population of women in their child-bearing years (usually defined as from 15 to 49 years of age). Birth rates are of interest in predicting crime trends since crime and age are closely correlated. *See also* **baby boom**; **fertility rate**.

Black Panthers A Black militant party, founded (1966) in Oakland, California, by Huey P. Newton and Bobby Seale. Originally encouraging violent revolution as the means of achieving Black liberation, the Black Panthers called on all Blacks to arm themselves for the liberation struggle. The Black Panthers were involved in many violent confrontations and several people were killed. Many of the Black Panthers brought to trial were eventually acquitted, and the killing by the police of two Black Panthers while in their beds confirmed that this group had been subjected to extreme police harassment.

Bloc Québeçois Formed in 1991 after the failure of the Meech Lake Accord which had proposed extensive constitutional changes. The Accord would have created increased powers for the provinces and a unique status for Quebec within Confederation. Federal Cabinet Minister Lucien Bouchard left the Progressive-Conservative government in protest at the failure and founded the Bloc Québeçois, with the main goal of promoting the agenda of a sovereign Quebec at the federal level of politics. The founding of the Bloc contributed to the electoral destruction of the Progressive-Conservatives in the 1993 election when they were reduced to two seats in the House of Commons. In that and subsequent elections, the Bloc has won a large majority of the parliamentary seats in Quebec.

block watch Also referred to as neighbourhood watch, a program usually sponsored by police departments to encourage residents of an area to share information about crime and crime prevention and to assume some responsibility for watching for unusual events in their neighbourhood.

BNA Act *See* **British North America Act.**

Bobbitt, Lorena An 1994 American criminal case in which Ms. Bobbitt was charged with cutting off the penis of her husband, John Wayne Bobbit, with a kitchen knife while he slept. Ms. Bobbitt was acquitted of this offence on the grounds of an "irresistible impulse defence." His penis was surgically reattached and he subsequently demonstrated its abilities in an X-rated video. In Canada, this defence is not available without also offering a mental disorder defence. A similar offence occurred in Canada in 1997 and the offender was acquitted.

Bonger, Willem (1876–1940) Bonger outlines a rather naive Marxist theory of criminality in his book *Criminality and Economic Conditions* (1916) in which he argues that in a capitalist society all people are encouraged to be self-centred and greedy, thus making crime more likely. However, the criminal justice system rarely harms the interests of the ruling class, so it is the inferior class that is accused and convicted of criminal wrongdoing. Reference: Bonger, Willem. (1916). *Criminality and Economic Conditions.* Bloomington, IN: Indiana University Press [1969].

booking The process of being admitted to prison or custody after arrest. Typically, this process involves recording the identity of the person, the reason for arrest, the arresting authority, and the time and place of arrest.

borstal An English institution for the reform of young offenders. Institutions fashioned on this model were opened in Canada during the post-war years. New Haven Borstal in British Columbia opened in 1947.

bourgeois class From the French, meaning a citizen of a city or burgh. In feudal time, the cities had become the place of business and residence for a growing class of merchants, professionals, and crafts persons. They were seen as having a social status between the peasant class and the land-owning or aristocratic class—hence the idea that they were the middle class. This new middle class came to feel oppressed by the traditions and restrictions of feudalism and aristocratic rule, and eventually were able to grasp power and transform social values. They are associated with the bloodless revolution of Great Britain in 1688 and the French Revolution in 1789. This new class also had a distinctive lifestyle that came to be referred to as "bourgeois." The term bourgeois class, or bourgeoisie, was used by Marx to refer to the corporate or capitalist class in modern societies that is thought, particularly in socialist ideas, to be also a ruling class.

Bow Street Runners A form of policing established by William Fielding in the early 1700s in London, England. Crime was widespread at this time, but there was no concerted attempt to control it or to catch serious offenders. Fielding was the justice of the peace for the Bow Street region and put together a disciplined group of "police" who were able to capture Jonathan Wild, a notorious criminal, in 1725. The Bow Street Runners remained in effect for most of the century.

Boyd gang Led by Edwin Alonzo Boyd, this small gang engaged in at least 11 dramatic bank robberies in the Toronto area in the late 1940s and early 1950s. On March 6, 1952, two members of the gang killed a Toronto police officer and were subsequently executed. A jury determined that Boyd was not involved in this death, but he received a life sentence for bank robbery and other crimes. During his sentence, he escaped twice from Toronto's maximum security Don Jail, and he was finally paroled in 1966. Reference: Vallee, Brian. (1998). *Edwin Alonzo Boyd.* Toronto: Doubleday.

Brave New World The title of a 1932 book by futurist and social critic, Aldous L. Huxley (1894–1963). In the "brave new world," Huxley imagines the authorities of society use new technologies, drugs, and instruments of propaganda like subliminal advertising to keep people happy and unaware or unconcerned about what is actually happening to them and their communities.

breach of probation A probationer who fails to comply with the conditions of their probation can be charged with breach of probation. This is a criminal offence with a maximum penalty of two years imprisonment.

Bre-X A mining company whose stocks soared on claims of an enormous gold find. The company went bankrupt in November of 1997 when it was found that the core samples taken from the area had been "salted" (gold was added to the samples after extraction) and the "gold deposit" was worthless. While billions of dollars were lost by investors, many people, including company executives, made millions on stock deals. Reference: Goold, D., and A. Willis. (1997). *The Bre-X Fraud.* Toronto: McClelland and Stewart.

bridewell *See* **house of correction.**

British Columbia penitentiary Opened in 1878, the British Columbia penitentiary served as the federal maximum security prison for the Pacific region for many decades. While it had its share of disturbances, perhaps the most serious occurred on June 9–11, 1975, when hostages were taken and a correctional worker, Mary Steinhauser, was killed. There were allegations that she had been shot because the custodial staff handled the situation badly and compromised her safety partly because of their dislike for the rehabilitation staff in the institution. The Farris report of 1976, held to investigate the disturbance, concluded that "there is conflict between correctional staff and classification staff of the penitentiary, making it impossible for either group to discharge its responsibility." This tension had been identified in the Ouimet report of 1969, but had not been fully acknowledged. It can, however, be seen as the end of a consensus about the rehabilitative goal of incarceration. This is made clear in the McGuiggan report of 1977, in which the current philosophy of incarceration is identified: Offenders are sent to prison as punishment, not for punishment. Opportunities for rehabilitation should be available, but rehabilitation is not a reason for incarceration, nor a goal of incarceration. *See also* **solitary confinement**.

British North America (BNA) Act Passed by the British Parliament in 1867, creating the nation of Canada. The BNA Act was the constitution of Canada as it provided the legal framework in which the political relations of the peoples of the nation were to be carried out. The most distinctive feature of the BNA Act is its division of powers between the federal and provincial governments. This Act provided no means for its own amendment; this could be only be done by Britain's Parliament at Canada's request. In 1982, Canada adopted a new constitution that established complete constitutional autonomy from Britain; the BNA Act was then renamed the Constitution Act, 1867. *See also* **constitution**.

broken window (theory) The title of a 1982 article by criminologists James Q. Wilson and George Kelling. This simple theory argues that a broken window left unrepaired will make a building look uncared for or abandoned, and soon attract vandals to break all the other windows. If this is so, then prevention of crime will be accomplished by steps like painting over graffiti, keeping buildings in good repair, maintaining clean streets and parks, and responding effectively to petty street crime. These actions make citizens feel safer, and when they frequent public places, criminal activity is less likely to occur. Many jurisdictions in North America have adopted practices based on this perspective. Reference: Kelling, George, and Catherine M. Coles. (1997). *Fixing Broken Windows: Restoring Order and Reducing Crime in Our Communities.* New York: Martin Kesslet Books/Free Press.

bulimia A mental disorder associated with food and body image. The person with this disorder will engage in binge eating, followed by periods of vomiting or laxative use. The late Princess Diana was a celebrity sufferer of this condition.

burden of proof The obligation to prove one's case. In North American criminal justice systems, the burden of proof is on the state. The state is obliged to prove its case. The accused does not have to prove that he or she is innocent. The state must prove that the accused is guilty. There is a standard of proof that must be met before guilt can be determined. *See also* **standard of proof**.

bureaucracy A formal organization with defined objectives, a hierarchy of specialized roles and systematic processes of direction and administration. Bureaucracy is found in earlier times in history (for example, in administration of agricultural irrigation systems, the Roman army, and the Catholic church), but it becomes most prominent in the large-scale administration of agencies of the modern state and modern business corporations. Max Weber (1864–1920) gave particular attention to bureaucracy and saw this form of social organization becoming dominant in modern society due to the commitment to the value of rationalization—the organization of social activity so as to most efficiently achieve goals. *See also* **rationalization**.

Burlingham case In the case of Burlingham, the Supreme Court of Canada established the test that must be met in determining if evidence resulting from a violation of the accused's Charter rights can be admitted in court. The Court declared that if the evidence would not have been discovered without the Charter violation, then the evidence cannot be admitted. Reference: *R. v. Burlingham* [1995] 2 S.C.R. 206.

Burnt Church In August 2000, violence erupted on the Burnt Church native reserve in New Brunswick over fishing rights recently recognized by the Supreme Court of Canada.

Butler case The debate around pornography and obscenity reached the Supreme Court with this case (1992) and the outcome was historic. The Court used the opportunity to examine and clarify the underlying rationale for the regulation of sexual expression. The Criminal Code states that obscenity is "the undue exploitation of sex or of sex and one or more of the following subjects; namely, crime, horror, cruelty and violence." The Supreme Court said that the meaning of "undue" must be determined by a community standard of tolerance and then added that "this determination must be made on the basis of the degree of harm that may flow from such exposure, harm of the type which predisposes persons to act in an anti-social manner." In explicitly finding pornography to be harmful, the court said it harms women's rights to be equal, their sense of self-worth, and their physical safety. This ruling made it clear that obscenity is not about the explicitness of sex nor is it about one morality versus another; rather it is about harm. Reference: *R. v. Butler* [1992] 1 S.C.R. 452.

Buxbaum, Helmut Buxbaum was a wealthy man who took out a $1-million insurance policy on his wife and then hired four men to murder her. She was dragged from her car and shot in the head on a highway near London, Ontario, in 1984.

C

Calder case A 1973 decision of the Supreme Court of Canada on a request by the Nisga'a peoples of British Columbia for a declaration that legal title to their land had not been lawfully extinguished. The decision considerably advanced the position of aboriginal peoples in their claims that aboriginal ownership of land had been continuous and had survived European colonization. Six of the seven judges agreed that aboriginal legal ownership of the land had existed prior to the arrival of Europeans.

In deciding whether this legal ownership still existed, three judges stated that the aboriginal peoples did still own the land, while the other three judges argued that they had ceded effective control to the Crown and implicit extinguishment had taken place (the seventh judge ruled on a technical matter, so did not address the question of legal ownership). In 1974, largely in response to this decision, the federal government established an office to deal with native land claims. In April 2000, after long and complex negotiations and intense public debate, the Canadian Parliament passed the Nisga'a Final Agreement Act, which settled land claims and established a limited sphere of self-government. Reference: *Calder v. Attorney General of British Columbia* (1973), 34 DLR (3rd) 145; Tennant, Paul. (1990). *Aboriginal Peoples and Politics: The Indian Land Question of British Columbia, 1849–1989.* Vancouver: University of British Columbia Press.

call girl A type of prostitute who waits to be called by a client rather than one who stands on a street corner or works in a bar or other location. Call girls tend to be more "up market" and expensive than street prostitutes.

Canada Assistance Plan (CAP) Federal legislation, passed in 1966 and considered by many as a keystone of the Canadian welfare state. The legislation required the federal government to shoulder half the cost of social programs undertaken by the provinces, chiefly social assistance (welfare programs). This policy enabled the federal government to set national standards for social programs and, backed by its right to withhold payments to provinces whose policies did not conform to federal standards, it was able to impose some consistency across the country. In 1991, the federal government imposed a limit on the funds it would pay out for social programs to more affluent provinces, and this led to the situation where the federal government was paying only approximately one-third of the actual costs. In 1996, CAP was replaced by the Canada Health and Social Transfer program, which combines federal funding for health, postsecondary education, and welfare, and transfers a designated amount of money to each province rather than transferring a percentage of actual costs. The replacement of the CAP was seen as the end of an era by many Canadians since it reduces the ability of the federal government to impose national standards and will encourage many provinces to reduce their social spending to fit within the transferred funds. Social programs that soften the impact of the free market on individuals are of interest to criminologists since research suggests that crime rates can be reduced by such programs. Reference: Currie, Elliott. (1985). *Confronting Crime: An American Challenge.* New York: Pantheon Books.

Canada Health and Social Transfer Program *See* **Canada Assistance Plan.**

Canadian Association of Chiefs of Police Established in September 6, 1905, this organization of police chiefs has become a powerful lobby group for issues around law and policing.

Canadian Centre for Justice Statistics (CCJS) A division of Statistics Canada, formed in 1981, with a mandate to collect national data on crime and justice. Most of the official figures on crime, including the useful publication *Juristat*, come from this agency. Reference: Haggerty, Kevin D. (2001). *Making Crime Count.* Toronto: University of Toronto Press.

Canadian Police Information Centre (CPIC) Opened in 1972, CPIC is a central pool of information on criminals (warrants, parolees, missing persons, unidentified bodies, and so on), vehicles, and property that can be accessed by policing agencies throughout Canada.

Canadian Security and Intelligence Service (CSIS) Developed in 1984 as a result of the McDonald commission, this group took away from the RCMP their previous national intelligence-gathering function. For years tension remained between the RCMP and the CSIS, and many believe this resulted in a difficult investigation of the Air India bombing. *See also* **McDonald commission.**

Canadians Against Violence Everywhere Advocating its Termination (CAVEAT) Established after the 1991 killing of Nina de Villiers by Jonathan Yeo while out on bail. Yeo had been stopped at American customs while transporting a rifle and was returned to Canada. Despite his violation of bail conditions preventing him from leaving the country, the Canadian police decided that they had no right to confiscate his firearms and released him. Just one hour after his release he abducted and subsequently murdered Nina De Villiers and soon went on to murder another woman. Yeo later shot himself during a police chase. CAVEAT was dedicated to the creation and maintenance of a just, peaceful society through public education, changes to the justice system, and ensuring the rights of victims. This organization has now ceased to function.

cannabis Also known as *marijuana, Mary Jane, dope, pot, grass, ganja,* and a wide variety of other terms, a drug derived from the leaves of the *cannabis sativa,* a member of the hemp plant family. Ingestion of this drug is known to decrease physical activity, change estimations of space and time, increase appetite, and frequently lead to euphoria. It is not known to be addictive, and in recent years its medicinal effects have been noted and are now being scientifically studied. Canada has passed regulations making the medical use of cannabis legal; the government has contracted with a company to produce the plant. The general use of cannabis remains forbidden under the Narcotics Act and is a criminal offence, although there have been several attempts to decriminalize possession and use of the drug. In September 2002, a Senate committee recommended that marijuana possession and cultivation be made legal (not just non-criminal), and that only behaviour causing demonstrable harm to others—illegal trafficking, selling to minors, and impaired driving—should be prohibited. The report also calls on the government to declare an amnesty for any person convicted of possession of cannabis under current or past legislation. *See also* **LeDain commission**. Reference: Special Committee of the Senate of Canada. (September 2002). *Cannabis: Our Position for a Canadian Public Policy.* Ottawa: Government of Canada; Alexander, Bruce K. (1990). *Peaceful Measures: Canada's Way Out of the "War on Drugs."* Toronto: University of Toronto Press.

capital An accumulation of goods or wealth used for the production of other goods and services rather than for immediate or personal use. If one just plays games on a computer, the computer cannot be considered capital. However, if it is used to produce reports or graphs that are then sold, the computer can be considered capital. Capital is central to a capitalist economic system. *See also* **capitalism**.

capital accumulation The process of accumulating resources for use in the production of goods and services. Private capital accumulation takes place when productive capacity exceeds the immediate needs for consumption. For example, a farmer can accumulate capital (stored grains, improved equipment, etc.) during years of good harvests and good farm revenues. Generally, accumulation is directly linked to profitability: the resources used to make commodities can be replaced and augmented when the commodity is sold for a profit. Capital accumulation can also take place in the public sector, where, from a structuralist approach within a conflict perspective, the state is seen as performing the function of aiding in the accumulation of private capital. This function may be performed by the state providing an educated work force (human capital), building rail lines into resource areas, maintaining a legal system to resolve contract disputes, and providing tax incentives or tax breaks. *See also* **structuralist approach**.

capital punishment Punishment of crime by execution of the offender. The word *capital* is from Latin, referring to the head, the locus of life. While capital punishment is still widely imposed in world societies, it has been abolished in the countries of western Europe and in Canada. The last hanging in Canada took place in 1962, after which the Canadian government routinely advised the Governor General to commute all death sentences. Capital punishment was formally abolished by changes to the law in 1976. A free vote was held in the House of Commons in 1987, and the majority supported the continued abolition of the death penalty. Reference: Archer, Dana, Rosemary Gartner, and Marc Ceittel. (1983). "Homicide and the Death Penalty: A Cross-National Test of the Deterrence Hypothesis." *Journal of Criminal Law and Criminology* 74: 991–1014.

capitalism An economic system in which economic activity is primarily directed toward the production of commodities for sale in the marketplace. The capital to carry out production (the goods or wealth used to produce other goods for profit) is privately owned and profit is reinvested so as to accumulate capital. Since the system is competitive, constant re-investment and development of the means of production are required to maintain a producer's market position and this leads to an unending process of technological development and transformation. *See also* **capital**; **labour theory of value**.

career In common use, this refers to the sequence of stages through which people in a particular occupational sector move during the course of their employment. It has also been applied to analyzing the various stages of an individual's involvement with criminal activity.

career criminal Those individuals whose criminality is like a career. They have gone through the minor leagues to the majors and devote many aspects of their life to criminality. These individuals tend to commit a large portion of the total amount of crime in a community. Career criminality is associated with an individual's exposure to deviant subcultures, especially those that exist in weakly controlled areas of society. These offenders are also referred to as "chronic offenders." Early valuable research was done by Marvin Wolfgang (1987) and David Farrington (1977). Reference: Sutherland, Edwin, and Chic Conwell. (1937). *The Professional Thief.* Chicago: University of Chicago Press; Wolfgang, M., T. Thornberry, and R. Figlio. (1987). *From Boy to Man, From Delinquency to Crime.* Chicago: University of Chicago Press.

carrier's case A legal case often pointed to as demonstration of the way in which the justice system serves the needs of the economically powerful. In this case, an English court (1473) decided that merchants holding or transporting (hence carrier) for another was guilty of theft if they kept the goods for themselves. This case extended the definition of theft. Reference: Hall, Jerome. (1952). *Theft, Law and Society.* Indianapolis: Bobbs-Merrill.

Carter, Rubin American boxer was convicted of the June 17, 1966 murder of three people. He spent 22 years in prison before a group, which had been moved by Carter's published story, was successful in having his indictment dismissed in February 1988. Carter gained a great deal of publicity and remains in the spotlight as an advocate for the wrongfully convicted. Carter now serves as the Executive Director of the Canadian Association in Defense of the Wrongfully Convicted. Reference: Chaiton, S., and T. Swinton. (1991). *Lazarus and the Hurricane.* Toronto: Penguin.

case law Equivalent to the expression "common law." Previous decided cases, or precedents, are an important source of Anglo-Canadian law. Precedent established by previous cases is binding on judges if the case is equivalent and if it has been decided in a superior court. *See also* **common law**; ***stare decisis.***

Cashel, Mount The abuse of children has a long history, much of it marked by silence. This silence was broken in Canada when victims of abuse at the Mount Cashel Orphanage in Newfoundland captured public attention. Between 1989 and 1992, eight Christian Brothers who had worked at the orphanage were convicted on charges involving assault and abuse. This case opened the floodgates of grievance from former residents of residential schools, training schools, and young participants in a variety of youth programs. Reference: Harris, Michael. (1990). *Unholy Orders: Tragedy at Mount Cashel.* Toronto: Penguin.

caste A status group, within a system of hierarchical social stratification, in which membership is hereditary. Caste differentiations are usually based on religious and mythical traditions, and caste membership determines occupational roles, place of residence, and legal and customary rights and duties. Caste is maintained from generation to generation by the practice of within-caste marriage (endogamy) and strict formality in social interaction with other castes. *See also* **class.**

caucus The members of a party group in a legislature. Each party forms an organized group to support or oppose a government. When a party is in office, the main role of the caucus is to organize support for the government, contribute to party discipline through peer pressure, and maintain party morale. An opposition party caucus allocates roles as government critics among its members corresponding to those of government ministers.

causality A relationship between two variables such that one (the independent variable) can be claimed to have caused the other (the dependent variable). In order to establish causality three conditions must be met: a) there must be a correlation or association between variables; b) the independent variable (the cause) must occur before the dependent variable (the effect); c) the relationship must not be spurious. *See also* **spuriousness**; **variables.**

cause Those features or characteristics with might produce a particular effect (e.g., features that might cause an individual to commit a crime). Causal analysis is a positivist approach to criminology. In order for something to be a cause it must meet four criteria: a) the cause must happen before the effect; b) there must be a correlation between the causal variable and the effect variable; c) all other possible reasons for the correlation must be examined and discarded; d) a theory should be available that links the cause to the effect. *See also* **theory.**

CAVEAT *See* **Canadians Against Violence Everywhere Advocating its Termination.**

CCF *See* **Co-operative Commonwealth Federation.**

celerity In deterrence theory, celerity refers to the swiftness with which an offender is discovered or punished.

Central Intelligence Agency (CIA) An arm of the US government, the CIA has a mission to protect US national security through the gathering of foreign intelligence.

Centre of Criminology Established at the University of Toronto in 1963 under the leadership of John J. Edwards, it provides a teaching and research program serving English-speaking Canada. The early focus was on law, but greater breadth has been developed over the years.

Chambliss, William Professor of sociology at George Washington University, he is associated with the development of conflict perspectives within criminology. He argues that people's social experiences as individuals and interactions with groups shape individual values and norms. In a complex society, there are many groups in a wide variety of social and economic situations, and, consequently, there is normative conflict between these groups and their members. Those groups that have more social and political power are able to have their norms and values enshrined within the law and reflected in the application of law. Consequently, the law reflects the norms and values of dominant classes and opposes the norms and values associated with the poor, criminalizing the behaviour of many poor and powerless citizens. Chambliss grounded this general theoretical approach in historical analysis of the law and policing and in participant observation work that led to a controversial exposure of political corruption, racketeering, and organized crime in Seattle. Reference: Chambliss, William. (1978). *On the Take: From Petty Crooks to Presidents.* Bloomington, IN: Indiana University Press; Chambliss, William, and Robert B. Seidman. (1982). *Law, Order and Power.* 2nd ed. Reading, MA: Addison-Wesley.

charge (1) A judge may charge (instruct) a jury. (2) To accuse a suspect or to state specifically which criminal offence a person is alleged to have committed.

Charlottetown Agreement An agreement between the federal government of Canada and the ten provincial governments to amend the constitution of Canada established by the Constitution Act, 1982. Major aspects of the agreement were the entrenchment of a right to aboriginal self-government, decentralization of power from the federal to provincial governments, and clauses recognizing the distinct character of Quebec society and culture. The agreement provided for a national referendum to be called before legislative change was made. The agreement was defeated in a national referendum in 1992. *See also* **referendum**. Reference: Curtis Cooke (ed.). (1994). *Constitutional Predicament: Canada after the Referendum of 1992.* Montreal-Kingston: McGill-Queen's University Press.

Charter decisions In 1982, Canada adopted a new Constitution Act, which, for the first time, included a Charter of Rights and Freedoms providing constitutional guarantees of civil rights. Included are fundamental freedoms of thought, belief, and opinion; democratic rights; mobility rights; legal rights (including the right to due legal process); equality and language rights; and aboriginal rights. All laws passed before or subsequently to 1982, by Parliament or a legislature, must be in conformity with these Charter guarantees. After the passing of the Constitution Act, 1982, and the Charter, Canada's courts began to deal with a stream of cases based on the Charter. These have included important cases on aboriginal rights, the abortion law (this was struck down as discriminatory against women and as offending the equality provisions), language rights, and access to medical use of marijuana. In some cases, Parliament or a legislature may enact that a law shall be valid notwithstanding provisions of the Charter. Where this takes place, the law must be renewed by additional legislation every five years. *See also* **Supreme Court of Canada**. Reference: Greene, Ian. (1989). *The Charter of Rights.* Toronto: Lorimer.

charter groups Groups, usually distinguished by ethnic identity, that have played a pioneering role in the opening and development of new territories and immigrant societies. In Canada, these groups have customarily been identified as the British and the French.

Charter of Rights and Freedoms Part of the Constitution Act of 1982, the Charter came into effect in April 1982. The Charter provides protection for a wide range of individual rights typical of liberal democracies but until this time not constitutionally protected in Canada. As a part of the

Constitution of Canada, the Charter cannot be changed without the consent of both Parliament and the provincial legislatures. The Charter includes provisions to protect mobility rights and minority language rights. The provincial legislature of Quebec did not support the Constitution Act of 1982, and its adoption without this consent increased nationalist support for sovereignty in Quebec. Several efforts have subsequently been made to make constitutional changes and achieve consensus with Quebec. *See* **Charlottetown Agreement; Meech Lake Accord; constitution; Bill of Rights.**

Chicago school Refers to the research and social theory that emerged in the first half of the 20th century from the world's first school of sociology at the University of Chicago. Due to its phenomenally rapid growth, the city of Chicago was seen as a laboratory for sociological research into the effects of urbanism on culture and social relationships. In criminology, it focused on the socio-cultural causes of urban crime and on crime prevention. Associated with the research of Robert Park (1864–1944), Ernest Burgess (1866–1966), Louis Wirth (1897–1952), and Frederick Thrasher (1892–1962). Canadian criminology was influenced by the Chicago school through Carl Dawson (1887–1964), who studied at the University of Chicago and brought the perspective of urban studies and social disorganization to McGill University in 1922. Reference: Shore, Marlene. (1987). *The Science of Social Redemption: McGill, the Chicago School, and the Origins of Social Research in Canada.* Toronto: University of Toronto Press.

child pornography *See* **Badgley report; online pornography; Sharpe decision.**

child sex tourism The practice of travelling to another country for the purpose of sexually exploiting children. A 1997 law gave the police the powers to prosecute Canadians engaging in this exploitation while travelling abroad.

church An institution composed of members sharing some common religious and ethical views and joining them together in religious celebration and social activities. Churches, as distinct from sects or cults, tend to be established, culturally accepted, and broadly supportive of the surrounding institutions of society; to be hierarchical; and to have a priesthood or set of authorized office holders. *See also* **cult; sect.**

CIA *See* **Central Intelligence Agency.**

circuit court Found mostly in northern Canada, a mobile court consisting of the judge, court clerk, defence lawyer, and Crown counsel, who travel from community to community "dispensing justice." Known by the locals as the *circuit circus.*

citizen Originally a status possessed by an individual in ancient Roman society, distinguishing them, as free individuals with full legal rights, from those, like slaves, who were in servitude and lacked civil rights. The term is used generally to refer to the individual as an active member of a democratic political community. It was not until the Canadian Citizenship Act of 1947 that the people of Canada became "Canadian" citizens. Prior to that date, immigrants and native-born people alike were simply British subjects.

civil code While the legal system in English Canada is dependent on common law and the principle of *stare decisis*, the Quebec Civil Code is derived from the French Civil Code and to some extent the Roman Code. In this system, law is codified; judges look to the written law to determine essential principles and then are free to apply those principles to a specific case. They are not bound by precedent, as is the case in a common law system. Quebec's civil code does not apply to criminal matters, as these still come under the federal criminal code. *See also* **common law; *stare decisis.***

civil death This term does not refer to physical death, but to the withdrawal of all rights of an offender, typically a prison inmate, to participate in the life of a citizen of the society. Not only are they isolated from society, but they are deprived of the right to vote, to have employment, go to school, to correspond freely, and to sue their holder. Throughout the 20th century, courts have found that most of these rights must be maintained for inmates, so the concept rarely applies in the western world. There is still some debate over the right of prisoners to vote, although in 2002, the Supreme Court of Canada ruled that federal prisoners had the right to vote.

civil society The concept of civil society captures that sphere of social life between the intimate bonds of the family and friends, the formal organizations of the state, and the restraining forces of the economy. As such it includes voluntary organizations, community groups, and organizations like unions and churches. If the role of the state is to shrink, then family life and civil society may come to play a larger role in society. The reverse may hold as well. Marxists see history as being made from the dynamics of civil society.

Clarke, Charles Kirk (1857–1924) A pioneer in Canadian psychiatry, Clarke formed the predecessor of the Canadian Mental Health Association; the Clarke Institute of Psychiatry is named after him. While Clarke gained international recognition, his belief in genetic engineering (eugenics) continues to haunt his reputation.

class The term is used in various ways in sociology. It usually implies a group of individuals sharing a common situation within a social structure, usually their shared place in the structure of ownership and control of the means of production. Karl Marx (1818–1883), for example, distinguished four classes in capitalist societies, a bourgeois class who own and control the means of production, a petite bourgeoisie of small business owners and professionals, a proletariat of wage workers, and a lumpenproletariat of people in poverty and social disorganization who are excluded from the wage-earning economy. In land-based economies, class structures are based on an individual's relationship to the ownership and control of land. Class can also refer to groups of individuals with a shared characteristic relevant in some socio-economic measurement or ranking (for example all individuals earning over $50 000 a year): it then has a statistical meaning rather than being defined by social relationships. While class is extensively used in discussing social structure, sociologists also rely on the concept of status, which offers a more complex portrait in which individuals within a class can be seen as having quite differentiated social situations. *See also* **lumpenproletariat**; **petite bourgeoisie**; **proletariat**; **status**.

class consciousness The awareness of individuals in a particular social class that they share common interests and a common social situation. Class consciousness is associated with the development of a "class-for-itself" where individuals within the class unite to pursue their shared interests. *See also* **class-for-itself**.

class consciousness, false Where members of a social class absorb and become committed to values and beliefs that serve and support the interests of other classes rather than their own. The concept assumes that there is an objective "class interest" of which its members are unaware.

class crystallization Where the divisions between social classes become obvious and somewhat fixed: it is difficult for individuals to change their social class because their whole life situation—income, wealth, education, status—is shaped by their class location.

class-for-itself A class of individuals conscious of sharing a common social and economic situation and who unite to pursue common interests. *See also* **class consciousness**.

class fraction Usually used by political economy theorists in discussions of the corporate class to acknowledge significant segmentation of this class. It is commonly linked to such distinctions as that between finance-based capital and industrial-based capital, each viewed as having different interests and perspectives. This is a useful concept in avoiding the simplistic view that the "corporate class" is a necessarily unified group.

class-in-itself A social class composed of individuals who objectively share class membership—they share a common social and economic situation—yet who are unconscious of their class membership or of shared interests that unite them.

classical conditioning A basic form of learning whereby a neutral stimulus is paired with another stimulus that naturally elicits a certain response; the neutral stimulus comes to elicit the same response as the stimulus that automatically elicits the response.

classical criminology Considered to be the first formal school of criminology, classical criminology is associated with 18th and early 19th century reforms to the administration of justice and the prison system. Associated with authors such as Cesare Beccaria (1738–94), Jeremy Bentham (1748–1832), Samuel Romilly (1757–1818), and others, this school brought the emerging philosophy of liberalism and utilitarianism to the justice system, advocating principles of rights, fairness, and due process in place of retribution, arbitrariness, and brutality. Critical criminologists see in these reforms a tool by which the new industrial order of capitalism was able to maintain class rule through appearing to apply objective and neutral rules of justice rather than obvious and direct class domination through coercion. Criminal law is stated in terms of moral universals rather than being seen as rules that simply protect the interests of property holders. The claims to fairness in the justice system provide a sense of legitimation for the state and the order it represents. *See also*

Positivist school. Reference: Mannheim, Hermann (ed.). (1972). *Pioneers in Criminology* (2nd edition). Montclair: Patterson Smith Publishing.

classical economic theory Known also as *laissez faire*, the theory claims that leaving individuals to make free choices in a free market results in the best allocation of scarce resources within an economy and the optimal level of satisfaction for individuals—"the greatest happiness for the greatest number." *See also* **classical liberalism**.

classical liberalism A political and economic philosophy emerging along with the growth of capitalism. The central beliefs are that unregulated free markets are the best means to allocate productive resources and distribute goods and services and that government intervention should be minimal. Behind this is an assumption about individuals being rational, self-interested, and methodical in the pursuit of their goals. By the end of the 19th century, the belief in free markets became moderated in some versions of liberalism to acknowledge the growing conviction that liberty or freedom for the individual was a hollow promise if the social conditions of society made liberty meaningless. It was believed that the state must become more involved in managing the economy in order to soften the negative effects of market economies and maximize the well-being of each individual. This new direction for liberalism is often referred to as "progressive liberalism." This newer philosophy supported the growth of the welfare state, but has come under attack in the past two decades. *See also* **classical economic theory**; **neo-convservatism**. Reference: Girvetz, Harry K. (1963). *The Evolution of Liberalism*. New York: Collier.

classless society A society that does not have a hierarchy of different social classes and in which individuals have similar resources of wealth, status, and power. Found in simple hunter-gatherer societies (like the pygmies of Congo) and also a socialist vision of a future society founded on collective ownership of the means of production.

claustrophobia An anxiety disorder exhibited by fear of being in confined spaces.

claw back A phrase used to describe Canadian government policy towards what were once considered universal benefits of the welfare state. While all senior citizens receive old age pensions from the government, it is now the case that if total income exceeds a certain amount, a portion, or all, of additional old age benefits is taxed back (clawed back) through annual individual income taxation. In the future, old age security pensions will be paid to individuals based on their income (or household income for couples). *See also* **means test**; **universality**.

Clayoquot Sound protest Located on Vancouver Island and the site of one of the largest stands of old growth temperate rain forest in the world, Clayoquot became the site of a prolonged battle between protestors, owners, loggers, and the government during the early 1990s. Before the conflict was resolved, 800 criminal convictions were achieved for acts of civil disobedience, the largest criminal prosecution for civil disobedience in Canada. In the end, the protestors partly won as large sections of the forest were saved from logging.

clearance rate The proportion of crimes reported to the police that are cleared by the police through conviction or identification of the perpetrator. Clearance rates are sometimes used as a measure of police effectiveness, so there is pressure to have a high clearance rate. These rates can be made to appear high by having offenders confess to a number of crimes for which they are not being tried. These confessions result in crimes being "cleared."

clink A prison located on the south side of the River Thames in London, England, dating from the 13th century and named after the district in which it was located. For many years the term "clink" stood for prisons in general throughout English Canada.

closed custody Also called *secure* custody, a sentence or disposition of a youth court, involving being detained in a facility that looks much like an adult prison. Approximately 16 percent of cases in youth court result in a sentence of secure custody. The Youth Criminal Justice Act no longer uses the terms "closed custody" and "open custody," but it does require each province to maintain two levels of custody and further mandates the courts to use the least restrictive form of custody unless certain requirements are met. It is anticipated that the rate of incarceration will decline under the new Act. *See also* **open custody**; **Young Offenders Act**; **Youth Criminal Justice Act**.

closed-class society The opposite of social mobility, this term refers to a society where it is improbable that individuals will be able to change their social class location usually because class location is ascribed. *See also* **class crystallization**; **status, ascribed**.

closure A procedural motion to end a debate in a meeting or assembly. Opposition parties usually accept reasonable limits on debate, but occasionally they will use all possible methods of delaying the legislative process. Closure is then used to terminate the debate and take an immediate vote on the legislation. In 1956, in a controversial use of closure, the federal Liberal government pushed through legislation to authorize construction of a natural gas pipeline from Alberta to Central Canada over opposition objections to what appeared to be American financial control of the project. The Liberals lost the subsequent election partly because of public distaste for what seemed to be dictatorial actions.

Cloward, Richard, and Ohlin, Lloyd American criminologists who developed differential opportunity theory, a development of Robert Merton's theory of anomie. The theory argues that for an individual to become involved in criminal acts, he or she must not only be denied access to legitimate means of attaining goals, but must also have access to illegitimate means of attaining them. They focus on delinquent gangs and argue that three types of gang subculture emerge: criminal, where the gang is organized effectively to pursue criminal activity; conflict, where the gang is less organized and the emphasis is on violence; and destructiveness and retreatist, where there is minimal organization and the gang is successful in neither legitimate nor illegitimate activities and retreats into a world of alcohol and drugs. Reference: Cloward, Richard, and Lloyd Ohlin. (1960). *Delinquency and Opportunity: A Theory of Delinquent Gangs.* Glencoe, IL: The Free Press.

cocaine First isolated in 1860, cocaine is an alkaloid derivative of the coca leaf. It was used in many popular medicines, and in 1886 was added to a new soft drink, called Coca-Cola (removed in 1906). As a powerful natural stimulant, cocaine produces euphoria, laughter, restlessness, and excitement. *See also* **crack**.

code of Hammurabi The first body of law that has survived for scholars to study. Hammurabi was the king of Babylon in approximately 2000 B.C. and prepared a legal system defending varying rights and based on a philosophy of retribution.

coercion The use of force or commands to gain obedience without willing consent of the individual.

Coffin, Wilbert On February 10, 1956, Wilbert Coffin, a prospector convicted of the murder of an American teenager bear hunting with two others in the Gaspé region of Quebec during 1953, was hanged in Montreal. All three hunters were killed by rifle shots, but no charges are ever laid in two of the murders. Locals were unconvinced by the evidence and felt the police were pressured by the government to settle the case quickly to appease the United States government. Coffin maintained his innocence until the end. Unease about this case and the fact that the current law provided no other penalty than the death sentence soon led to the development of the legal distinction between first- and second-degree murder with only the former involving the death penalty. The distinction remains in the present Criminal Code, although both offences are now punishable with terms of imprisonment.

Cohen, Albert (1918–) American sociologist known for his study of the origins and dynamics of male juvenile gangs. Combining the differential association theory of Edwin Sutherland with the strain or anomie theory of Robert Merton, he argues that delinquent subcultures emerge that have norms and values opposed to those of the outer community and that juveniles attach themselves to these subcultures as a result of class and status differentials and parental and school socialization. Boys from less favourable backgrounds experience status frustration within the wider community and gravitate to gangs to gain feelings of enhanced status within a subculture. Their criminal acts become principally motivated not by gain, but by a desire to achieve and maintain high status within the gang peer group. Reference: Cohen, Albert. (1955). *Delinquent Boys.* Chicago: University of Chicago Press.

cohort All people sharing a similar experience or event at a particular time. For example, all children born in Toronto in 1963 or all students graduating from high school in 1980. Cohorts are frequently used in longitudinal research. Marvin Wolfgang, for example, established a research project to follow all male children born in Philadelphia in 1940 in order to determine their encounters with the police. *See also* **longitudinal studies**.

Cold War The name given to the mutually hostile relations after the end of World War II in 1945 between the now fallen communist systems of Eastern Europe, the Soviet Union, and Asia, and the world's capitalist societies and their allies led by the United States. While this was a war of propaganda, spying, sabotage, and political and economic subversion on both sides, it avoided the "hot war" of direct conflict between the world's dominant military powers. The Cold War reflected the new realities of the nuclear age and the catastrophic consequences of armed superpower conflict. The economic and political collapse of communism has now ended this era in international relations.

collective solidarity Similar in meaning to Émile Durkheim's term "mechanical solidarity," this refers to a state of social bonding or interdependency that rests on similarity of beliefs and values, shared activities, and ties of kinship and cooperation among members of a community.

colonialism Political domination of one nation over another that is institutionalized in direct political administration by the colonial power, control of all economic relationships, and a systematic attempt to transform the culture of the subject nation. It usually involves extensive immigration from the colonial power into the colony and the immigrants taking on roles as landowners, business people, and professionals. Colonialism is a form of imperialism. Canadian society can itself be seen as a colonized nation with regard to Britain and the United States, but can also be seen as a colonizing nation in relation to First Nations peoples. *See also* **dependent development**; **imperialism**.

Columbine high school In April 1999, two students of this US high school, using firearms from their homes, killed 12 students and a teacher by sniping them from the area around the schoolyard. All of North America was shocked by this event and Canadians were doubly shocked when a copycat shooting occurred a week later in a Taber, Alberta school, resulting in the death of one student and critical wounding of another. *See also* **Taber, Alberta**. Reference: Fox, J.A. and J. Levin. (2001). *The Will to Kill: Making Sense of Senseless Murder*. Boston: Allyn and Bacon.

command economy An economy directed by state authorities, rather than market forces. There are a variety of command economies. In the ancient world, command was found in agricultural economies, especially those dependent on large-scale systems of irrigation requiring extensive regional planning and coordination. The power to control water resources gave central authorities immense social and economic dominance. Mesopotamia (modern Iraq) and Egypt are examples. Large sectors of the economy were also commanded in other ancient and medieval societies like Rome, China, and among the Inca. In modern times, command economies were dominant in the Soviet-style communist societies, where state central planning agencies allocated capital and resources, established production targets, and fixed the levels of prices. Command economies, because they rely on centralized bureaucratic administration, appear to be inherently less efficient than market mechanisms in allocating resources and stimulating economic growth. Soviet-style central planning has now been generally abandoned as a method of economic management. *See also* **state capitalism**.

Commission on Systemic Racism in the Ontario Criminal Justice System Growing tension between the police and the Black community of Toronto and a destructive "riot" in the summer of 1991 led to the 1992 report to the premier of Ontario. This lead to the creation of a Commission of Inquiry and to several published reports from the Commission. *See also* **racial profiling**. Reference: Commission on Systemic Racism. (1994). *Racism Behind Bars*. Toronto: Queen's Printer of Ontario.

commitment The degree to which an individual pursues conventional goals. In Travis Hirschi's 1969 work, aspects of the *social bond*.

commodity A good or service that is exchanged or sold in the marketplace.

common law The common law tradition found in English Canada derives from feudal England where it had become the practice for the king to resolve disputes in accordance with local custom. Customs that were recognized throughout the country were called common custom, and decisions made by the king and by subsequent courts set up to settle disputes became known as common law. Common law is considered a source of law, which means that the cases settled over the past 600 years themselves become part of the law, and these precedents become binding on present and future judges.

Another source of law is statutes. *See also* **case law**; **civil code**; ***stare decisis***; **statutes**.

commonsense reasoning A term used by ethnomethodologists, derived from Alfred Schutz (1899–1959), referring to the practical or everyday reasoning used by members of society to create and sustain a sense of social reality as being objective, factual, predictable, and external to themselves. Since the objectivity of the world as a practical accomplishment is the focus of ethnomethodology, this kind of reasoning is a primary topic of investigation. Also referred to as *mundane reasoning*. *See also* **ethnomethodology**. Reference: Pollner, M. (1987). *Mundane Reason: Reality in Everyday and Sociological Discourse*. Cambridge: Cambridge University Press.

communism A political theory that advocates collective ownership of the means of production (resources, land, and capital), abolition of private property, and equalization of incomes. Communism differs from socialism because it contemplates revolutionary social change rather than just electoral politics. The first modern communist society was established in Russia after the revolution of 1917, and this political system was imposed by the Soviet Union, after World War II, on many countries of Eastern Europe. In Asia, a successful communist-led revolution in China in 1949 led to the growth of communist regimes and political movements in other areas, including Korea, Vietnam, and Malaysia. These centralized and dictatorial communist systems were far from the model societies envisaged by Karl Marx and Frederick Engels, who believed that a communist revolution would create cooperative collective ownership, a true community-based democracy, and a weakening of the role of the state. *See also* **socialism**.

communitarianism A philosophy or belief system that places priority on the community or on social values. Often contrasted to individualism or libertarianism. It claims that meaning in individual life and individual liberty are only possible within a strong and vital community so government policies and individual choices should be responsive to social values. *See* **community**; **libertarianism**.

community A society where people's relations with each other are direct and personal and where a complex web of ties link people in mutual bonds of emotion and obligation. In the social sciences, especially sociology, the idea of community has provided a model to contrast to the emergence of more modern, less personal societies where cultural, economic, and technological transformation has uprooted tradition, and where complexity has created a less personal and more rationalized and goal-directed social life. *See also* ***gemeinschaft***; ***gesellschaft***.

community corrections At the end of the 1950s, the primary form of punishment was a prison term. Most offenders under the supervision of the state were in provincial reformatories or federal penitentiaries. Just as there was a move to reduce the population of chronic patients in psychiatric institutions, there was a move to reduce prison populations. Forms of community correction, allowing offenders to serve their sentence within the community, began to emerge. Probation sentences were developed, along with community work orders, restitution, and eventually electronic monitoring. Criminologists have been interested in the fact that these new services did not reduce the size of prison populations. Rather, the number of people under the surveillance of the state expanded. These new people had been diverted from the justice system in the past, but as services emerged, the police and prosecutors appeared to bring more people into the justice system. *See also* **net widening**.

community crime prevention A general category of prevention strategies that focus on the community itself. This general category includes strategies such as development crime prevention, effective guardianship, or situational crime prevention.

community notification The practice of informing the community that a high-risk offender has been released into the area.

community policing Seen as an alternative to the traditional policing model of enforcement and isolation from the community, community policing attempts to integrate policing into the community through programs like community police stations, neighbourhood watch, decentralization of policing functions, working with social service agencies, beat policing, and other strategies. Reference: Normandeau, Andre, and Barry Leighton. (1991). "Police and Society in Canada." *Canadian Journal of Criminology* (special issue) 33.

community psychology A perspective that analyses social problems, including crime, as largely a product of organizational and institutional characteristics of society. It is closely related to sociology.

community service order Usually a condition of a probation order for a young offender, but it can be a sentence in itself. Since young people are usually unable to pay a fine, they may be ordered to do some service to the community. They may be required to do things like work for a charitable organization, help with cleaning up the environment, or assist work at a food bank.

commutation The Governor General has the ability under the Criminal Code to apply clemency (or pardon) and is thus able to commute a death sentence to a sentence of life imprisonment. The government of John Diefenbaker commuted 52 of 66 death sentences during its time in office (this is no longer necessary in Canada). In general terms, it is the changing of a penalty from a greater one to a lesser one.

comprador elite The members of a national business class of senior corporate managers who derive their position and status from connection to foreign corporations of developed nations. The term is used in critical theories of the sociology of development to imply that a foreign-allied national business class tends to encourage local economic development that benefits other nations rather than their own. *See also* **metropolis-hinterland theory**.

comprehensive land claims Claims to land made by native peoples not covered by a treaty with Canada or the British Crown. Comprehensive claims are most significant in the north and in British Columbia, two regions with few treaties. Since the establishment of the land claims process in 1974, some claims have been resolved in the north, and the principles of a treaty with the Nisga'a in British Columbia were signed in 1996 and passed into law in April 2000. *See also* **Calder case**.

compulsive disorder A form of mental disorder in which a person exhibits recurrent needs to perform certain actions. They may repeatedly wash their hands, wipe doorknobs, repeat certain words, or rearrange objects to put them into a certain order.

concurrent sentence The legal practice of sentencing an offender found guilty of more than one offence (either through trial or through a plea of guilty) to serve two or more sentences concurrently or at the same time. For example, if an offender is found guilty of separate assaults on two people, the sentence may be five years for each assault. These terms are not added together but served at the same time. This model is the most typical way of handling multiple offences in Canada. *See also* **consecutive sentence**.

conditional discharge Since 1969, Canadian courts have been able to use what is called a conditional discharge. Rather than convicting an offender, the court may discharge him or her from the authority of the court if certain conditions are met that are typically spelled out in a probation order. If the offender meets the conditions imposed, he or she is then discharged and will have no criminal record.

conditional release There are a number of conditional release programs in Canada. These are ways in which an offender may be released from prison early and may remain in the community as long as the conditions of the release are met. The following conditional release programs may be used: temporary absence, day parole, full parole, or statutory release.

conditional sentence Section 742 of the Criminal Code allows a judge to impose a conditional sentence of imprisonment on a convicted offender who would otherwise receive less than two years imprisonment. This conditional sentence allows offenders to serve time in the community rather than in prison. They must comply with a set of conditions on behaviour. They can also be required to submit to treatment against their will. In the event that the conditions are violated without reasonable excuse, offenders may be sent to prison for the time remaining on the sentence.

conduct norms Specifications of proper and appropriate behaviour generally supported and shared in by members of a group. Societies contain different groups whose conduct norms are to some extent divergent.

confederation The joining together of territories with separate political systems into a political union that establishes a federal government. The federal government is constitutionally permitted to exercise specific powers, while others are reserved for the exclusive jurisdiction of provincial or state governments. Canadian Confederation was established by the Constitution Act of 1867 (originally the British North America Act, 1867), which joined Ontario and Quebec (the "Province of Canada") with Nova Scotia and New Brunswick. Six provinces later joined Confederation: Manitoba (1870), British Columbia (1871), Prince Edward Island (1873), Alberta and Saskatchewan (1905), and Newfoundland (1949). The Yukon, Northwest

Territories, and the territory of Nunavut do not have provincial status and exercise limited powers of government under the authority of the government of Canada. Within Confederation can be found three distinct visions of the nation of Canada. One sees Canada with a strong federal or central government and weaker provincial governments; the second sees Canada with a weak federal government and strong provincial governments; and the third sees Canada as the federation of a French-speaking nation and an English-speaking nation. These three visions have created tensions within Canada that continue to influence Canadian politics. *See also* **national policy**. Reference: Moore, Christopher. (1997). *1867: How the Fathers Made a Deal*. Toronto: McClelland and Stewart.

conflict perspectives Sociological perspectives that focus on the inherent divisions of societies with social inequality and the way these social divisions give rise to different and competing interests. The central assumption is that social structures and cultural ideas tend to reflect the interests only of some members of society rather than society as a whole. This contrasts with consensus or functionalist perspectives, which assume a foundation of common interest among all members of society. Marxism and feminism are examples of conflict perspectives. *See also* **critical perspectives**; **Marx, Karl**; **feminism**.

conjugal visit The practice of many penitentiaries to allow inmates to have a private visit with their spouse or common-law partner with the intent of continuing the intimacy felt to be necessary to maintain a relationship and assist rehabilitation.

conscience, collective A concept associated with Émile Durkheim (1858–1917), referring to the common norms, values, and beliefs shared in by members of a community. It consists of beliefs and ideas that shape the structure and direction of community life, rather than just the personal interactions of individuals.

conscription crisis A major division in Canadian public opinion about the enforced drafting of individuals into the armed forces during World War II (1939–45). During World War I (1914–18), the use of conscription was generally supported in English-speaking Canada, but there was widespread opposition to it in Quebec. In the late 1930s, when a new European war seemed increasingly likely, Canada's prime minister, Mackenzie King, promised that if Canada became involved in war, there would be no conscription of individuals for service overseas. Once the war began in 1939, it became obvious that Canada could not avoid conscription if there was to be major involvement in the war against Germany. Conscription for service in Canada was introduced in 1940, and in 1942, the government asked the Canadian people to release it from the pledge not to introduce conscription for service overseas. In a national vote—a plebiscite—English-speaking Canada strongly supported a change in policy, but Quebec was strongly against. As a result of this split in opinion, the government adopted a cautious policy and not until November 1944 did it finally send conscripted armed forces to Europe. By that time there was a more supportive opinion in Quebec. Reference: Granatstein, J.L., and J.M. Hitsman. (1977). *Broken Promises*. Toronto: Oxford University Press.

consecutive sentence The legal practice of sentencing an offender found guilty of more than one offence (either through trial or through a plea of guilty) to serve two or more sentences consecutively. That is the sentences are added together so that an offender may receive a total sentence lasting several lifetimes. This practice is commonly used in the United States, but is relatively rare in Canada.

consensual crime Any crime in which the "victim" is a willing participant (drug use, prostitution, etc.). Also known as *victimless crime*.

consensus perspective Also known as *functionalism*, the foundation of this perspective is the assumption that societies have an inherent tendency to maintain themselves in a state of relative equilibrium through the mutually adjustive and supportive interaction of their principal institutions. The approach also assumes that effective maintenance of a particular form of society is in the common interest of all its members. This perspective has its roots in Émile Durkheim (1858–1917). *See also* **Durkheim, Émile**; **functionalist explanation**; **structural functionalism**.

conservatism It is important to think of conservatism as a set of ideas that is not necessarily the same as those upheld by political parties calling themselves "Conservative." Some modern "Conservative" parties are strongly associated with the idea of a reduced role for government (privatization, reduced social programs) and promotion of free markets. This perspective, however, is based on classical liberalism rather than conservatism. Conservative ideas do not welcome the unrestricted operations of a free market, but value social stability and the maintenance of traditional community bonds and social hierarchies. Conservatives assume that institutions and values that have lasted a long time embody the collective experience of the community. They have persisted because they have played a valuable and positive role in society. *See also* **classical liberalism; neo-conservatism.**

Conservative Party of Canada This new federal party was created in December 2003 from a union of the Progressive Conservative Party and the Canadian Alliance Party (successor to the Reform Party). The joining of the two parties is seen as a way to end the division of the political right in Canada and to create a more nationwide support base than either of the individual parties was able to achieve in recent elections.

conspicuous consumption The public display of individual possession and consumption of expensive goods and services. The term, used by Thorsten Veblen (1857–1929), has been used to convey the idea of a society where social status is earned and displayed by patterns of consumption, rather than by what an individual does or makes. Reference: Veblen, Thorsten. (1899). *The Theory of the Leisure Class.* New York: Mentor [1933].

constitution The set of arrangements by which a nation governs itself. In Canada the core of the constitution is the BNA Act and its amendments (now called the Constitution Act, 1867) and the Constitution Act, 1982. Most of what we take to be the Constitution, however, is not contained in these documents: things like responsible government, political parties, Cabinet, and the bureaucracy are absent. Some of these matters are covered by laws like the Elections Act, the House of Commons Act, the Legislative Assembly Acts, and the Public Service Acts. In Canada, constitutional convention, embodying political traditions and practices, is unusually important and Canada's system of government cannot be understood simply from the written laws. For example, it is constitutional convention, but not law, that ministers must be members of the House of Commons or the Senate, or that the Governor General must appoint the leader of the largest party in the House of Commons as prime minister. It is appropriate to also include court judgments interpreting constitutional Acts and formal agreements between federal and provincial governments as parts of Canada's constitutional arrangements.

Constitutional Act, 1791 Passed by the Parliament of Britain under pressure from the United Empire Loyalists who had arrived in Canada (many into the old province of Quebec) and wished to continue to live under British institutions, this Act divided the old province of Quebec into Upper Canada (now Ontario) and Lower Canada (Quebec). A powerful British minority remained in Lower Canada and these people were given significant representation in the legislative assembly (30 percent of the seats for 10 percent of the population). Upper Canada elected to develop British institutions, while Lower Canada choose to retain the arrangements it had been granted under the Quebec Act of 1774. *See also* **United Empire Loyalists.**

constitutional monarchy *See* **monarchy, constitutional.**

constructive murder This category of murder was struck down by the Supreme Court in 1987 (*Queen v. Vaillancourt*). Constructive murder (section 213 of the Criminal Code) said that if a person caused the death of a person in the process of committing a serious offence and had a weapon, then that person was guilty of murder. There was no need to prove intent of the accused, so there was no real defence. The particular case involved an appeal by one of two men who had robbed a poolroom, one of whom carried a gun that the other (the appellant) thought was not loaded and assumed was not going to be used. In the course of events, a customer of the poolroom was shot and killed. According to this section of the Criminal Code, both men were guilty of murder. The Supreme Court found that intent, or *mens rea*, was a necessary component for the commission of a crime as serious as murder, that the Criminal Code provisions thus violated the Charter, and allowed the appeal ordering a new trial on reduced charges. Reference: *R. v. Vaillancourt* [1987] 2 S.C.R. 636.

consumer culture A culture in which the attainment of ownership and possession of goods and services is presented as the primary aim of individual endeavour and the key source of social status and prestige. *See also* **audience**; **popular culture.**

content analysis A research method involving the gathering of data capturing one or more variables descriptive of the content of a cultural expression such as movies, newspaper stories, speeches, cartoons, or advertisements. A researcher may, for example, analyze stories of sexual assault to determine how blame is allocated in such stories, or may examine the covers of popular magazines such as *Time* or *Maclean's* to see which sex or racial group is typically depicted, or to observe differences in the depiction of men and women. Reference: Voumvakis, S.E., and R.V. Ericson. (1984). *News Accounts of Attacks on Women*. Toronto: Centre of Criminology.

continuance commitment Adherence to a criminal or other identity arising from the unattractiveness or unavailability of alternate lifestyles.

contradictions of capitalism The term is associated with Karl Marx (1818–1883), who claimed that capitalist societies suffered from two irresolvable problems that would prevent both social harmony and a stable economic life. First, Marx assumed that the competitive processes of a capitalist market society would lead to a concentration of capital ownership in fewer and fewer hands. Marx built this claim on the assumption, which he held in common with *laissez faire* economics, that a competitive economy must lead inevitably to the elimination of some producers by others; there must be winners and losers and the winners would grow increasingly large. Capitalism, Marx argued, contrary to the general assumption of *laissez faire* economics, had an inherent tendency towards concentration of capital in oligopolies and monopolies. The concentration of capital involved, first of all, the displacement of the handworker and the craftsworker and increasing domination of factory-based technology. An industrial proletariat of wage workers emerged, and grew larger, as independent producers were eliminated by factory-based competition. As capitalist corporations grew more concentrated and larger, the number of individuals owning the means of production became fewer. The class structure became polarized, and the economic and social conditions of the two opposed main classes more strongly contrasted, leading to political activation of the working class and prolonged conflict with the dominant bourgeois class through political and industrial organization. It is this development of social polarization that provides the unsolvable social or relational contradiction of capitalist society. The social organization of a capitalist society also presented an inherent structural contradiction in the economic dynamics of capitalism. While capitalism revolutionized the means of production by promoting the greatest economic development in human history, its class structure focused the capacity to consume in a tiny minority of the population. The mass social scale of production could not remain compatible with the concentration of wealth in fewer and fewer hands. As a result, there must be inherent instability, or anarchy, in the whole capitalist system of production. The social effects of such instability in turn must intensify the political struggle of social classes hastening the event of socialist revolution. *See also* **communism**; **dialectical**; **dialectical materialism**; **monopoly**; **oligopoly**.

control variable In causal analysis, in order to test for spuriousness, researchers use one or more control variables. These are variables, which may be related to the independent variable or the dependent variable, that may produce confusing results. To avoid this confusion, the researcher holds these variables constant (they do not vary), allowing the investigator to determine if the original relationship between the independent variable and dependent variable still holds. For example, if looking at the relationship between race and sentence severity in court it would be necessary to hold prior criminal record constant since prior record may be related to both sentence severity and to race. *See also* **variables**.

conventional crime Those traditional, illegal behaviours that most people think of as crime, such as property offences and assaults. Most crime is conventional crime. Non-conventional crime might include organized crime, white-collar crime, or political crime.

conviction An act or process of finding an accused (one charged) guilty of an offence. To have a conviction is to have been found guilty of an offence. The term has different meanings in ordinary language. For example, to have a conviction may mean to hold some belief firmly. *See also* **charge**; **guilty**.

Co-operative Commonwealth Federation (CCF) Founded in 1932 in Calgary, this party adopted a radical socialist political program at its first convention in Regina, Saskatchewan in 1933. At the federal level, the party built popularity during World War II and briefly led in public opinion polls in 1943. In 1945, 28 Members of Parliament were elected. Although the party had limited success in federal politics, it gained power in Saskatchewan in 1944 to become North America's first social democratic government. The main support for the party came from farmers' movements, labour unions, and from socialists in many spheres of society, especially the churches. In 1961, the party was dissolved and was re-established as the New Democratic Party. Reference: Lipset, S. (1950). *Agrarian Socialism: The Co-operative Commonwealth Federation in Saskatchewan.* Berkeley, CA: University of California.

CORCAN The federal prison industries corporation, established in 1977, provides skills training to federal inmates in "businesses" producing goods and services sold to the public sector.

corporal punishment Physical punishment of an offender; may range from spanking to flogging or branding. By the end of the 18th century there were attempts to curtail or prevent this form of punishment, but it was occasionally used in federal prisons until the late 1960s. It was officially abolished in 1972.

corporate crime A crime committed by corporate employees or owners to financially advantage a corporation. It may involve acts like fraud, environmental pollution, creation of unsafe products, and dangerous work environments. *See also* **white-collar crime**.

corporate elite The owners, directors, and senior executives of the largest and most important of a nation's business corporations. They can be variously defined according to criteria of corporate size and type of enterprise. *See also* **comprador elite**.

corporatism A political ideology historically associated with fascism. It upheld strong political leadership and strict social hierarchy, and attacked the democratic system as inefficient, indecisive, and disorganized. The main idea was that the major sectors of industry, organized in groups called syndicates, should have direct political representation in the political system as a part of legislatures. In theory, labour as well as capital has representation, but labour's voice is controlled because free unions are suppressed. As a political doctrine, corporatism has had only a marginal influence in Canada, but the idea of giving corporations a direct role in shaping public economic policy is evident in the modern globalization process, where corporations acquire rights to sue governments and where international bureaucratic organizations set trading and investment rules that strictly limit the actions of elected governments of nation states.

corpus delicti Does not refer to the body of anyone. Rather it is the body of crime, meaning the legal foundation of the offence itself. In short, the particular statutory elements of a crime must be established. It is somewhat similar to the term *actus reus*.

Corrections and Conditional Release Act The Act that sets out the purposes of parole, the principles of conditional release programs like parole, and establishes the types of early release programs available to inmates.

correlate Any variable which is correlated (the relationship between the two variables is one of correlation) with another variable. Age and sex are the two strongest correlates of crime. *See also* **correlation**.

correlation Criminologists from an empiricist perspective tend to look at the social world in terms of variables (anything that varies within a population or group rather than being constant). Everyone in your class is a student, so that is a constant; however, there is a great deal of variation by factors like sex, age, income, program, GPA, religion, and ethnic heritage. If one gathers information from the whole class on these variables, we might begin to see that some variables vary in patterned ways. People with a particular ethnic heritage may tend to be more religious than those from other heritages. This would suggest a correlation: as one variable varies, so does the other. If there were more students of that particular ethnic heritage in the class, then religiosity for the group would also increase. As one goes up, so does the other. This is referred to as a positive correlation or relationship. If one variable goes up as the other goes down, this is called a negative relationship. For example, as age goes up, the crime rate goes down: this is a negative (or inverse) correlation. A correlation does not mean that one variable causes the other. For example, research done for the Marshall inquiry attempted to determine if there was a correlation between being Black and receiving a harsh sentence. A causal relationship has to be determined by further research work.

correlation, zero order A correlation between two variables that does not include a control variable. A first-order correlation, then, would include one control variable as well as the independent and dependent variables.

counterculture A set of cultural ideas that, to some extent, differ from and conflict with those generally upheld in the society. A counterculture develops when members of groups identify common values that distinguish them from others. These groups may be based on common appearance, ethnic group, sexuality, status, or social behaviour. The term is close in meaning to subculture, but the concept of counterculture stresses the idea of an open and active opposition to dominant cultural values.

court of last resort The last court to which an offender can appeal his or her case, usually the Supreme Court of Canada. It is often suggested as well that the "public" may be the court of last resort, suggesting that citizens themselves have to decide the morality of an issue. *See also* **Supreme Court of Canada**.

court reporter An individual, usually working under contract to the court, who produces verbatim transcripts of court proceedings.

court martial A military court mandated to try members of the defence forces for service offences as defined in the National Defence Act.

crack A form of cocaine produced by using ammonia of baking soda to remove the hydrochlorides from street cocaine, in order to create a crystalline form of cocaine that can be smoked. This is not a pure form of cocaine, however, as it contains residues from the baking soda and hydrochloride. Crack provides a powerful high, and users become addicted quite quickly. Also known as *rock*, *gravel*, and *roxanne*. *See also* **cocaine**.

craft unions A structure of labour unions that brings together workers within the same area of craft or skill (typographical unions, carpenters, stoneworkers, iron moulders, boilermakers, railway engineers, etc.). These unions, because their members possessed crucial knowledge and physical and conceptual skills, had considerable influence in the workplace and struggled to maintain control of their work process and standards of training and apprenticeship. They became uneasy about the rise of industrial unions, which brought together all workers in a single industry regardless of their craft or level of skill. In this way, they were somewhat elitist and perhaps cautious. Elizabeth Comack (1985) argues that 19th century Canadian industrialists, with the assistance of the federal government, exploited this tension within the union movement and used craft union fears of the threat of competition from Asian immigrants to transform concern about labour problems into a race issue. The government introduced legislation to control narcotics, which they linked to the Asian community, and this encouraged suspicion of Asians from other workers, thus splitting and weakening the union movement. It took many decades for some of the rifts within the union movement to be healed. *See also* **syndicalism**.

Cressey, Donald, R. (1919–87) Professor of sociology at the University of California, Santa Barbara, known for his investigations and analysis of organized crime and financial crime. His most well known book was only slightly facetious in its conclusion that since the Cosa Nostra was so powerful, the authorities should negotiate with them and agree to legalize their gambling rackets provided they pay taxes on the profits and give up involvement in politics and political funding. Reference: Cressey, Donald, R. (1969). *Theft of the Nation: The Structure and Operations of Organized Crime in America*. New York: Harper and Row.

crime Any form of human behaviour that is designated by law as criminal and subject to a penal sanction. While crime is the central focus of criminology and a major topic of the sociology of deviance, there is no consensus on how to define the term. While the everyday use of the term seems to refer to intentional violations of criminal law or public law in general, many sociologists look at crime as a social construction, or a label, and look at crime being created through the passing of laws and the application of those laws. *See also* **classical criminology**; **criminology**; **critical criminology**; **deviance**; **labelling theory**.

crime-control model An ideal type used to capture one side of a debate about the central values or practices of the criminal justice system: should the central value be the protection of the liberty of the individual citizen or should the central value be the maintenance of social order? This model gives emphasis to values and practices that would exert or enhance the system's capacity to control crime, and thus maintain social order, through police action, prosecution, conviction, and punishment. *See also* **due process model**. Reference: Parker, H.

(1968). *The Limits of Criminal Sanctions.* Stanford: Stanford University.

crime funnel The image of a "funnel" refers to the much lower number of crimes detected and punished by the criminal justice system than the number actually committed. This model implies that crime is an objective occurrence; it is thought to exist in the qualities of certain acts without needing to be recognized, identified, and officially responded to. This is what is called a *realist* assumption about crime. Symbolic interactionists and phenomenologists, however, see "crime" as something created and defined by processes of social interaction and interpretation and reject both the "realist" assumption and the concept of the crime funnel. *See also* **crime net.** Reference: Brannigan, A. (1984). *Crimes, Courts and Corrections: An Introduction to Crime and Social Control in Canada.* Toronto: Holt, Rinehart and Winston.

crime net A model of the relationship between crime and the resources employed in its detection and punishment by the criminal justice system. In this model, the agents of the criminal justice system (the law makers and law enforcers in particular) are thought to operate like fishers: they can use nets of varying dimensions or with varying sizes of mesh, and the "net" will determine how much crime is caught. This model tends to be favoured by critical criminologists, as they are interested in understanding how the state can use the criminal justice system to support particular interest groups in society or to legitimize the political and economic arrangements of the society. Like the crime funnel, it reflects realist assumptions about crime. Crime is assumed to exist objectively; the net simply determines what quantity of it will be revealed. Symbolic interactionists and ethnomethodologists would reject this model and insist that crimes are only those events that are recognized, identified, or categorized as crime. *See also* **crime funnel**; **net widening**. Reference: Brannigan, A. (1984). *Crimes, Courts and Corrections: An Introduction to Crime and Social Control in Canada.* Toronto: Holt, Rinehart and Winston.

criminal definitions Refers to the fact that crime is socially defined and that these definitions will vary from society to society.

criminal identity A social category, imposed by the community, that correctly or incorrectly defines an individual as a particular type of criminal. The identity will pervasively shape their social interactions with others. It is similar in concept to *master status.*

criminal injuries compensation Begun in Saskatchewan in 1967, every province now has a program to provide financial compensation for injuries or death resulting from being a victim of crime or attempting to prevent a crime.

criminal insanity *See* **mental disorder defence.**

criminal justice studies While related to criminology, the field of criminal justice studies tends to be less theoretical and more focused on the administration of justice and acquiring the detailed knowledge of how the justice system works in preparation for employment in the field of justice. *See also* **criminology**. Reference: Griffiths, Curt, and Alison Cunningham. (2003). *Canadian Criminal Justice: A Primer.* Toronto: Nelson.

criminogenic Those conditions or structures that themselves seem to create crime. Just as, for example, hospitals create disease (e.g., infection), it is possible that prisons or even courts or youth correction centres are "criminogenic."

criminology A social science studying crime and related phenomena such as law making, criminal behaviour, victimization, and punishment. In North America, this social science emerged from sociology, while in Europe, it is more related to law. There is some debate as to whether it is an independent social science or if it is a field of interdisciplinary study. As with many social sciences, it contains many competing perspectives. *See also* **classical criminology**; **Positivist school**. Reference: Siegel, Larry, and Chris McCormick. (2003). *Criminology in Canada* (2nd ed.). Toronto: Nelson.

criminology abstracts Found in academic libraries and larger public libraries, criminology and other social science abstracts are indexes that provide information on all articles published in a specified array of journals. Typically these indexes are organized alphabetically by author, title, and subject. A valuable resource for everyone interested in criminology or criminal justice topics.

critical criminology A form of criminology (the study of crime) using a conflict perspective of some kind: Marxism, feminism, political economy theory, or critical theory. In all of these, the focus is on locating the genesis of crime and the interpretation of what is "justice" within a structure of class and status inequalities. Law and the definition and punishment of crime are then seen as connected to a system of social inequality and as tools for the reproduction of this inequality. Reference: Fleming, T. (ed.). (1985). *The New Criminologies in Canada: State, Crime, and Control.* Toronto: Oxford University Press.

critical perspectives Refers to perspectives within sociology that uncover and analyze the sources of social inequality and advocate social change. Two examples are Marxism and feminism. Marxism examines class inequality and advocates collective ownership of the means of production as a foundation for establishing social equality. Feminism examines gender inequality and advocates a transformation of gender roles in society and a systematic uprooting of cultural attitudes that support and encourage the social subordination of women. The term is closely associated with conflict perspectives. *See also* **conflict perspectives**; **feminism**. Reference: Taylor, Ian, Paul Walton, and J. Young. (1975). *Critical Criminology.* London: Routledge.

critical theory A sociology developed by the Frankfurt school that is influenced by divergent intellectual ideas, including Marxism and psychoanalysis. It starts from two principles: opposition to the status quo and the idea that history can be potentially progressive. Together, these principles imply a position from which to make judgments of human activity (rather than just describing) and provide the tools for criticism. Sometimes associated with highlighting the "dark side" of modernity, critical theory attacks social ideas and practices that stand in the way of social justice and human emancipation (the rational organization of society as an association of free people). Critical theory is opposed to "bourgeois liberalism".

Crofton, Walter Crofton was head of the Irish prison system in the 18th century. He built on the ideas of Alexander Maconochie to develop a system of early release from prison organized on a progressive system of moving toward less intense forms of incarceration until deemed worthy of full release.

cross-cultural analysis Also known as *comparative analysis.* A method central to many social sciences involving the comparative examination of differing cultures. This method is crucial for distinguishing universal aspects of human culture and social organization from those that are particular to individual societies. By observing the range of variation in culture and organization between societies, a deeper understanding of individual development, family, gender, crime control, social inequality, etc. can be developed.

cross-sectional research Research that makes observations at only one period in time (for example, conducting a survey or opinion poll). It is analogous to taking a still picture of the population or group being investigated. Longitudinal research, on the other hand, makes more than one set of observations and can be compared to a simple moving picture. *See also* **longitudinal studies**.

Crown caution The Youth Criminal Justice Act allows the Crown to issue a formal caution to a young offender and, with this, terminate prosecution.

crown counsel A public official (i.e., a government employee), typically a lawyer, who conducts criminal proceedings on behalf of the Crown and against the accused. Also called a Crown attorney or prosecutor. Reference: Grosman, B. (1969). *The Prosecutor: An Inquiry into the Exercise of Discretion.* Toronto: University of Toronto Press.

culpable To be blameworthy or responsible for a wrongful act. This concept is not the same as "guilty."

cult This concept was originally developed as one component of a typology: churches, denominations, sects, and cults. Churches and denominations are seen as established forms of religious organization, while sects are groups that have broken away from established groups in order to preserve what they thought were central traditions or orthodoxy. Cults, on the other hand, are religious forms and expressions that are unacceptable or outside cultural norms, and thus seen as the first stage of forming a new religion. However, the term now has a rather negative meaning, suggesting strange beliefs, charismatic leadership, manipulation of members, strong emotional bonding, and slavish devotion to the group. *See also* **church**; **sect**.

cult of domesticity The belief that family and individual life are most fulfilling when experienced in a private household where women are the chief homemakers and caregivers. Also associated with the idea that women have moral and temperamental qualities that are best expressed in the personal and domestic sphere of life. The cult of domesticity has been given emphasis at various times in Canadian history, most recently in the period from 1945 to approximately 1960. *See also* **baby boom**.

cultural capital As used by P. Bourdieu (1973) in the sociological analysis of education, this term refers to the way that the schools reflect standards of cultural expression and definitions of valued abilities that are characteristic of the socially and economically dominant class in society. Students who bring this cultural capital (a form of human capital) to the school are apt to be most successful in meeting criteria set by the schools; the result is that the school system supports and justifies the privileges of children of the wealthy and powerful. The school can alternately be seen as bestowing cultural capital on students, improving the equality of opportunity for those groups not already in possession of this capital essential for maintaining an open class society. Reference: Bourdieu, P. (1973). "Cultural Reproduction and Social Reproduction," in R. Brown (ed.), *Knowledge, Education and Cultural Change*. London: Tavistock.

cultural construction A perspective on a subject that is shaped by cultural assumptions, rather than having a natural or objective basis. For example, marriage is a cultural construction: it is not biologically necessary for men and women to marry. Another example is gender: we have concepts of masculine and feminine that suggest to us how men and women should behave, but few of these gender differences are determined by biological sex.

cultural explanation An explanation for crime (such as homicide) that is phrased in terms of the culture of the offender's nation or sub-group. John Hagen (1984) for example, has argued that Canada has a lower homicide rate than does the US because Canada's culture (its values) is more traditional than that of the US. Canada's culture, he argues, tends to focus on respect for authority and communitarianism, and is more elitist than American culture. Reference: Hagan, John. (1977). *The Disreputable Pleasures: Crime and Deviance in Canada*. Toronto: McGraw-Hill [1984].

cultural genocide Comes from the word *gens*, meaning a clan or community of people related by common descent. The idea of cultural genocide implies the process of undermining, suppressing, and ultimately eliminating, cultures. In Canada, the term has been used to refer to the government policy of using residential schools to separate native children from connection with their own cultures and languages and to impose European culture upon them. *See also* **potlatch**; **residential schools**.

cultural imperialism The practice of systematically spreading the influence of one culture over others by means of physical and economic domination. Usually involves an assumption of cultural superiority (ethnocentrism). In Canada, the term is associated with the concern that the power of the United States' entertainment and communications media tends to marginalize Canadian stories and Canadian experience and reduce Canadians' ability to communicate with each other. With the spread of satellite television, cultural imperialism is seen as a global problem. *See also* **ethnocentrism**; **imperialism**.

cultural studies Associated with the Frankfurt school in the early decades of the 20th century and the writings of the Birmingham Centre for Cultural Studies (begun in 1964). Both of these groups began to look at culture as a force shaping lived human experience, rather than at the level of abstract generalization. Their focus was on examining the function of culture in everyday life and its role in a system of social hierarchy and domination. These studies eventually began to build on Antonio Gramsci's (1891–1937) concept of hegemony to demonstrate how class or gender rule is supported not only by overt mechanisms of law and the exercise of power, but is pervasively dispersed throughout society in institutional structures and cultural beliefs and values. Cultural studies now include a substantial portion of sociological work. Cultural studies is now associated with the Birmingham School in the U.K. and the work of Stuart Hall. *See also* **hegemony**. Reference: Davis, Helen. 2004. *Understanding Stuart Hall*. London: Sage Publishing.

culturally prescribed aspirations A rejection of the notion that aspirations are entirely a matter of self-creation; rather they are defined by culture and transmitted by other members of the society. Sociologist Robert Merton (1910–2003) assumes that everyone within a culture shares the same cultural goals or aspirations and that the primary goal in modern capitalist society is wealth. It should be noted that Merton wrote during the Great Depression, and his idea may be appropriate for an age of scarcity. Do they apply to an age of prosperity? Other sociologists have argued, and demonstrated, that groups of people may have quite different aspirations or goals.

culture The generally shared knowledge, beliefs, and values of members of society. Culture is conveyed from generation to generation through the process of socialization. While culture is made up of ideas, some sociologists also argue that it is not exclusively ideational but can be found in human-made material objects. They define a separate "material culture." This distinction appears weak, since human-made material objects must embody human ideas. Culture and social structure are considered as the two key components of society and are therefore the foundation concepts of sociology.

culture of poverty thesis The theory that certain groups and individuals tend to persist in a state of poverty because they have distinct beliefs, values, and ways of behaving that are incompatible with economic success. The thesis is controversial and is opposed by situational theory, which locates the genesis of poverty in economic and social structures of society rather than in the value orientations of individuals or groups. Reference: Lewis, Oscar. (1966). "The Culture of Poverty." *Scientific American* 215: 19–25.

culture shock Where an individual encounters a new and different culture and experiences a major disruption of their normal assumptions about social values and behaviour. Their old values seem unable to provide guidance in the new situation, yet the new culture seems strange and unacceptable. It is experienced by individuals who travel to a very different society and discover cultural ideas and practices that differ very much from their own. It is common among immigrant groups and can sometimes affect whole societies if they are swept up in rapid social change. The concept has been applied to the experiences of aboriginal peoples following colonial contact.

D

Dalkon shield An IUD used by women as a form of birth control and produced by A.H. Robbins. During the 1970s, women began to suffer health problems as a result of the use of this device; investigation determined there was a design fault that could have been corrected by the maker.

damages The resolution in a civil suit involving the awarding of money to compensate another. The court can award compensatory damages or punitive damages.

dangerous offender An offender sentenced under Part 24 of the Criminal Code of Canada and receiving an indeterminate prison sentence. Introduced in 1977 to replace the habitual offender legislation. This sentence is available to specific offences (serious personal injury offences) and is determined by a special sentencing hearing in which the Crown must prove a future threat to members of society. Dangerous offender sentencing is not used often, but there are significant variations across the provinces. While determination of "dangerousness" usually occurs after conviction and before sentencing, Parliament has made it possible for a prison inmate to be declared a dangerous offender if he or she is close to the end of a sentence and is deemed to be a threat to the community upon release. *See also* **indeterminate sentence**. Reference: Bonta, J., A Harris, and D. Carriere. (1998). "The Dangerous Offender Provisions: Are They Targeting the Right Offenders?" *Canadian Journal of Criminology* 40 (4): 377–400.

dark figure of crime The amount of crime that is unreported or unknown. The total amount of crime in a community consists of crimes that are known or recorded and the dark figure of crime. Criminologists have used differing methods (like victimization surveys) to try to decrease the amount of unknown or unrecorded crime. The notion of a dark figure of crime is based on a positivist approach to criminology and assumes that crime is real or objective.

date rape drug Rohypnol is a drug used in the short-term treatment of some sleep disorders and came to be used by those attending raves as it causes euphoria rather quickly (it may also cause drowsiness). Since this state of euphoria also reduced inhibition and memory loss, it also came to be used to dope the drinks of women in order to get them to have sex. The drug is also known as *ropies*, *ruffies*, *R-2*, *rib*, and *rope*.

Davis Inlet A Mushuau Innu population of approximately 535 living in Davis Inlet of Labrador gained international attention in 1993 when video pictures spread across the nation showing young people openly sniffing gasoline and talking to the interviewer about their hopelessness and the suicides of many of their friends. The community became a symbol of the plight of many aboriginal nations within Canada. While government aid was provided, problems continued for many years. The community has now been relocated to a more accessible area (now called Natuashih) with richer resources to support traditional occupations of fishing and hunting.

Dawson, Charles A. (1887–1964) Dawson trained at the University of Chicago and established the first sociology program at McGill University, Montreal, in 1922. Being shaped by the Chicago school, he educated students in the areas of urban studies, social reform, and the development of crime and deviance in the urban community. *See also* **Chicago school.**

day parole A form of conditional release from prison that allows the inmate to reside in a community-based facility and participate in community programs. This type of release is used to provide inmates with gradual release into the community and in preparation for full parole.

debt The total amount owed by governments to lenders who have bought bonds and Treasury bills sold by the government to cover past deficits and operating expenses. A substantial portion of Canadian government debt is now held by investors outside of the country. Criminologists are interested in the level of debt since some theories claim that as national debt rises, there is pressure to cut social spending, and this may result in an increase in spending on social control.

decarceration *See* **deinstitutionalization.**

deconstruction A concept central to postmodernism, this is a process of rigorously analyzing and making apparent the assumptions, judgments, and values that underlie social arrangements and intellectual ideas. Authors such as J. Derrida reject the idea that texts (e.g., the writing of Marx or Plato) have an objective link to external events and represent truth. Rather they suggest that texts contain within them material that undermine the claims or arguments the text itself is presenting. This being so, these texts cannot be used to learn about the external events of the social world or to evaluate those events. The text can only be examined internally to search for the hidden assumptions, or subtext, that give it meaning. *See also* **postmodernism.** Reference: Milovanovic, Dragan. (1988). *A Primer in the Sociology of Law.* New York: Harrow and Heston.

decriminalization Removing a prohibited activity from the Criminal Code, thus making it non-criminal. The activity may continue to be regulated or controlled through other legal mechanisms. Today, demands for decriminalization are mostly associated with drug use and possession. Critics of these laws argue that they create social problems and promote crime by defining victimless activity, engaged in by millions of Canadians, as criminal. They claim that drugs like marijuana are harmless and argue that even use of hard drugs is a health and social issue and should not be a focus of criminal law.

defence counsel A trial lawyer hired by the accused or appointed by the court to defend the accused in criminal proceedings or to represent him or her before a court of law. *See also* **legal aid.**

defendant In a criminal case, this is the accused. In a civil case, it is the person responding to the claims of the plaintiff.

defensible space A concept from environmental criminology, suggesting that public spaces should be designed to create a sense of ownership among residents or users. The general philosophy is that environmental design can make a space easier to defend from potential criminal activity. Reference: Newman, Oscar. (1973). *Defensible Space: Crime Prevention Through Urban Design.* New York: Macmillan.

deficit The gap between governments' revenues, from taxes and charges, and their expenditures, on programs, infrastructure, and debt financing. Canada ran a deficit from the 1970s until approximately 1998 when the Liberal government of Jean Chrétien brought in a balanced budget. This long-term deficit left Canada with a substantial debt that is now being reduced from an emerging budgetary surplus. *See also* **debt.**

defining the situation Refers to the process through which humans go when trying to comprehend the social situations in which they find themselves and deciding on what values and norms are relevant in guiding social interaction. If one contrasts macro-structural studies and symbolic interactionism, this concept is associated with the latter. The structural view tends to focus on the situation individuals are in, not on their definition of the situation. The term was first used by W.I. Thomas (1863–1947).

definition of the situation In symbolic interactionism, sociologists reject the notion of objective social structures existing independently of the actor; it is assumed that actors behave in accordance with how they have defined the situation. Definitions of the situation can be negotiated by two or more actors. For example, when a 911 operator receives a call, the operator and the caller interact in negotiating the definition of the caller's situation. This definition then determines how the caller will be received, what message may go out over the radio, and what action may be taken. If a situation is defined as real, it is real; a subjective approach to the study of social phenomena. *See also* **symbolic interactionism**.

deinstitutionalization Reduction in the size of populations held in institutions of involuntary confinement, primarily mental hospitals and prisons. This movement began in the 1970s and was very successful in reducing the size of mental hospitals. It was thought that patients would be better off in the community, and that community care would be cheaper than institutional care. But many communities found that support resources were inadequate, leaving uncared for and confused former patients to wander the streets of Canada's towns and cities. In the United States, the program was applied to prisons, and for a short time prison populations appeared to decrease, but there was a subsequent increase of unprecedented dimensions. Reference: Chan, J.B.L., and R.V. Ericson. (1981). *Decarceration and the Economy of Penal Reform.* Toronto: Centre of Criminology, University of Toronto; Scull, A.T. (1977). *Decarceration: Community Treatment and the Deviant: A Radical View.* Cambridge: Polity.

Delgamuukw A major case on aboriginal rights decided by the Supreme Court of Canada in 1997. The court held that aboriginal title to land was not extinguished by the establishment of sovereignty by the Crown. It also stated that Crown ownership of lands was a separate issue from jurisdiction over those lands. Where aboriginal title to land was established by long-term exclusive and continuous occupation, the Crown may still infringe on aboriginal title for valid legislative objectives like settling foreign populations or for economic development. The Court specified that groups with aboriginal title should be involved in the decision-making process regarding their lands. Depending on the nature of any proposed infringement, fair compensation would normally be required. Reference: Persky, Stan. (1998). *Delgamuuk.* Vancouver: Douglas and McIntyre.

demand characteristic As used in experimental psychology, refers to unintended features of the experiment that affect the results, thus compromising the internal validity of the study. The term is also used in the sociology of deviance to refer to those organizational features of work settings, other than the formal goals of the organizations or principles such as due process or fairness, that shape arrest decisions, plea bargaining, or jury deliberations. Examples of demand characteristics that police officers may attend to in making decisions on the street are the informal expectations of police culture, their work load, their need to accumulate overtime, or organizational rules. Reference: Blumberg, A. (1967). "The Practice of Law as a Confidence Game." *Law and Society Review* 1 (1): 15–39.

demand mobility A form of social mobility that takes place over time. It is not caused by individuals ascending or descending in class or status, but rather by changes in the occupational structure of the economy. It results from there being greater demand for some kinds of labour and a shrinking demand for others, and not from the openness of the society. In a situation of high demand mobility, with little openness, one might find that workers occupy the same relative positions in social and economic position as their parents although performing quite different kinds of work. *See also* **equality of opportunity**; **social mobility**.

Demeter, Peter Demeter, a wealthy real estate developer, was not home at the time of his wife Christine's brutal murder in 1973. However, a witness declared that Demeter had discussed his wife's murder with him. Another witness said that the man who had killed Demeter's wife had been shot by the police in another incident, but that he had been contacted by Christine to murder her husband. When she changed her mind and would not pay, the "contractor" murdered her. The jury, which had not heard this evidence, convicted Demeter. In 1985 he was charged again, while in prison, for counselling two convicts to murder the son of his cousin. Again in 1988, a jury found him guilty of conspiring to murder the daughter of his former lawyer. Reference: Jonas, George, and B. Amiel. (1983). *By Persons Unknown: The Strange Death of Christine Demeter.* Toronto: Macmillan of Canada.

democracy In the original Greek literally "rule by the people." In the Greek world, political organization was usually centred around "city states," and male citizens had equal rights to participate in government. The Greek concept of citizenship implied that citizens must become actively involved in government, not just vote for representatives. In modern usage, the term has become narrowed to mean a system of government where citizens have equal legal rights to vote in free elections. *See also* **autocracy**; **meritocracy**; **plutocracy**.

democratic deficit The gap between the principle of democratic control exercised by citizens of a nation and the actual amount of democratic control available to them. This control may be limited by government's executive domination over elected assemblies because of the system of strict party discipline or from the transfer of decision making to non-elected agencies. Many social scientists are of the belief that this deficit has increased substantially because of free trade agreements, the deregulation of corporate activity, the growth of multinational corporations, which are now beyond the ability of any one nation to control, and the growth of super bureaucracies designed to coordinate cross-border activities.

demographic transition The transformation of the structure of a population accompanying the change from an agrarian economy to an industrial economy. The former society is characterized by high birth rates and high death rates, providing some stability to population size. The transition period typically involves declining death rates while birth rates remain high, leading to population growth. Stability is found in mature industrial societies with low death rates and low birth rates, a situation that creates rising average age of the population. *See also* **demography**.

demography The study of populations, including their size, structure, and transformations. Studying the structure of a population provides some predictive power about crime rates. For example, a community with a high ratio of young males will have more crime than a community with a high retirement population.

dependency ratio The proportion of the population that is outside the labour force and thus dependent on the economic activity of those working. This is typically calculated as the proportion of the population between the ages of 0 to 16 plus those over 65 to those between the ages of 16–65. As industrial societies have matured, and particularly in those with a large baby boom such as Canada, the dependency ratio has increased significantly (for example, from 1 dependent to 20 workers to 1 dependent for 3 workers). *See also* **baby boom**; **demographic transition**.

dependent development A central concept of dependency theory. Rather than seeing the world's nations dividing economic labour and interacting as equal partners, dependent development suggests that some nations are able to impose unequal exchanges on others, and thus retard the economic development of these nations or make their development dependent on stronger or more economically advanced nations. Dependent development has typically involved the exporting of primary resources. *See also* **colonialism**; **imperialism**; **metropolis-hinterland theory**.

dependent variable In a causal analysis, the dependent variable is that variable considered to be the effect; it depends on the independent variable. For example, if examining the relationship between race and sentence length, sentence length would be the dependent variable. *See also* **independent variable**.

descriptive statistics Statistical tools or techniques used to describe a sample or a population. For example, a mean, median, or mode is a descriptive statistic. *See also* **inferential statistics**.

desert-based sentencing Court sentencing that reflects solely the seriousness of the offence committed by the convicted offender. An offender's previous convictions play only a limited role in this model. Sentences do not reflect an interest in rehabilitation nor the deterrence of future offenders, only that the punishment fit the particular crime. This model was clearly articulated by the American Quaker Society's report, *Struggle for Justice*, 1971. The Quakers are the same society that brought North America the rehabilitation-based penitentiary. *See also* **proportionality**. Reference: American Friends Service Committee. (1971). *Struggle for Justice: A Report on Crime and Punishment in America.* New York: Hill and Wang.

determinate sentence A sentence (usually one of incarceration) by the court for a fixed period so the offender knows exactly when he or she will be released from prison or supervision. Canada has a system of determinate sentencing, but also has parole, which allows the inmate to be released to the community prior to the expiration of the sentence. *See also* **flat time sentencing**; **indeterminate sentencing**.

determinism The theory that examination of one or more definable factors allows for a complete explanation and prediction of the characteristics of society or the individual. For example, to argue that societies gain all their central characteristics from the psychological drives of human beings is a form of psychological determinism; to explain the social roles and behaviour of men and women by reference chiefly to their sex is biological determinism. *See also* **economic determinism**; **methodological individualism**; **psychological reductionism**.

deterrence The attempt to control crime by creating a threat of punishment; this is directed to specific individuals (individual deterrence) or other, potential offenders (general deterrence). The sentencing system attempts to prevent crime through the fear of punishment. *See also* **general deterrence**; **specific deterrence**. Reference: Gibbs, Jack. (1968). "Crime, Punishment and Deterrence." *Social Science Quarterly* 48: 515–30.

developmental crime prevention An approach to crime prevention that assumes that known factors are likely to place people, particularly young people, at risk of becoming offenders. This being so, it is argued that resources should be directed at those factors that lead to the motivation to commit crime. In general, this approach to crime prevention tries to prevent the development of a motivated offender. Reference: Tonry, Michael, and David Farrington. (1995). *Building a Safer Society*. Chicago: University of Chicago Press.

deviance Commonly refers to violations of social norms (including legal norms), but many sociologists reject this behavioural or normative definition of deviance and see deviance instead as simply a label. Deviance in this view is that which we react to, through social control responses, as deviance. *See also* **labelling theory**.

deviance, primary Where the individual commits deviant acts that do not emanate from a deviant or criminal sense of self. Lemert (1951) postulates that a person may commit many deviant or criminal acts in this manner, but if caught and labelled by agents of control, the "offender" may come to see him or herself in a different manner and become a secondary deviant. *See also* **deviance, secondary**.

deviance, secondary Where the individual commits deviant acts after being identified and perhaps labelled by agents of social control. Although recognizing that these acts are socially defined as deviant, he or she remains committed to continue them. The deviant acts flow from the adoption of a deviant self-identity that confirms and stabilizes the deviant lifestyle. Reference: Lemert, Edwin. (1951). *Social Pathology*. New York: McGraw-Hill.

dialectical The belief that social organization, culture, and intellectual ideas change because of the development of contradictions that create challenges to the existing state of affairs and lead to the emergence of something new from this tension. Georg Hegel (1770–1831) developed this idea in western philosophy when he claimed that every existing social arrangement or intellectual belief system represents a "thesis"—a way of doing or thinking about things—that gives rise to a contradictory, or opposing, "antithesis." From the contest between "thesis" and "antithesis" emerges something new and unique: a "synthesis." There is some element of this conception in the writing of Karl Marx (1818–83), when he claims that contradictions arise in capitalism and the resolution of these contradictions produces a new type of social and economic system. This suggests that the seeds of capitalism's demise or transformation are located within capitalism and are not generated from outside. *See also* **contradictions of capitalism**; **dialectical materialism**.

dialectical materialism A concept linked to Marx's ideas, but an expression never actually used in his writing. In general, this concept suggests that the process of social change is not attributable to changes in culture or ideas, but arises within the material conditions of people's lives, in the way they are organized around economic activity. *See also* **contradictions of capitalism**; **dialectical**.

Dick, Evelyn The dismembered body of John Dick was found in Hamilton in 1946. Evelyn, who claimed to have slept with 150 men, many of them prominent, was charged with her husband's murder. Police also found the body of a young child encased in cement in the Dick home. In October of 1946, Evelyn Dick was sentenced to death. This conviction was appealed and lawyer J.J. Robinette succeeded in having a new trial at which time she was acquitted. However, she was also charged with the murder of the child and was given a sentence of life imprisonment. Robinette went on to become one of Canada's most famous trial lawyers. Reference:

Campbell, Marjorie Freeman. (1976). *Torso.* Scarborough: Signet.

differential association Developed by Edwin Sutherland (1883–1950) in the 1930s, this was a radical explanation for criminal behaviour, since it argues that crime, like any social behaviour, is learned in association with others. The phrase "differential association" simply means that people have different social situations and thus learn different things. What is learned is cultural material. If an individual regularly associates with criminals, and is relatively isolated from law-abiding citizens, then he or she is more likely to engage in crime. First, he or she learns some specific skills needed to commit crime (how to open a locked vault), and, second, learns ideas that justify and normalize crime. This concept leads directly to a subcultural theory of crime that asserts that not all groups in society uphold the same values or norms and for some groups crime is normative. Reference: Sutherland, Edwin. (1939). *Principles of Criminology.* Philadelphia: Lippincott.

disclosure The principle that the prosecution must give all evidence gathered by the police to the defendant in order to permit an adequate defence. This principle was established in the R.V. Stinchcombe case of 1991. The Supreme Court ruled that evidence gathered by the Crown in the course of an investigation was not its own property to use to get a conviction, rather the evidence was the property of the public and must be used to support the fair and equitable administration of justice.

discourse analysis An important theme in postmodernism especially in writers like Michel Foucault (1929–84) for whom it is important to analyze how people talk about the world around them. The central idea is that the way people talk about the world does not reflect some objective truth about that world, but instead reflects the success of particular ways of thinking and seeing. These ways of thinking and seeing tend to become invisible, because they are simply assumed to be truthful and right, and in this way people's thought processes themselves can come to represent and reinforce particular regimes of power and coercion.

discrimination The unequal treatment of individuals on the basis of their personal characteristics, which may include age, sex, sexual orientation, and ethnic or physical identity. Discrimination usually refers to negative treatment, but discrimination in favour of particular groups can also occur. *See also* **prejudice.**

disenchantment of the world *See* **rationalization.**

disenfranchised To be without the right to vote. More commonly the term is used to describe groups that have little power or representation in the political process. Young people could be called disenfranchised, since they have a low rate of voting and, more importantly, they have little representation in the political process or institutions that concern them. *See also* **enfranchisement**; **suffrage**.

disparity The lack of uniformity of sentencing. It has long been know that judges, using their discretion and their own philosophy of sentencing, impose vastly different penalties for offences that to the outsider look very similar. Reference: Roberts, J.V., and D. Cole. (1999). *Making Sense of Sentencing.* Toronto: University of Toronto Press.

dissociation This phrase can be used in a psychological way or in a sociological way. For psychology, it refers to the tendency for people in crisis to dissociate their experiences from aspects of their personality or identity. This can lead to multiple personalities. For the sociologist, it refers more to social isolation from others for a variety of reasons.

dissociative disorders A form of mental illness in which the person becomes dissociated from his or her life. Examples of this would be amnesia (other than that form caused by trauma or organic disease) and multiple-personality syndrome.

distributive justice One of two key categories of justice or fairness, the other being retributive justice. Distributive justice refers to fairness in the allocation of the rewards or benefits of society or of an institution within society. For example, it is seen as "fair" that those student essays that best meet the criteria of academia should receive the best grades. When Karl Marx asserts that workers produce value in a commodity that they do not receive and are thus exploited, he is concerned about distributive injustice. Retributive justice, on the other hand, refers to fairness in the administration and imposition of punishment on those who have brought harm or negative consequences on individuals or society. It is seen as fair, for example, that those who violate the law should receive punishment. The criminal justice system can be thought of as the institutionalization of this type of justice.

diversion Generally, the term means to keep someone away from something or to "steer" them past something. In the justice system, the term has taken on several meanings. (1) To divert offenders from the trial process. Those who plead guilty, or for whom there is sufficient evidence to convict, may be given the chance to avoid legal penalties. For example, the police or crown counsel are permitted to send a letter of warning to the parents of a young offender rather than proceed to court. Or, offenders may be given the chance to do some form of restitution rather than having a legal punishment imposed. They may apologize to their victim, pay for the repairs of vandalism, etc. (2) To divert offenders from the prison. Various forms of community corrections have been developed to allow for this form of diversion. For example, community service orders, restitution, treatment programs. Reference: Church Council on Justice and Corrections. (1996). *Satisfying Justice: Safe Community Options that Attempt to Repair Harm From Crime and Reduce Use or Length of Imprisonment.* Ottawa: Correctional Service of Canada.

Divorce Act Until the Divorce Act of 1968 divorce was difficult to obtain in Canada, and in Quebec and Newfoundland, where no legislation existed, divorce could only be obtained through a private Act of Parliament. The 1968 Act created two grounds for divorce: fault (adultery, mental and physical cruelty, homosexuality, imprisonment, or addiction) and marriage breakdown (which included separation for at least three years). The divorce rate jumped considerably after the passage of this Act. The 1986 Divorce Act removed the fault grounds and provided that divorce could be obtained when marriage breakdown could be proven by a separation of one year.

dizygotic twins Commonly known as *fraternal twins*, they are from two separate fertilized eggs, consequently, they share no more genetic material than any other siblings and may be of different sexes. Twin studies have been a valuable research tool for sorting out the effects of heredity and environment. *See also* **monozygotic twins**.

DNA matching It was not until 1985 that it was realized that DNA could be used for the purpose of identification, a tool that has become increasingly useful to the police. DNA stands for deoxyribonucleic acid, is found in the centre of human cells, and is the principal component of chromosomes, the structures that transmit hereditary characteristics. Since genetic material is unique to each individual (with the exception of identical twins), offenders can be identified by matching the DNA of the offender with a sample of material containing DNA found at the scene of a crime. Since 1995, Canadian police have been able to obtain DNA samples from suspects with a warrant. DNA matching has since led to the freeing of several people wrongfully convicted of serious crimes; opponents of the death sentence in the United States have named DNA, Do Not Annihilate. A DNA bank was established in Canada in 1998. *See also* **Legere, Allan**.

documentary method of interpretation This term was used by Karl Mannheim (1893–1947) and Alfred Schutz (1899–1959), but its current meaning derives from Harold Garfinkel, the founder of ethnomethodology. He asserts that the documentary method is a method that lay persons and sociologists alike use in commonsense reasoning about the world. The method consists of treating an actual appearance as the document of, or as pointing to, a presupposed underlying pattern. The child's choice of toys (a boy choosing a truck or a girl choosing a doll) is seen as an indication of an underlying pattern of biological preferences (or for the sociologist, of gender socialization). Further, there is a reciprocal relationship between the "document" and the underlying pattern: the underlying pattern is now given some legitimacy because of the observation of the individual "document"—the child's choice of toys. *See also* **ethnomethodology**.

doing gender A concept derived from a theory to explain crimes by men. It postulates that all cultures have an ideal of manliness and failure to meet this is perceived as effeminate. This being so, men need opportunities to "do gender," to make their manliness apparent. Abuse of women and crime itself may be seen as way to assert manliness. Reference: Messerschmidt, James. (1993). *Masculinities and Crime.* Lanham: Rowman and Littlefield.

dominant ideology thesis Associated with Karl Marx and his claim that each historical era is dominated by the intellectual ideas of its economically and politically ruling class. The institutions and culture of a society are widely permeated by this ideology, which provides the key institutions and values of the society with an appearance of naturalness and inevitability. It is not claimed that there is only one ideology present within a society, or that this ideology is without challenge. Marx's envisages a process of class conflict in society that develops the contest between dominant ideology and the ideas or counter ideologies that challenge them. *See also* **class consciousness, false; ideology**.

domination *See* **authority**.

Don Jail Built between the years of 1858 and 1865 on the banks of the Don Valley overlooking central Toronto, the Don Jail served as the primary prison for the region. The prison has been condemned many times, and as late as 2004 was found not to meet the minimum standards set by the United Nations. *See also* **execution, public**.

double blind procedure A method of enhancing internal validity in an experiment. Neither the researcher nor the subjects are made aware of which group is the experimental group and which is the control group. This prevents the researcher from communicating expectations and the subjects from acting in ways they think to be expected of them.

double burden A term used to describe the situation of women who perform paid work outside the domestic sphere as well as homemaking and child-care work inside the home. Since domestic work is private and outside the cash economy, it is not remunerated; this causes it to appear as something less than real work and as part of the natural gender role of women. Canadian studies have consistently demonstrated that women perform by far the largest share of this domestic work. Men, however, spend considerably more hours at paid work; recent data suggests that total hours worked by men and women are roughly comparable. However, the demands of providing and arranging child care, which fall primarily on women, lead to many women being subjected to demands greater than those imposed on male workers. Some feminists have advocated wages for housework to gain recognition for this work that women do in the private world of family and household.

double jeopardy A principle that states that normally an offender cannot be tried twice for the same offence. In Canada, however, an offender can be retried even if acquitted the first time if the Crown successfully appeals the first acquittal (although this is not considered as double jeopardy).

double marginality A theory used to explain why women tend to commit fewer crimes than do men. The theory argues that women are isolated within the family and are denied access to male-dominated street crime. Hence, they are doubly marginalized, and this only leaves avenues toward less serious crimes and victimless crimes like drug abuse. Reference: Messerschmidt, James. (1986). *Capitalism, Patriarchy and Crime.* Totowa: Rowman and Littlefield.

double standard A cultural practice that accords less freedom and choice to one sex than the other. The term is usually used to refer to different norms of sexual morality for women than for men. Men's sexual activity is viewed positively as natural, right, and normal, whereas women are seen as diminished in status if they engage in free sexual relationships outside marriage. This double standard of conduct was once severely oppressive to women (and still is in many non-western societies), but has reduced relevance in western societies today where pre-marital sexual activity is normative for both sexes. *See also* **status offence**.

Doukhobors Of Russian origin, a pacifist sect rejecting both the orthodoxy of established religion of the 17th and 18th century (they believed that God dwells in each person and not in the church) and secular governments. After many years of persecution, a group of 7400 sailed to Canada in 1898–99 and settled in Saskatchewan. When it became clear that they would have to take an oath of allegiance in order to homestead the land, most objected and moved to British Columbia in 1908. Here the group established a complex pattern of communal living. Extremists among the group (the Sons of Freedom) continued to reject government regulation and were in conflict with the government over compulsory schooling, registration of births, and taxes for several decades. Many were arrested, a special prison was established and many children taken into care. Some stability returned to the community in the 1970s, and the Sons of Freedom and the more orthodox Doukhobors live in the interior of British Columbia in relative harmony. In 1996, the government of British Columbia made it possible for Doukhobor communities to hold land without paying taxes. In place of taxes, they would pay a fee for government services. Reference: Woodcock, George, and Ivan Avakumovic. (1968). *The Doukhobors.* Toronto: McClelland and Stewart [1977].

dramaturgical model As used by Erving Goffman (1922–82) and symbolic interactionists since, this is a *metaphor* for understanding human interaction and how humans present their self in society. All the world is conceived as a stage and individuals are seen as actors who present a show of their self by putting their "best foot forward." The metaphor is extended by Goffman through concepts such as "front stage," "back stage," and "presentation of self". *See also* **Goffman, Erving**. Reference: Goffman, Erving. (1959). *Presentation of Self in Everyday Life*. New York: Doubleday Anchor.

drift A psychological state of weak normative attachment to either deviant or conventional ways. David Matza developed this idea to demonstrate that delinquents are not fundamentally different from non-delinquents and but they drift in and out of delinquency and may become committed to this way of life. Reference: Matza, David. (1969). *Delinquency and Drift*. Engelwoods Cliff: Prentice-Hall.

drug court A court that handles only drug offences. There is growing interest in this type of court, as it is believed that these courts can spend more time on cases and offer treatment as an alternative to punishment. Toronto began a drug treatment court in December 1998. Addicts apply for the program after they have been charged, and the screening process is very rigorous. Participants remain in the program for approximately one year, and research now shows that those who complete the program have a significantly lower rate of recidivism. Reference: Chiodo, L.A. (2001). "Sentencing Drug-Addicted Offenders and the Toronto Drug Court." *Criminal Law Quarterly* 45(1/2): 53–100.

due process model This model gives priority to values and practices that protect the rights of the offenders from the coercive power of the state. This protection would include strict regulation of police enforcement, independent and impartial judicial process, and imposition of proportional and justifiable punishment. The Canadian Charter of Rights and Freedoms in the Constitution Act, 1982, contains various guarantees of legal rights that support due process. *See also* **crime-control model**; **disclosure**. Reference: Parker, H. (1968). *The Limits of Criminal Sanctions*. Stanford: Stanford University.

duress A legal defence available to an accused for lesser crimes than treason or murder. The accused must prove to the court that he or she was coerced by someone into committing the charged crime by fear of immediate and unbearable harm. For example, the accused smuggles drugs into Canada to prevent the murder of a child who has been abducted by the drug dealers.

Durkheim, Émile (1858–1917) French sociologist associated with the Positivist school and functionalism. In criminology, Durkheim's principal influence has come for his concepts of anomie, or normlessness, and of mechanical and organic solidarity. In Durkheim's sociology, high levels of crime reflect weakness in society's integrative mechanisms. If normative regulation and structural integration can be strengthened this suggests that rates of crime will be correspondingly reduced. *See also* **anomie**; **anomic division of labour**; **mechanical solidarity**, **organic solidarity**.

duty counsel The duty counsel system exists to ensure that an accused person will receive legal advice and procedural assistance when appearing before the Court without a lawyer. The counsel meets with defendants prior to their court appearance and may represent them for some specific purposes before the court. Usually duty counsel are available to defendants without charge.

dyslexia A form of cognitive impairment associated with learning difficulties in school. Dyslexia has been shown to correlate with elevated levels of criminal offending, but it is unclear if this is a direct result of dyslexia or a result of the economic and social marginalization that may occur as a result of school failure. This cognitive impairment is often associated with a person reversing letters or an inability to grasp a number sequence.

E

echo generation Children born to the baby boomers, or those Canadians born between 1980 and 1995. *See also* **baby boom**. Reference: Foot, David. (2001). *Boom, Bust & Echo: Profiting from the Demographic Shift in the 21st Century*. Toronto: Stoddart.

ecofeminism A set of ideas within the environmental movement. A basic assumption of this set of ideas is that patriarchal societies tend to associate women with nature, and debase, or rape, both. Thus it is necessary for the environmental movement to overthrow patriarchal structures and ideologies in order to protect or enhance the natural environment.

ecological fallacy An error made in reasoning about differing units of analysis. Specifically, it is the error of using data generated from groups as the unit of analysis and attempting to draw conclusions about individuals. For example, if neighbourhoods with high rates of unemployment also have high crime rates, it is an error to conclude that it is necessarily the unemployed people in these neighbourhoods that commit crime. *See also* **units of analysis**.

ecological studies Developed by criminologists in the early part of the 20th century, this research looks at the relationships of various areas of a community to each other and the ways in which particular forms of behaviour may flourish in some communities and not in others. *See also* **Chicago school**.

ecology The study of living beings relationships to the world around them, including other living beings. The study of the interdependence of living beings.

economic determinism A form of determinism that explains social structure and culture as a product of the social and technical organization of economic life. Karl Marx has been described, many claim incorrectly, as an economic determinist. *See also* **determinism**.

effective guardianship An aspect of the routine activities approach to understanding crime and in particular victimization. This approach argues that three key factors are required for crime to happen: a motivated offender, a suitable target, and ineffective guardianship of that target. Effective guardianship would include having locks on bikes, security lights in the backyard, or putting goods in the trunk of the car. Measures like this should reduce the risk of being victimized.

egalitarian A shortening of the word *equalitarian*, suggesting a commitment to, or a state of, equality. Egalitarian societies or groups are contrasted to hierarchical or class-based societies or groups.

ego In anthropology, this refers to the individual from whom the networks of kinship and family relationship and descent are reckoned and traced. In psychology, the term is used to refer to the self of the individual, and the way he or she has constructed a personality and identity in society. In Freud's psychoanalytic theory, the ego is the outcome of the individual's struggle to adapt basic drives (the "id") to the imperative control of society and culture (the "superego"). Between drives and the coercive influence of social expectation, an individual creates a sphere of unique personality.

electrodermal activity Electrical activity of the sweat glands in the skin. Tests of electrodermal activity have indicated correlation between skin conductivity and tendency to delinquency, aggressiveness, and recidivism. *See also* **lie detector**. Reference: Loeb, J., and S.A. Mednick. (1977). "A Prospective Study of Predictors of Criminality: Electrodermal Response Patterns. In S.A. Mednick, K.O. Christainsen, (eds.), *Biosocial Bases of Criminal Behaviour*. New York: Gardner Press.

electronic monitoring Begun in 1987, electronic monitoring is a form of home confinement using new technologies. Offenders serving a probation sentence, home confinement, and those on parole may be monitored using a system allowing supervisors to determine if the person is at home. Often used for those charged with drinking and driving, those serving a short sentence, or those for whom it is desirable that they remain in the community (to keep a job, continue schooling, etc.). *See also* **conditional sentence**. Reference: Bonta, James, S. Wallace-Capretta, and T. Rooney. (1999). *Electronic Monitoring in Canada*. Ottawa: Solicitor General of Canada.

Elmira reformatory Built in Elmira, New York, in 1876, this institution reflected the new philosophy of rehabilitation of inmates articulated by the National Prison Association in 1870. Reformation was to replace the goal of punishment; to aid in achieving this, the state government passed an indeterminate sentencing bill to allow for early release for good behaviour.

embourgeoisement thesis The argument that, contrary to the class conflict theory of Karl Marx (1818–83), increasing numbers of the working class will come to assume the lifestyle and individualistic values of the middle class and will reject commitment to collective social and economic goals. The opposite would be *class consciousness*.

empirical evidence Evidence that can be observed through the senses. As a minimum, it must be sensed by at least one faculty of sight, hearing, touch, smell, or taste and, to some extent, be measurable. This is the only form of evidence acceptable to positivism, which describes social science as the study of a social world deemed to be external to the observer and proceeding with the researcher being a neutral "observer" of that external world.

empiricism The philosophical belief that sensory input (seeing, touching, hearing, etc.) is the sole source and test of knowledge. *See also* **empirical evidence**; **epistemology**; **positivism**.

employment equity Equity can be thought of as a state of being equal or fair, and fairness in dealing with people. Employment equity has come to have several dimensions. First, it suggests equal pay for equal work or equal pay for work of equal value. The goal of both these principles is to establish equality between men and women, or able-bodied and physically challenged persons, or "whites" and people of colour. The term has also come to imply proportionate hiring of various minority groups.

enfranchisement Acquiring the right to vote in the elections of the nation. Women, for example, were federally enfranchised in 1918. Many groups in Canada were denied the right to vote and thus were disenfranchised, being without the vote. The right to vote is now constitutionally guaranteed and the last large adult group to achieve this right was the federal prison population (although this still remains controversial). *See also* **suffrage**.

enlightenment (project) In order to understand what postmodernism is about, it is essential to understand what modernity means for the social sciences. This is linked to what is deemed to be the "enlightenment project." The age of enlightenment ushered in human rationality as the source of knowledge, thus encouraging the rejection of previous authorities such as the church or custom. This new acceptance of human rationality became linked to science as the key to understanding the natural and social worlds, and led to a search to understand causality and to the belief that human rationality would lead to a more enlightened, progressive age characterized by human liberation. These beliefs shape social sciences by giving science a privileged position in the pursuit of truth, encouraging the search for sets of concepts to provide a framework for understanding social life regardless of particular social situations or time and the acceptance of "metanarratives" (large and abstract social theory including sociology) as superior to other narrative accounts about society. Much of this is apparent in some of the works of Karl Marx. Marxian theory is a large metanarrative about the historical development of western societies; it includes all stories about society, and because of its claim to be based on scientific observation and its use of a conceptual framework (modes of production, relations of production), it claims a privileged position and a universal nature (it is to apply to all capitalist societies). Further, it is claimed that by using the metanarrative, the consciousness of workers can be enhanced (corrected) and an age of liberation will follow. Modernity or the enlightenment project is reflected in "positivism," the importance of the "scientific method," the belief that social science can be used to better society (Émile Durkheim is very explicit about this), and the sweeping away of the subjective beliefs of "ordinary actors." *See also* **deconstruction**; **meta-narrative**; **positivism**; **postmodernism**.

entrapment A legal defence available to the accused. The accused must prove to the court that he or she was induced by law enforcement agents to commit a crime that would not otherwise have been contemplated. Courts have indicated that entrapment must be separated from the issue of the guilt or innocence of the accused. Reference: *R. v. Pearson* [1998] 3 S.C.R. 620.

epidemiology A term used largely in medical sociology to describe the study of the occurrence and distribution of diseases. Such investigations look for changes in the frequency of occurrence (or incidence) and association of diseases with particular physical or social locations. Epidemiological research can be conducted on crime—viewed as analogous to a disease of society—and a host of social problems. For example, a researcher may map the distribution of youth crime in relation to race, social class, school success, or family structure in the hope of finding those factors that appear to be associated with delinquency.

epistemology The study of knowledge and of how we know. All science, since it is concerned with verification and proving or disproving, must make assumptions about how we know. All science then adopts an epistemology. In sociology, there has been a long debate about the sources of knowledge and this can be seen in the differences between positivism and postmodernism, or between positivism and phenomenology. For sociologists, this debate is most frequently engaged over the methods to be used for learning about the world: the survey or experimental method on one side, and participant observation or using one's own "member's" understanding to analyze conversations. *See also* **empiricism**; **ethnographic research**; **member**; **positivism**; ***verstehen***.

equality of condition Where there is very little difference in individuals' possession of wealth, status, and power. Does not exist in any complex society.

equality of opportunity Where differences in individual's wealth, status, and power are not so great as to create advantage and disadvantage in the pursuit of personal achievement. Liberal ideology and consensus theory claim that broad equality of opportunity exists in modern societies. Criminologists since Durkheim have been interested in inequality of opportunity since it is believed that people's commitment to the norms and rules of society are diminished as inequality rises.

equalization payments Funds transferred from the government of Canada to some of the provinces to compensate them for having a smaller per capita tax base than other provinces. The intent of the payments is to support a comparable level of provincial government services across all of Canada. Historically, Ontario has been the chief net contributor, via federal taxation, and Quebec the chief net beneficiary. The Atlantic provinces, Manitoba, and Saskatchewan have also been recipients, while Alberta and British Columbia have been net contributors.

essentialism *See* **feminism, difference**.

esteem Refers to honour or positive evaluation within a group or community. Some sociologists have thought of esteem as a form of status that can operate independently of income, wealth, or power. *See also* **class crystallization**; **status**.

ethnic group A group of individuals having a distinct culture—a subculture—in common. The idea of "ethnic group" differs from that of "race" because it implies that values, norms, behaviour, and language, not necessarily physical appearance, are the important distinguishing characteristic. Usually, ethnic groups are thought of as minority groups within another culture.

ethnic identity An individual's awareness of membership in a distinct group and of commitment to the group's cultural values. This is the subjective aspect of ethnicity, but for many people their ethnic heritage has little subjective meaning although it can be objectively determined.

ethnocentrism The assumption that the culture of one's own group is moral, right, and rational, and that other cultures are inferior. When confronted with a different culture, individuals judge it with reference to their own standards and make no attempt to understand and evaluate it from the perspective of its members. Sometimes ethnocentrism will be combined with racism, the belief that individuals can be classified into distinct racial groups and that that there is a biologically based hierarchy of these races. In principle, however, one can reject a different culture without in any way assuming the inherent inferiority of its members. *See also* **racism**; **xenophobia**.

ethnographic research Uses participant observation as a tool for gathering information and is a form of what is termed qualitative research in contrast to quantitative research which focuses on measurement and formal analysis. As participant observer, the researcher becomes actively immersed in the chosen setting in order to gain understanding through experiencing aspects of the life of an individual or group. Ethnographic research is the foundation of anthropology, which has been principally concerned with the descriptive recording and analysis of the group life of traditional, generally pre-literate, societies. Until the 1950s, anthropologists would often resist close involvement in community life and maintain quite formal and narrow relations with the host society in order to do better "objective science," but today anthropologists generally seek active involvement as a source of understanding. Ethnographic research is also central to symbolic interactionism, phenomenological sociology, labelling theory and ethnomethodology, where the goal is to comprehend the subjective perspectives of individuals. Ethnographic research is linked to a reaction to positivism that distrusts subjectivity in research and attempts to treat human "subjects" as an object that can be scientifically investigated. *See also* **epistemology**; **positivism**; **qualitative research**. Reference: Le Compte, M.D., and Jean J. Schensul. (1999). *Designing and Conducting Ethnographic Research*. Lanham, MD: Roman & Littlefield Pub Inc.

ethnomethodology (1917–) A sociological theory developed by Harold Garfinkel, building on the influence of phenomenologists such as Edmund Husserl and Alfred Schutz and more recent linguistic philosophers. Roughly translated, the term means the study of people's practices or methods. There are three central strands to ethnomethodology: mundane reason analysis, membership categorization, and conversational (or sequential) analysis. This is a micro-perspective; it does not see the social world as an objective reality, but as something that people must build and rebuild constantly in their thoughts and actions. Rather than treating ordinary members of society as "cultural dopes" driven by society, it tries to uncover the methods and practices that are used by people as they create the taken-for-granted-world. *See also* **sequential analysis**; **commonsense reasoning**. Reference: Garfinkel, Harold. (1967). *Studies in Ethnomethodology*. Englewood Cliffs: Prentice-Hall.

etiological factors Those factors that encourage or cause a particular outcome; for example, addiction to hard drugs is a factor that can lead people into prostitution or criminal behaviour. Being raised in a violent home is a factor that can lead to violent behaviour or being victimized by violence.

etiology The study of the origins or causes of things. Typically used in medical research to describe the study of the causes of disease, but the term is also used in the social sciences in reference to social problems like crime and deviance.

eugenics Translates roughly as "good genes." The eugenics movement, active in many parts of the western world, was driven by the belief that social intervention should occur in order to protect the best gene pool. This was achieved by encouraging people who were considered to represent "good" genes to breed, and, more importantly, to support interventions by the state to prevent those considered to have "bad" genes from breeding. In Alberta, for example, the Sexual Sterilization Act, in force from 1928 to 1972, allowed the state to sterilize 2832 people—most, or all, without their consent. Reference: McLaren, Angus. (1990). *Our Own Master Race: Eugenics in Canada, 1885–1945*. Toronto: McClelland and Stewart.

euthanasia Literally, "a good death." The painless killing of a person, at his or her request, to escape from the indignity and suffering of an incurable medical condition. Some societies make legal provision for such deaths; Canada does not. *See also* **Latimer, Robert**; **mercy killing**.

evolutionary psychology A relatively new paradigm for understanding human social behaviour, which argues that attributes such as altruism, romantic love, protection of children, pair-bonding, coyness in females, sexual aggression, sexual attraction, or conscience, have a genetic basis. Applying Darwinian principles to the understanding of human behaviour, it is claimed, provides insights into things such as human kinship structures, male–female relationships, family formation, sibling rivalry, and domestic violence. Reference: Evans, Dylan. (2000). *Introducing Evolutionary Psychology*. New York: Totem Books.

exceptional state This arises when a liberal democratic society adopts government policies that rely on the coercive power of the state, rather than trying to maintain compromises that balance conflicting interests. This is a departure from the usual role of democratic states and is therefore exceptional. Stuart Hall used the term to describe what happened in Britain in the 1980s, as economic failure led to mass unemployment, a government fiscal crisis, and a loss of support among important groups; there was a crisis of legitimacy. The British government fostered a sense of an enemy within the society and claimed that social instability was caused by rampant crime and militant unionists. This "threat" then justified giving the state coercive powers that it used to control the crisis. *See also* **fiscal crisis**; **legitimation crisis**.

exchange theory A theory associated with the work of George Homans and Peter Blau, built on the assumption that all human relationships can be understood in terms of an exchange of roughly equivalent values. These exchanges are seldom monetary; rather they are frequently intangibles like intimacy, status, and connections.

exchange value In Marxian analysis, the theoretical value of any commodity exchanged or sold in the marketplace is the amount of socially necessary labour time embodied in it. In actual market conditions, the money or equivalent paid for a commodity (the price) may differ from the value of the commodity, although, in a perfectly working market, price and value would be identical. It is the unique characteristic of capitalism that the great majority of goods and services are produced to be sold, rather than for their immediate use value to the producer. In less modern economies, the production of commodities took place only in limited sectors and most production was for use values. *See also* **labour theory of value**.

exclusionary rule A rule of evidence that declares that evidence gathered illegally will not be admitted in court. Also known as the *fruit of the poisoned tree doctrine*. This rule was given constitutional recognition in 1982 in the Charter of Rights and Freedoms Section 24 (2). Reference: *R. v. Stillman* (1997). I.S.C.R. 607.

execution, last On December 11, 1962, Ronald Turpin and Arthur Lucas, found guilty of murdering a police officer, became the last people executed in Canada. Prime Minister John Diefenbaker, an experienced trial lawyer who had seen many miscarriages of justice, never liked the death penalty, and after this case the Cabinet routinely advised the Governor General to commute all death sentences into life imprisonment. Of the 710 people to be executed since Confederation in 1867, there were 697 men and 13 women. The death sentence was finally abolished by Act of Parliament in 1976.

execution, public The last public execution in Canada was in 1869 when Patrick Whelan was hanged for the murder of prominent Irish-Canadian politician D'Arcy McGee. A crowd of over 5000 people assembled in Ottawa to witness the event. Semi-public executions continued to be held in prison yards, easily observable from buildings, lamp posts, and telephone poles around the prisons, which people would climb to observe the spectacle. The last of these semi-public executions was in March 1902, when Monsieur S. LaCroix was hanged. The execution was conducted by Canada's first public hangman, John Robert Radclive. *See also* **McGee, Thomas D'Arcy.**

execution, women The last woman ever to be executed in Canada, Marguerite Pitre, was hanged in Montreal on January 9, 1953. On September 9, 1949, a Quebec Airways airplane exploded in mid-air halfway from Quebec City to Baie Comeau; 23 people were killed. Rita Morel Guay, wife of a Quebec jeweller, Albert Guay, was among them. Albert Guay's affection for his wife had cooled dramatically since a new affair with a 17-year-old waitress. This new girlfriend threatened to end the relationship unless he divorced his wife—almost impossible in 1953, especially in Catholic Quebec. Guay decided that this inconvenient wife must be removed. He knew a watchmaker, who owed him large sums of money, and he offered to forgive the debt in return for the making of a timed-detonating device. Marguerite Pitre, sister of the watchmaker, became involved. On August 18, 1949, she bought seven sticks of dynamite and some detonating caps at a Quebec hardware store, signing a false name to the bill. On September 9, she took a taxi to the airport. On her lap was a parcel. The parcel, described as a "religious statue" and labelled "fragile," was loaded onto the plane for Baie Comeau. Forty minutes after takeoff, the plane exploded. Wreckage showed that the cause was a bomb. Police soon discovered the unusual fact that Guay had taken out a $10 000 life insurance policy on his wife just minutes before she boarded the plane. On September 19, police were called to the scene of an "attempted suicide" in Quebec City's old town. There, they found a distraught Marguerite Pitre. She told them that Guay had admitted that the parcel she took to the airport was a bomb, and he has demanded that she write a suicide note and take some pills he has given her. Police then seized Guay, but thought Pitre and her brother were innocent dupes in the crime. In March 1950, Guay was tried, found guilty, and sentenced to hang. As his date of execution came close, Guay decided to make a detailed confession and he named Pitre and her brother as paid co-conspirators. The two are arrested and tried. Damning evidence was given by the driver of Pitre's taxi to the airport. He testified that she told him to drive carefully because the parcel was "dangerous." Both were found guilty and sentenced to death.

executive disengagement The detachment of senior executives of large corporations or other institutions from the day-to-day work and work situation of lower-level employees. It develops both because lower-level employees will customarily assume that executives are best left uninformed of certain decisions and actions of employees, and because of the assumption that executives cannot be legally expected to have complete control over their individual staff. This concept of separation from daily responsibility has been challenged in Canada, and executives can be found liable, for example, for sexual harassment committed within their institutions. A legal responsibility has been established to create an environment in which harassment is not tolerated and where, if it occurs, it is promptly disciplined and eliminated.

explanation All science aims to provide explanation of phenomena or behaviours. Once can think of two ways to provide a useful explanation. First, a causal explanation can be offered if research can clearly establish that one variable is caused by another. Second, and more powerful, a theoretical explanation locates the phenomena or behaviour in question within a theory, a conceptual model of how some aspect of the world works. It should be noted that explanation in history in particular is somewhat different than other explanations. *See also* **theory**.

exponential growth Growth that follows a geometric progression (e.g., 1, 2, 4, 8, 16, 32) rather than a linear progression (e.g., 1, 2, 3, 4, 5, 6).

external validity Refers to the accuracy of scientific results when generalized beyond the laboratory or survey situation to the real world. If it is thought that the researcher could expect to find confirmation of research results in the ordinary life of the community, the results would be said to be externally valid. *See also* **internal validity**.

extra-chromosome theory *See* **XYY**.

extra-judicial measures The Youth Criminal Justice Act allows for the imposition of non-court measures on a young offender, and thus avoids formal court sanctions being imposed. If the extra-judicial measures are not met by the offender, the Crown may then take the offender to court and have judicial measures imposed. A form of diversion.

extraversion A personality characteristic associated with sociability, impulsiveness, and aggression.

Exxon Valdez A tanker carrying oil for Exxon (the oil company) hit a reef near the Alaskan city of Valdez on March 24, 1989, on its way to California. Ten million gallons of oil spilled into pristine Prince William Sound. This incident drew worldwide attention to the tremendous actual and potential harm from the movement of oil around the world. Reference: Keeble, John, and N. Fobes. (1999). *Out of the Channel: the Exxon Valdez Oil Spill*. Washington: University of Washington Press.

F

faint hope clause A section of the Criminal Code dealing with sentencing for first- and second-degree murder where the offender is given a life sentence with no eligibility for parole for 15 years. Persons convicted of multiple murders are not eligible for this provision. To provide some possibility of recognizing offender rehabilitation, the Act allows for an appeal to the courts to request that they be allowed to make application for parole after 15 years. This is the faint hope provision. The offender can be turned down by the court, or, if accepted, can then move on to a judicial review hearing composed of a jury of community residents. If the inmate is given permission to apply for early parole by this review, the case then goes to the parole board where again it can be accepted or rejected. There is a strong public demand to remove this section of the Criminal Code.

false consciousness *See* **class consciousness, false**.

false positives When trying to identify dangerous offenders (or other things as well), researchers often make mistakes. One of these mistakes is known as a false positive. The error is identifying someone as dangerous (and possibly keeping him or her incarcerated or denying parole) when he or she is not dangerous. The other type of error would be a false negative: identifying someone as non-dangerous when he or she in fact goes on to commit a dangerous act.

falsifiability (or refutability) A central tenet of science that demands that all claims or assertions investigated by science must be open to being proven false. If a researcher cannot define what would count as empirical or experimental disproof of a claim then the claim itself must fall outside the domain of science. This tenet is consistent with the belief that in science it is possible to prove something false, but not to prove something true. In fact it is assumed that we can never prove something to be true, we can only fail to disprove something and therefore accept its truth for the time being. Science does not simply try to illustrate or demonstrate its theories or hypotheses, rather, it actively tries to disprove them.

familism Refers to core values of a family type that emphasizes commitment to the family as a unit. Staying together for the sake of the children would be an indication of this value. Found in the "bourgeois family," which reflects the cultural belief that it is the family that is the foundation of society and the source of human identification and moral discipline. The modern conjugal family, by contrast, is typically described as having a central value of individualism that de-emphasizes the importance of the family unit. *See also* **individualism**; **family, bourgeois**.

family, bourgeois A family system based on private family life and in which women are separated into the domestic sphere and men act as family heads in the social and economic sphere.

family, conjugal A nuclear family of adult partners and their children (by birth or adoption) where the family relationship is principally focused inwardly and ties to extended kin are voluntary and based on emotional bonds, rather than strict duties and obligations. *See also* **family, nuclear**.

family, consanguineal A family system of nuclear families linked through shared descent from a common ancestor. The individual nuclear families are bound into complex ties of obligation and daily activity with each other. Consanguineal families can be linked either matrilineally or patrilineally.

family, egalitarian A family system based on the equality of the participants and in direct contrast to the patriarchal family. It usually refers to an equal relationship between the adult partners, though it can mean permissive, rather than authoritarian, parent-child relationships. In North American families, this family form is most likely to be found among young and well-educated couples. The term "symmetrical family" is sometimes used as an equivalent. The concept is in many respects an ideal, rather than descriptive of typical or usual family relationships. *See also* **double burden**.

family, nuclear This has the same composition as the conjugal family, but the term "nuclear" does not imply that the family is inwardly focused and relatively autonomous from extended kin as in the case of the conjugal family. Extended, or consanguineal (based on shared blood descent), families can be thought of as composed of linked nuclear families. *See also* **family, conjugal**.

family class immigrant *See* **sponsored immigrant**.

family court A provincial court with jurisdiction over some aspects of family law. Usually involved in child custody matters and support payments. At some times the family court has also served as a youth court.

fascism A political doctrine opposed to democracy and demanding submission to political leadership and authority. A key principle of fascism is the belief that the whole society has a shared destiny and purpose that can only be achieved by iron discipline, obedience to leadership, and an all-powerful state. Fascism first developed in Italy, under the leadership of Benito Mussolini (dictator of Italy from 1922 to 1943), and later influenced the development of German fascism in the Nazi movement led by Adolf Hitler (dictator of Germany from 1933 to 1945). While fascism increases the power and role of the state in society and suppresses free trade unions and political opposition, it preserves private ownership and private property.

fatalistic suicide A type of suicide, identified by Émile Durkheim (1858–1917), occurring in social conditions where the individual experiences pervasive oppression. For example, the condition of slavery may make an individual feel the only way to find escape is suicide.

Fattah, Ezzat Moved from the University of Montreal to Simon Fraser University in British Columbia to establish the School of Criminology in 1975. His perspective is radical in advocating decriminalization of drugs, almost total abolition of prisons, and a focus on restorative justice centred on processes of healing, reparation, and restitution.

Fauteux commission Commissioned by the federal government to inquire into the principles and procedures of the remission service (to become the parole service) in connection with the exercise of clemency. The members defined their tasks very broadly and reported on the philosophy of corrections, the goals of the court, and the parole service. Reporting in 1956, the Fauteux commission clearly articulates a philosophy of rehabilitation, seeing prison inmates as persons who have been damaged in the life process of growing up. Among their specific recommendations were an extensive system of adult probation, a concentration of treatment and training, specialization of institutions, creation of minimum security prisons, recruitment and training of professional staff, parole as an integral part of the rehabilitative process, and the development of a quasi-judicial parole board.

FBI *See* **Federal Bureau of Investigation**.

fecundity Refers to the potential number of children a woman can have. Fertility rate, on the other hand, refers to the actual number of children a woman has.

Federal Bureau of Investigation (FBI) This agency of the United States government was created in 1908 to investigate violations of federal law. Its most famous director was J. Edgar Hoover who served from 1924 to 1972 and systematically used the power the organization gave him to promote his own personal and political perspective.

federal court The federal courts of Canada have no jurisdiction over criminal cases. Rather, they are involved in such federal matters as tax law, copyright law, civil cases against the federal government, and review of federal government decisions.

federal prison Normally called penitentiaries, these are federally financed and operated institutions housing offenders with sentences of two years or more. Although the federal government is solely responsible for criminal law, there is a division of responsibility around the administration of that law. The federal government of Canada operates 10 maximum security institutions, 20 medium security institutions, 12 minimum security institutions, 7 women's institutions, and 15 community correctional centres. *See also* **provincial prison**.

federalism, asymmetrical Where a federal system of government does not accord precisely the same legal powers and areas of jurisdiction to all its constituent states or provinces. In Canada, this form of federalism has been advocated as a way to reconcile Quebec to the federal system by awarding the province specific additional powers connected to the protection and promotion of French language and culture.

federalism, centripetal A federal system where there is a strong federal government and weaker provincial governments. Its opposite is centrifugal federalism, where power would be dispersed from the centre to the provincial governments. In Canada, the debate over these visions of federalism has continued since before Confederation and is still unresolved. *See also* **confederation**.

felony An older term, although still used in the United States, now replaced in Canada with the term *indictable offence*.

femicide Since technically the term homicide refers to the killing of a man, the term femicide has been used to refer to the killing of a woman.

feminism A diverse political and intellectual movement chiefly developed by women, but having increasing influence with both sexes, that seeks to criticize, re-evaluate, and transform the place of women in social organization and in culture. Common to feminists is the assumption that social organization and culture have been dominated by men to the exclusion of women and that this exclusion has been accompanied by a diverse pattern of devaluation and disadvantagement that have marginalized women's status in most known societies. Consequently, a major area of concern to feminism is the recovery and articulation of women's experience in history and in contemporary societies and a wholesale reconstruction of the fundamental intellectual assumptions of social practices and of many areas of study including especially sociology, psychology, history, and other social and humanistic disciplines. *See also* **patriarchy**; **liberal feminism**; **radical feminism**; **ecofeminism**.

feminism, cultural A feminist perspective that reverses the assumption that men exhibit the normative form of behaviour and that women are different and thus "the other." This view makes female cultural characteristics the norm. The characteristics of women are positively evaluated and those of men, as the "other," seen as bad or evil. For example, women are cooperative (and that is good), while men are aggressive and competitive (and that is bad).

feminism, difference A form of feminism that rejects the belief that the differences between men and women are socially constructed or are established through socialization. Rather, it believes men and women are different in essence, and that these differences arise from differing human natures. Cooperation and competition, therefore, are not just values that have been socially assigned to women and men respectively, but are values that arise from the fundamentally different character of the two sexes.

feminism, standpoint A perspective influenced by the sociology of knowledge that claims less powerful members of society are able to achieve a more complete view of social reality than are others. Less powerful groups, like women and minorities, may be less incorporated into the reward system of society and more clear-sighted and critical about its inequalities and deficiencies. The sociology of knowledge assumption behind this is the idea that knowledge is socially constructed and shaped by the social position occupied by the knower. It follows then that the point of view of the researcher is also shaped by his or her position in society, and standpoint feminism acknowledges this and claims for it a positive role in contributing to a rounded understanding of the character of the society. This acknowledgment is a rejection of traditional notions of objectivity. *See also* **sociology of knowledge**.

feminist criminology While there has always been a criminological interest in the criminal behaviour of women, it was not until the early 1970s that a plethora of literature appeared clearly revealing the sexist assumptions behind most criminological theory and calling for a reorientation of criminology. Through including women in the academic study of crime and developing a realistic understanding of women, the whole field of criminology would need to rethink much of its theory about men and women. Reference: Smart, Carol. (1976). *Women, Crime and Criminology: A Feminist Critique.* London: Routledge and Kegan Paul.

feminist movement A social movement whose goal has been, and continues to be, the elimination of the patriarchal nature of society. Two large waves of feminist organization can be identified, the first following the French Revolution and extending the principles of liberty and freedom to women. This period is associated with Mary Wollstonecraft (1759–97). The second can be identified with French writer Simone De Beauvoir's *The Second Sex* in 1952, and, in North America, with the publication of Betty Friedan's book, *The Feminine Mystique*, in 1963. *See also* **social movement.**

feminist theory While there is not a single feminist theory, central to all such theories is an attempt to understand the social, economic, and political position of women in society, with a view to liberation. Feminist theory has challenged the claims to objectivity of previous social science, and, by examining society from women's position, has called much social science into question as being male-centred and a component of the hegemonic rule of patriarchy. *See also* **liberal feminism; radical feminism; Marxist feminism; ecofeminism.**

feminization of poverty A social process in which the incidence of poverty among women becomes much higher than among men. Changes in social policy, the structure of the family and the workplace, social security provisions, life expectancy, and other aspects of society have had the unintended result of increasing the female proportion of the population on low incomes or in poverty. In Canada, poverty rates are particularly high among female single parents and among elderly women. The feminization of poverty is often cited as an explanation for an increase in women's involvement in crime and contrasted to a "liberation" explanation.

fence A person or a shop dealing in stolen goods. They do not steal property but buy it for resale or distribution. Reference: Klockars, Carl. (1976). *The Professional Fence.* New York: Free Press.

feral child A child who, in legend or in fact, has been raised and protected from infancy by animals. The most famous example is the "Wild Boy of Aveyron" who was discovered in 1800 at the age of 11 or 12 after having apparently been raised by animals. Although considerable effort was made to "civilize" the young man, there was little success and only a few words were mastered. The case is offered in the social sciences to emphasize the importance of socialization and the social nature of the human species. A more recent example of a child growing up in isolation from human contact is found in the story of Genie (Curtiss 1977). *See also* **socialization.** Reference: Curtiss, Susan. (1977). *Genie: A Psycholinguistic Study of a Modern Day "Wild Child."* New York: Academic Press; Shattuck, Roger. (1980). *The Forbidden Experiment: The Story of the Wild Boy of Aveyron.* New York: Washington Square Press.

Ferri, Enrico (1856–1929) Ferri was a student of Lombroso and a member of the Italian school of criminology or the Positivist school. Ferri pushed the notion of determinism further than others of this school and argued that while offenders could be held socially responsible, they should not be held morally responsible because the behaviour was caused by forces they were not aware of and could not control.

fertility rate The number of children born to women in their fertile years within a given population. Usually expressed as the average number of children born to women over their lifetime. Not to be confused with the birth rate. *See also* **birth rate.**

fetal alcohol syndrome This term was first used in 1973 when two scientists noticed similar deformities in the infants of six mothers with a history of alcohol abuse. The consumption of alcohol during pregnancy is now known to result in brain abnormalities and other deformities in some children. It is now believed that this syndrome may account for the criminal behaviour of many offenders.

fetishism A form of disorder in which the person becomes sexually aroused by inanimate objects such as someone's underwear, a piece of fur, or a rubber doll, or is fixated on non-sexual parts of the body like the feet or knees.

feudalism A system of economic and social organization found historically in several areas of the world including Japan, China, other parts of Asia, the Americas, and many countries of eastern and western Europe. In western Europe, feudalism was at its height between about 1000 and 1500. The system was founded on a web of military obligations between powerful overlords and their vassals. Vassals, who were usually landlords of knightly rank, owed duties of military service in return for grants of land (fiefs) from the overlord. The land, and the military obligations, was usually passed from father to son. The usual economic foundation of the system was the feudal manor, an agricultural organization that included a central farm owned by the landlord and small land holdings for a class of bonded farm labourers (serfs). The serfs were required to work the central manorial farm and to provide the lord with produce and money payments in return for their own rights to land use. The system gradually declined as cities and towns grew, money became the basis for economic transactions, and power became centralized in nation states under monarchies. Loss of rural population from plague also hastened the end of this system of economic organization, especially in England.

Firearms Control Act An Act that resulted from pressure of lobby groups responding to the "Montreal Massacre" demanding tighter gun control. The Firearms Act required all firearms to be registered by January 1, 2001 and owners to have a license. These policies have been hotly debated and there has been much resistance, much of it coming from rural areas of Canada as well as from the National Firearms Association. In 2000, the Supreme Court of Canada unanimously dismissed an action brought by Alberta, four other provinces, and two territories to have the law struck down on constitutional grounds of invasion of an area of provincial jurisdiction. The Court ruled that the federal government's exclusive jurisdiction over criminal law entitled it to regulate gun ownership, since guns are clearly connected to the commission of serious crime. Reference: *The Attorney General for Alberta v. The Attorney General for Canada*, (2000) I.S.C.R.

first-degree murder *See* **murder, first-degree**.

First Nations This term emerged in the mid 1980s to describe Canadian aboriginal individuals and communities. The traditional term "Indian" has fallen into disfavour as it is both mistaken (it was applied only because European explorers had expected to find India across the Atlantic Ocean) and ignores the great variety of history and culture among First Nations societies. The name is also politically significant, since it implies possession of rights arising from original historical occupation of Canadian territory. Canada's principal national organization of aboriginal (but not including Inuit) people is the Assembly of First Nations.

first reading In parliamentary procedure, a bill (a request to the Crown that a matter become law) has three readings. The first reading usually just introduces the bill and is not debatable. Agreement at this stage just gets the bill into the process, and it is sent to committee. When the bill appears for second reading, it is debatable and can be defeated, amended, or approved. If it is approved, it goes to third reading, which is normally a vote of formal approval to send it to Senate and not a time for extended debate.

fiscal crisis Refers broadly to a long-term situation where government expenditures exceed government revenues. Within modern Marxist theory (neo-Marxism), the term has been used more specifically to refer to a situation where governments have increased their role in society in serving the needs of private capital, but have not been able to adequately tax private capital to support the expenditures. For example, technical employment training has now largely become a preserve of the state (rather than the private employer), leaving the state with additional expenditures, but without corresponding revenues. According to neo-Marxism, this tendency is linked to the development of economic concentration and monopoly and inbuilt in the capitalist economic system. The fiscal crisis of the state is thought to drive much contemporary government policy on social programs. Reference: O'Connor, James. (1973). *The Fiscal Crisis of the State*. New York: St. Martin's Press.

fiscal policy Government economic policies that rely on economic regulation and control exercised through government taxation and budgetary policy. These policies are in contrast to monetary policy, which seeks to influence the direction of the economy and regulate levels of economic activity and inflation by control of both the rate of interest (the cost of borrowing money) and the amount of money available within an economy (the money supply). *See also* **monetary policy**.

flapper Adolescent girls and young women who rebelled against the rigid Victorian sexual standards for women. While the age of consent had been raised to 18 in many North American jurisdictions in the later half of the 19th century, the open expression of sexual interest by women in the early 20th century set off alarm bells. The Juvenile Court movement of the early 20th century should be seen as one aspect of a strategy to control the sexuality of young women.

flat tax A tax structure that has gained significant public support in North America in which all citizens would pay the same percentage of taxation on their income. This would simplify tax law and the completion of a tax return but would make income tax regressive. *See also* **regressive taxation**.

flat time sentencing A sentence of imprisonment all of which is served in prison; the offender may not spend any portion of it in the community or on parole. *See also* **determinate sentence**; **indeterminate sentencing**.

flogging To beat a person with a whip or a stick. Commonly found in naval services, this form of punishment is not common in the western world. Attempts were made as early as 1850 to stop this practice in the US navy. It can still be found in nations such as Singapore.

folk society A society of primary communal relationships with little complexity, minimal division of labour, and largely insulated from contact with other societies. The term is an ideal type associated with American anthropologist/sociologist Robert Redfield (1897–1958) and it is closely related to F. Tonnies' (1855–1936) concept of *gemeinschaft*. *See also* ***gemeinschaft***.

forces of production In Marxian terms, the essential component of the economic system of society. Refers to the materials used in the production of goods as well as the tools, knowledge, and techniques used to transform these materials. Does not include the class structure or relations of society, known as the *relations of production*. *See also* **mode of production**; **social relations of production**.

Ford Pinto After the 1973 world oil crisis, American carmakers rushed to design compact cars with greater fuel efficiency. Ford manufactured the Pinto and, wishing to retain a large trunk, they repositioned the gas tank. Their crash tests showed that the tank was apt to explode. However, the car was marketed, and approximately 500 people died in fires. It was later learned that Ford had done a cost analysis: They compared the cost of recalling and redesigning the car with the cost of lawsuits for death and injury. It was determined that paying for lawsuits was the cheapest option. Ford became the first corporation charged with murder, a charge of which the company was acquitted.

fordism Refers to the system of mass production (e.g., the assembly line) pioneered by Henry Ford to meet the needs of a mass market.

Foucault, Michel (1926–84) Foucault represents French intellectual tradition, and, through his studies of the prison, has had an influence on criminology. In his book, he studied the new body of knowledge represented by penology and criminology, the new architecture of the penitentiary, and the new form of regulation of the body these two combined. *See also* **postmodernism**. Reference: Foucault, M. (1975). *Discipline and Punish: The Birth of the Prison*. New York: Vintage.

four pillars A co-ordinated strategy to reduce negative impacts on society from the trading and use of addictive drugs. The pillars are prevention, treatment, harm reduction, and enforcement. Prevention involves interventions with individuals and families. Treatment helps people to emerge from the drug lifestyle and regain integration into society. Harm reduction involves programs like safe injection sites, supplies of clean needles, and rapid health-care responses to overdose crises. Enforcement focuses on police action to reduce the role of organised crime and maintain safety in neighbourhoods.

fourth estate The news and journalistic media: newspapers, magazines. The term suggests that the media represents a powerful force within a society and can shape political events and opinions as well as being watchdogs over the use of authority by political and corporate authorities. The intimate connection between media and corporate capital is pointed out by skeptics. The origin of the term is from medieval France where, on rare occasions, the Crown consulted a constituent assembly representing the French people. The assemblies were composed of representatives of the three "estates" of French society: the clergy composed the first estate; the aristocracy composed the second estate; and the middle class merchants, professionals, state administrators, and wealthier farmers composed the third estate. In modern societies, the media is seen as another base of social power and described as the "fourth estate." It is now argued that the electronic media of radio, television, and the Internet have created a fifth estate.

Frankenstein Title of book written by Mary Wollstonecraft Shelley (1797–1851), the daughter of Mary Wollstonecraft. This book, published in 1818, depicts the creation of a man through the application of science, who subsequently gets out of control and kills his creator. Taken as a metaphor of the limited vision but overwhelming arrogance of scientific "man" or rational "man," the book is now seen as an indictment of the modern society emerging in the 18th and 19th centuries.

Frankfurt school A group of chiefly German social theorists associated with the Frankfurt Institute of Social Research founded in 1923. Authors associated with the school are T.W. Adorno, Max Horkheimer, Herbert Marcuse, and Friedrich Pollock. The underlying philosophy of this group can also be found in the more recent work of Jurgen Habermas, a student of Adorno. The school developed critical theory, an extension and development of the ideas of Karl Marx and Sigmund Freud. Much important work flowed from this school examining culture as a lived experience and its role in modern societies. *See also* **critical theory**; **cultural studies**. Reference: Wiggerhaus, R. (1995). *The Frankfurt School: Its History, Theories and Political Significance*. Boston: MIT Press.

Fraser report A 1985 report titled, Report of the Special Committee on Pornography and Prostitution, commissioned by the federal government of Canada and chaired by John Fraser.

fraud Receiving benefit on the basis of misrepresentation or intentionally misleading information. Fraud can range from false promises of home repairs to false claims of stock market values. *See also* **Bre-X**.

free trade Trade between nations that is conducted on free market principles, without tariffs, import quotas, or other restrictive regulations. Free trade, especially with the United States, has been controversial throughout post-Confederation Canadian history and has been widely distrusted as likely to lead to Canada playing the role of resource provider to a more advanced US manufacturing and service economy. Since 1989, when a free trade agreement with the United States was introduced, Canadian opinion has tended to become more supportive of this policy, especially in light of the general globalization of trade and international communication. Since the initial free trade agreement, there is growing consensus that there has been an economic (and to some extent social) integration of the two nations. In 1993, Canada, the United States and Mexico entered into a trilateral free trade agreement: the North American Free Trade Agreement. *See also* **dependent development**; **metropolis-hinterland theory**; **staples trap**.

free trade election The Canadian federal election of 1988 was contested largely on the issue of entering into a free trade agreement with the United States. The governing party, the Conservatives, were in favour of such an agreement, while many groups organized in opposition. The conservatives won the election and the Canada–U.S. Free Trade Agreement was entered into in 1989.

free will In the criminological debate over the causes of criminal behaviour, the philosophy of free will argues that all individuals are conscious, willful, rational, and goal directed, so rejects that idea that individuals' behaviours are caused (or determined) by factors outside of their consciousness. To treat individuals as though their behaviour is determined is to treat them as objects, but if we accept the philosophy of free will we must treat individuals as subjects and attempt to understand how they make the social world meaningful. The criminal justice system of course is built on the philosophy of free will, since it adjudicates individual responsibility.

freebase A chemical produced from street cocaine by removing the hydrochloric acid bonded to pure cocaine. The free cocaine (or pure cocaine) is then dissolved in a solvent that crystallizes the pure cocaine. It then produces an immediate and powerful high. The production of this drug is dangerous as the ingredients are apt to burst into flame.

French Revolution The French Revolution brought the ideas of liberty, equality, and democracy to continental Europe and set off a profound and irreversible historical transformation. The Revolution began in 1789, and some historians have traced the end of the Revolution to the overthrow of Robespierre, its most radical leader in 1794, others to the seizure of power by Napoleon Bonaparte in 1799, and yet others to the final defeat of Napoleon Bonaparte at the Battle of Waterloo in 1815. From 1789 to 1815, France was transformed by revolution. It began with the overthrowing of the monarchy and soon became a reign of revolutionary terror. The king and queen and many of the aristocracy were executed, and there were mass executions of political opponents. Attempts were made to export the Revolution to the rest of Europe as the French armies moved east and forced monarchs to give up power, granted freedom and land to the serfs, and recruited thousands of the ordinary people into the French army to help carry forward the message of equality and liberation. This initiated a period of international wars with Britain and the old powers of Europe, finally leading to ultimate defeat of the French forces at the Battle of Waterloo in 1815. For the social sciences, the French Revolution is important for representing the triumph of the liberal claim that all humans are essentially equal and all have a right to liberty and freedom of choice. Along with the Bloodless Revolution in England of 1688, which irreversibly established the principle of a limited constitutional monarchy; the Industrial Revolution, which gained momentum in the mid 1700s; and the American Revolution of 1776, this event ushered in the social, economic, and political transformation of western societies and helped create the age of modernity, democracy, economic development, and legal equality for all citizens. The history of the French Revolution has fascinated social scientists since the early 19th century and continues to shape modern culture and intellectual ideas.

Freud, Sigmund (1856–1939) Freud was the founder of psychoanalysis, the theory that adult personality is shaped in early infancy and is especially influenced by the individual's experiences in sexual exploration and development.

Freudian slip Psychoanalyst Sigmund Freud argued that our hidden or suppressed thoughts have a tendency to emerge unexpectedly in what appear to be ordinary mistakes of language or errors of memory. These errors reveal our hidden wishes and desires.

Front de liberation du Québec (FLQ) In English, Front for the Liberation of Quebec. The FLQ was founded in 1963 and inspired by the terrorist war being waged against French colonial domination of Algeria. The Front was dedicated to the use of terrorism and violence to promote the establishment of a separate and socialist Quebec state. In 1963, Front groups set off bombs in mailboxes and other location in Quebec; in 1964, they conducted a hold-up resulting in the theft of military equipment and some $50 000 in cash. Between 1963 and 1970, over 200 bombings were carried out including one at the Montreal Stock Exchange, which injured 27 people. The terrorist activities of the group ceased after the October crisis of 1970. *See also* **October crisis**.

fruit of the poisoned tree doctrine *See* **exclusionary rule**.

Fry, Elizabeth (1780–1845) An English Quaker who devoted her life to penal reform. Like John Howard, she visited prisoners and worked to make prison life more humane. Her name was first used in the title of the Elizabeth Fry Society by a Vancouver, British Columbia, group in 1939. There are now many such groups dedicated to penal reform and providing service to women inmates and offenders. Reference: Fry, K. (1974). *Memoir of the Life of Elizabeth Fry*. N.J.: Patterson and Smith.

functionalist explanation The explanations offered by functionalists or structural functionalists have a property referred to as teleology—explaining things in terms of their end results or purposes. Functionalists tend to explain features of social life in terms of their function (the part they play) in social life. These kinds of explanations are found in biology as well, and it is not surprising that functionalists like Durkheim adopted an organic metaphor. The lungs, for example, are explained in terms of what they do in and for the human body. The classic example of this reasoning is found in Durkheim's discussion of the functions of crime in any society. He argues that as darkness needs light, a moral society needs immorality as a way to make morality visible. Others have argued that crime or deviance also help the society by clarifying the moral boundaries of the group. Many would argue that these are not explanations at all, but are logically circular. *See also* **structural functionalism**.

G

gang legislation Canada passed anti-gang legislation (criminal conspiracy) in 1997 to be applied to any or all of the members of a criminal organization engaging in criminal offences for the benefit of the organization. This legislation allows the courts to seize all proceeds of crime, including property. Several attempts to use this legislation against large numbers of offenders at one time have not met with much success.

Garofalo, Raffaele (1852–1934) A member of the Italian school of positivism associated with

Lombroso. Among other things Garofalo postulated that criminals could be distinguished by the ability to withstand pain. His evidence for this was the frequency with which prisoners displayed tattoos. Given the current popularity of tattoos, we know this claim to be incorrect. *See also* **Positivist school**; **Lombroso, Cesare**.

gemeinschaft A German word, translated as "community," used by sociologist Ferdinand Tonnies (1855–1936) to define an "ideal type" or model society where social bonds are personal and direct and there are strong shared values and beliefs. Characteristic of small-scale, localized societies, it is in contrast to *gesellschaft*, which refers to complex, impersonal societies. American sociologist Talcott Parsons (1902–79) amplified the contrasts of *gemeinschaft* and *gesellschaft* with his "pattern variable" value alternatives. *See also* ***gesellschaft***; **pattern variables**.

gender gap The gap between the political party preferences of men and women. During the 1990s, this gap became significant, with women in most western societies more likely to support liberal or socialist parties favouring public welfare programs and men more likely to support conservative or right-of-centre parties. All political parties now give some attention to positioning their policies and advertising to appeal to both women and men.

gender roles Social roles ascribed to individuals on the basis of their sex. The term *gender* differs from sex because it refers specifically to the cultural definition of the roles and behaviour appropriate to members of each sex, rather than to those aspects of human behaviour that are determined by biology. Thus giving birth is a female sex role, while the role of infant nurturer and caregiver (which could be performed by a male) is a gender role usually ascribed to females. *See also* **sex**.

general deterrence As used in criminal justice, refers to crime prevention achieved through instilling fear in the general population through the punishment of offenders. *See also* **specific deterrence**.

generalized other A term used by George Herbert Mead (1863–1931) to refer to an individual's recognition that other members of their society hold specific values and expectations about behaviour. In their behaviour and social interaction, individuals react to the expectations of others, thus orienting themselves to the norms and values of their community or group.

genocide The systematic killing of an entire ethnic community. In Canadian history, the complete physical elimination of the Beothuk aboriginals of Newfoundland as a result of disease and deliberate killing is perhaps an example. *See also* **cultural genocide**; **Holocaust**; **Armenian genocide**; **Rwandan genocide**.

gentrification A process of change in the social and economic condition of urban neighbourhoods where poorer original residents are replaced by newcomers from the middle class and professional groups.

George, Dudley In 1995, the Chipewyan peoples of Kettle Point and Stony Point in Ontario protested against the tardy return of land taken from them many years previously for a military base. During a confrontation, a member of the Ontario provincial police shot an unarmed protestor, Dudley George. A commission of inquiry was established, and rumours circulated about the possible involvement of the provincial government in directing the activities of the police. Reference: Edwards, Peter. (2001). *One Dead Indian: The Premier, the Police and the Ipperwash Crisis.* Toronto: Stoddart.

gerontocracy Rule by elders; a society in which power, wealth, and prestige flow upwards within an age pyramid. While authority or power was in the hands of elders in many small-scale societies and great reverence was paid to them, in modern society wealth may flow toward the elders, but there is little positive evaluation or prestige bestowed on the elderly, and they are seen as having little authority.

gesellschaft A German word, translated as "society-association," used by Ferdinand Tonnies (1855–1936) to refer to an "ideal type" or model of a society where social bonds are primarily impersonal, instrumental, and narrow. Characteristic of large-scale, complex societies, with a strict division between private and public spheres of life, it contrasts to the community-oriented life of the *gemeinschaft*. American sociologist Talcott Parsons (1902–79) amplified the contrast of *gemeinschaft* and *gesellschaft* with his "pattern variable" value alternatives. *See also* ***gemeinschaft***; **pattern variables**; **ideal type**.

Giant mine *See* **Warren, Roger**.

Gini coefficient Developed by Italian statistician Corrodo Gini (1884–1965) to provide a mathematical expression of the degree of concentration of wealth or income. While it has been criticized over the years, it continues to be used by social scientists describing inequality or comparing inequality among nations. A Gini coefficent of approximately 0.400 is normal for most developed economies. For a fuller grasp of how the coefficient is determined, *see also* **Lorenz curve.**

Gladue case A precedent-setting case regarding aboriginal offenders. The court determined that in passing sentence in cases where a term of incarceration would normally be imposed, judges must consider the unique circumstances of aboriginal people and are under an obligation to consider alternatives to prison. Reference: *R. v. Gladue* [1999] 1 S.C.R. 688.

glass ceiling In the analysis of women in the workplace, this concept is useful for describing the invisible barriers that block the promotion of women. It refers to barriers that are not explicit, but are inherent in the social organization and social relationships of the workplace. For example, women may find their corporate careers obstructed because they are excluded from the recreational and social associations created by male fellow workers and lack the social contacts that are important in gaining status and recognition.

globalization A comprehensive world-wide process of the internationalization of communication, trade, and economic organization. In the economic sphere, it can be seen in international trade agreements, vast increases in the volume of international trade, and growing economic interdependency. It is also marked by the expansion of the size and power of multinational corporations and the development of the American entertainment industry's domination of international cultural communication. Generally the process is seen as driven by the growth of international capitalism and involving the transformation of the culture and social structures of non-capitalist and pre-industrial societies. *See also* **free trade**. Reference: Giddens, Anthony. (2000). *Runaway World: How Globalization is Reshaping Our Lives.* New York: Routledge.

Goffman, Erving (1922–82) Canadian-born sociologist associated with the Chicago school of symbolic interactionism and later professor of anthropology and sociology at the University of Pennsylvania. Perhaps his most important book, *The Presentation of Self in Everyday Life*, developed a "dramaturgical" model of people's interactions with society. In private, "back stage," they express their spontaneous identity, but in public, "front stage," they manage their social presentation to create an impression that will cause their audience to define them in the desired way. They behave as actors as they manage the impression they are creating. For criminology, his most important work is *Asylums*, which examines the transformation of identity that takes place when individuals enter total institutions like mental hospitals or prisons, where their previous sense of self is stripped away and they are resocialized to a new identity. This transformation can be so powerful that prisoners become incapable of recovering their previous sense of self. Reference: Goffman, Erving. (1959). *The Presentation of Self in Everyday Life.* New York: Doubleday; Goffman, Erving (1961). *Asylums: Essays on the Social Situation of Mental Patients and Other Inmates.* New York: Anchor/Doubleday.

golden triangle Areas within Thailand, Laos, and Burma (now called Myanmar) that produce and export heroin. In recent times, Mayanmar has also become the region's main source of amphetamine drugs.

goods producing economy An economy whose central method of capital accumulation is the manufacture of goods for consumers (televisions), for public consumption (trains), or for private economic use (robots for building cars). It has been claimed for several years that western societies have passed through this goods producing, or industrial, stage and have now entered a new economy founded on the delivery of services and the production and dissemination of knowledge. *See also* **service economy**.

Goodwin, Ginger Goodwin was a union organizer in British Columbia who caused trouble in the workplace of Dunsmuir, the Vancouver Island coal baron, and in the Cominco smelter in Trail. In 1918, his earlier exemption from conscription due to poor health was reversed. Goodwin went into hiding, and when an order went out to arrest those who did not show up for their conscription duties, he was hunted down and shot by a local police officer in a wooded area near Cumberland, B.C. Reference: Stonebanks, Roger. (2004). *Fighting for Dignity: The Ginger Goodwin Story.* St. John's: Canadian Committee on Labour History.

Gouzenko case Igor Gouzenko (1919–1987) was a Soviet citizen working as a clerk in the Soviet embassy in Ottawa from 1943 to 1945. When he discovered that he and his family were to be returned to the Soviet Union, he defected and reported to Canadian authorities that a Soviet spy ring was operating in Canada. This was the first of several "spy scares" to emerge in the west after World War II. After much controversy, the Canadian government acknowledged that such a spy ring was operating, and Gouzenko was given protection and a new identity; he and his family remained in Canada. As a result of this case, there was an escalation of repressive measures against potential dissidents in Canada. For American equivalents, *see also* **Hiss, Alger**; **McCarthyism**. Reference: Witaker, R., and G. Marcuse. (1994). *Cold War Canada: The Making of a National Insecurity State, 1945–1957.* Toronto: University of Toronto Press.

Green River killer In 2003, Gary Ridgway, resident of the United States, confessed to the killing of approximately 50 women beginning in the early 1980s, making him the worst mass-murderer in North American history. Ridgway escaped the death penalty by providing information on the location of many of the bodies and by pleading guilty.

Grits A name used to refer to the Liberal Party of Canada, this derives from the mid-1800s when it was first applied to members of a radical farmers' movement in southwestern Ontario. In the early 1870s, this and other movements joined together to establish the Liberal Party, which then inherited the name.

gross counts of crime A count of the total amount of crime in a given community, making no distinction between crime categories. It is usually better to talk about the number of crimes within a specific category, say "violent crime." Even here, however, one finds that a majority of violent crimes are "assault level 1" crimes, the least serious form of assault, and not classed as violent crime in the US.

gross domestic product Gross domestic product is the value of all goods and services including the value of dividend, interest, and other payments made to overseas investors, produced by a nation over a one-year period.

grounded theory A theory that has been derived through inductive reasoning, thus giving it a firm grounding in data or observations of the world. This was an attempt to avoid sociological theory, which was overly abstract and for which the references to the real world were unclear. Such abstract theory would be simply a logical construction deduced from assumptions and propositions.

group An aggregate of individuals having some characteristic in common. They may be distinguished from others by appearance, language, socio-economic status, or cultural values and practices. A group is often characterized by a sense of common identity and shared interests and goals among its members, but a group may exist simply because its members share some objective characteristic and are defined as a group by others.

group, primary A circle of individuals with whom a person is extensively involved: they have bonds of common activity and emotional commitment. People interact in primary groups as whole person to whole person: relationships are comprehensive and emotionally charged. Examples include the family and small traditional communities. The term was developed by C.H. Cooley (1864–1929) and contains echoes of *gemeinschaft. See also* ***gemeinschaft***.

group, secondary A number of individuals jointly linked by some common instrumentally related characteristic. The members of the group have some specialized and specific relationship to each other. Examples include a professional association, colleagues in the workplace, a political party, or a tennis club. The term was developed by C.H. Cooley and contains echoes of *gesellschaft. See also* ***gesellschaft***.

guilty To have been found responsible of a criminal offence either by pleading such or by a court of law. It may also mean conscious of or feeling badly for an offence for which one knows he or she is responsible. Thus, one may feel guilty, look guilty, and so on.

Gun registration *See* **Firearms Control Act**.

H

habitual offender First introduced in 1947–48 to protect the community from those who repeatedly offend and also those determined to be sexual psychopaths. Research found that many offenders incarcerated under this legislation were minor offenders and spent many years behind bars. It was replaced with the dangerous offender provisions of the Criminal Code in 1977.

Hagan, John (1946–) Professor of criminology and law at the University of Toronto and known for his development of structural criminology and power control theory. The power control theory seeks to explain why there is a greater crime rate among males than females; the explanation is located in the power relations of the family and the patterns that arise in relational positions of spouses in the workplace and within the family and their relations with children of both sexes. Reference: Hagan, John. (1989). *Structural Criminology.* New York: Rutgers University Press.

halfway house Usually a housing facility developed as part of a corrections policy to permit gradual release from prison. While the offender is living in the community, he or she remains under some degree of supervision.

hallucinogens Those chemicals having the effect of causing the apparent perception of objects not really present.

Haney correctional institution Opened in 1957 in British Columbia, Haney was the first or second Canadian institution that was purposely built and fully dedicated to the rehabilitative ideal. It was modelled on Californian experiences and shaped and directed by American psychologist Kim Nelson, who had come to British Columbia to participate in the criminology program at the University of British Columbia. The institution appeared when the rehabilitative ideal was already under attack, and thus had a very short life. It was closed in 1974.

harm reduction A term often used in the discussion of drug users, prostitutes, etc. Rather than taking a moralistic approach, perhaps focusing on punishment or rehabilitation, the system tries to reduce the harm that comes to such offenders. For example, it provides drug users with clean needles or perhaps with a safe place to shoot-up, or even provides them with standardized heroin. The community might also provide a safe area for prostitutes to work, provide free testing for infectious diseases, etc. All of this will reduce harm to the "offenders," but in the long term should also reduce harm to the community. *See also* **four pillars**. Reference: Ericson, P.G., D.M. Riley, and I. W. Chung. (1997). *Harm Reduction: A New Direction for Drug Policies and Programs.* Toronto: University of Toronto Press.

Harper, John Joseph Harper, a Manitoba native leader, was mistaken for a car thief and shot by the Winnipeg police on March 9, 1988. His death was one among many instances of mistreatment of aboriginal peoples in the province and led to the Report of the Aboriginal Justice Inquiry of Manitoba: The Deaths of Helen Betty Osborne and John Joseph Harper (1991). Reference: Sinclair, Gordon, Jr. (1999). *Cowboys and Indians: The Shooting of J.J. Harper.* Toronto: McClelland and Stewart.

hashish A concentrated form of cannabis made from the resin of the female plant.

hate crime There is no such thing as a hate crime, but a 1995 amendment to the Criminal Code made motivation by hatred for a designated group an aggravating factor to be considered in sentencing. Sexual orientation has been added as a designated group. *See also* **hate propaganda**.

hate propaganda In 1970, it became a criminal offence to promote hate against identifiable groups. There have been few convictions under this provision, among them Jim Keegstra and Ernst Zundel. Both cases involved anti-Semitism and denial of the Holocaust. Reference: *R. v. Zundel* [1992] 2 S.C.R. 731.

Hawthorne effect An increase in worker productivity observed at the Chicago Hawthorne plant of General Electric in the 1920s and 1930s, attributed to improvements in worker–management communication and increased involvement of workers with each other. The term is now used more generally to refer to improvement of worker productivity that does not result from any objective change in working conditions or work organization, but seems to arise from workers having more positive psychological feelings about the workplace.

hearsay rule The rule that hearsay evidence (or second-hand evidence) cannot be used in court. Instead the court must hear from the person who was the original source of the information in order for cross-examination of the witness to take place.

hegemony A concept of Italian Marxist Antonio Gramsci (1891–1937) that refers to the way that the political and social domination of the bourgeois class in capitalist society is pervasively expressed not only in ideologies, but in all realms of culture and social organization. The comprehensive expression of the values of class-divided society in social life lends this form of society an appearance of naturalness and inevitability that removes it from examination, criticism, and challenge. While arising in the analysis of a class-divided society, the term is also used in discussion of a patriarchal society or a colonial society.

heritability The extent to which a characteristic of a living organism is genetically determined, rather than shaped by the surrounding environment. In the social sciences, this term is chiefly associated with debate about the heritability of characteristics such as intelligence, criminality, gender behaviour, and aggressiveness: Are each of these (however measured) shaped most by biological (genetic) inheritance or by the influence of environmental factors like culture, socialization, and physical nutrition?

heroin First produced from morphine in 1875, heroin was found to have powerful painkilling abilities and was used to replace morphine, because it was thought to be non-addictive.

heuristic device An abstract concept or model useful for thinking about social and physical phenomena. For example, sociologists use the concept of social structure to help them to define and analyze aspects of society that create patterns and regularity in the everyday roles and activities of individuals. Sociologists do not imagine that individuals mechanically and automatically act in precisely prescribed ways within social structures, or that social structures are unchanging or fixed, but the concept of structure and regularity is an essential tool for understanding how social life itself is possible.

hierarchy A structuring of social statuses and roles within an organization or society ranked according to differentiations of power, authority, wealth, income, etc. Related terms are ranking or stratification.

hinterland *See* **metropolis-hinterland theory**.

Hirschi, Travis Professor of sociology at the University of Arizona. He is associated with the development of social control theory, which has a focus on the strength of social bonds, rather than on the idea of individual pathology. According to this theory, delinquency arises when there are weak bonds of social attachment, since commitment to others reduces the chance of deviant behaviours. He later elaborated a theory with a different emphasis that focused on self-control and the idea that effective internalization of control must occur at an early stage of individual social development. In this theory, the quality and orientation of early parental socialization is crucial. Thus, observed differences in crime rates between groups based on race, gender, and ethnicity are reflective of contrasted early socialization patterns, rather than of later differential associations etc. He thus advocates a focus of public policy on strengthening families and improving child rearing practices. Reference: Hirschi, Travis, and Michael R. Gottfredson. (1990). *A General Theory of Crime.* Stanford, CA: Stanford University Press.

Hiss, Alger A lawyer who rose to become a significant public official in the United States through the 1930s and 1940s. In 1948, a magazine editor, who confessed to being a communist, accused Hiss of assisting in the transmittal of documents to the Russians. Hiss denied any involvement, but was found guilty in his second trial and sentenced to five years in prison. Many did not believe his pleas of innocence, and the case stimulated support for Senator McCarthy and the hunt for communists in places of influence in American society. Some believed that Hiss was the scapegoat for the loss of China to the communists and the Russian development of the atomic bomb. Americans found it difficult to believe that either of these events could have happened without duplicity and thus looked to subversion, spies, lack of loyalty, and moral degeneration as explanations for these world developments. However, recent evidence tends to suggest that Hiss was indeed guilty. *See also* **McCarthyism**.

historical materialism The central concept of social analysis in the work of Karl Marx (1818–83) and Frederick Engels (1820–95). The core idea is that the political and intellectual history of human societies is shaped most importantly by the social and technical organization of economic production and exchange. This view suggests that it is not principally intellectual ideas and knowledge that shape the structure and cultural values of social life, but rather the shape of social life, especially in the social organization of economic production, that chiefly shapes intellectual ideas and knowledge. *See also* **dialectical materialism**.

Holocaust Originally a term from ancient Greek referring to a human sacrifice by burning the victim. In modern times, however, it has come to refer to the attempted genocide of Jews by the German Nazi regime during World War II and the resulting systematic murder of 6 million Jews between 1941 and 1945. *See also* **genocide**.

homicide The killing of a person by another person. Not all homicides, however, are classified as murder or as manslaughter. *See also* **murder**.

homogamy Marriage between individuals who are, in some culturally important way, similar to each other. The similarity may be based on ethnicity, religion, or socio-economic status. Canadians, for example, tend to be homogamous, with marriage partners usually having quite similar social and economic status and ethnic affiliation. This is a descriptive concept only and does not refer to rules or customs about mate selection.

Homolka, Karla *See* **Bernardo, Paul**.

homophobia Literally an uncontrollable fear of homosexuals and of homosexuality, but the term is generally used for a negative and contemptuous attitude to same-sex sexual relationships and to those who participate in them.

homosexuality Homosexuality has long been tangled in the law, but only when involving sexual relations between men. Lesbian sex has rarely been given legal attention, and there has been no law against it in Canadian history either before or after Confederation. Gay sex has a quite different history. The term *homosexual* was first used in 1869, and by the beginning of the 20th century, although there was a consensus developing among intellectuals that homosexuality was best understood simply as sexual variation, there were clear indications of growing official hostility towards it. Under the Nazi regime some 100 000 to 400 000 homosexuals were murdered in the concentration camps. In Canada, male homosexuality remained punishable by up to 14 years in prison until legal reform in 1969. In 1974, the American Psychological Association removed homosexuality from its catalogue of illnesses, and, in 1996, protection against discrimination based on sexual orientation was added to Canada's human rights legislation. The Charter of Rights and Freedoms has also been expanded by courts to include protection against discrimination. Recently, courts have decided that benefits for married couples must be equally accessible to same-sex couples, and same-sex marriages are now performed in several Canadian provinces.

horizontal integration The expansion of a corporation to include other previously competitive enterprises within the same sector of goods or service production. For example, one candy maker may take over another candy maker. This process is characteristic of capitalist economies, which have a marked tendency to sectoral concentration into fewer and fewer enterprises and business conglomerates.

house of correction Linked to the development of mercantile capitalism, the first house of correction emerged in Amsterdam. This institution did not serve as punishment for criminal offence; rather, it was accessible to employers and parents and state officials to deal with those who were unwilling to work in the new economy or did not have the attitudes and dispositions required for this work. Typically, inmates of these houses worked long hours at tasks that aided the productivity of the nation. The first house of correction (also called a workhouse) appeared in England in 1555, it was known as the Bridewell. These institutions eventually became prisons, serving the purpose of holding those awaiting trial, awaiting transportation, or unable to pay fines. The penitentiary emerged from these institutions as nations sought to replace transportation with more humane ways to confine people and to make incarceration become a sentence of the courts. Reference: Morris, N., and D.J. Rothman. (1995). *The Oxford History of the Prison: The Practice of Punishment in Western Society*. New York: Oxford University Press.

Howard, John (1726–90) Howard, an English prison reformer, clearly articulated the belief that prisoners should be treated humanely and that there was hope of their rehabilitation. He believed that prisoners and all offenders were "children of God," just like everyone else, and thus should be treated as such. By equating crime with sin, he believed that offenders could be rehabilitated through religious education and being given the opportunity to reflect upon God. In 1777, he published a review of prisons in Europe, discovering that the Roman Catholic Church was using single cells, based on a monastic model, to incarcerate young offenders. Howard championed this form of incarceration among other reforms. The John Howard Society, while no longer religious, does reflect Howard's commitment to service to inmates and offenders, and runs programs to help prisoners while in prison and on re-entry to society. Reference:

Howard, Derek. (1963). *John Howard: Prison Reformer.* New York: Archer House.

Hudson's Bay Company The Hudson's Bay Company was incorporated in 1670 by Royal Charter of the King of England to exercise political and economic control over all the lands and the sea around Hudson Bay and the entire area that drained its lakes and rivers into Hudson Bay. The Bay's main interest was to monopolize the extraordinarily profitable fur trade, particularly in the beaver pelts that were prized by European hat makers. The extent of the Bay's territory ran from Edmonton in the west to north of Ottawa in the east, and from areas south of the present border with the United States to Baffin Island in the north. Over this vast territory, the Bay wielded unchallengeable political and economic power, and was, for almost 200 years, the effective government of this area. After Confederation, the new government of Canada determined immediately that the Bay must be shorn of its monopoly domination of trade and resources and of its quasi-governmental powers. In 1869, under pressure from the British government, Canada and the Bay reached an agreement by which the Bay surrendered almost all its territory. The company retained great tracts of land, however, and for another hundred years exercised extensive powers and influence in Canada's remote northern communities. In 1987, this role in the north was ended when the Bay sold its northern stores, and the company then became similar to any large corporate retail organization.

hulks Abandoned ships anchored and configured to imprison offenders. This practice arose in Britain as crime rates rose and transportation to the American colonies was curtailed by the War of Independence. The practice of transportation was resumed in 1787 after the British government designated the eastern coast of Australia as a new destination for convicts.

human capital The talents and capabilities that individuals contribute to the process of production. Companies, governments, and individuals can invest in this "capital" just as they can invest in technology and buildings or in finances.

human rights *See* **Bill of Rights**; **Charter of Rights and Freedoms**; **rights, human**; **Universal Declaration of Human Rights**.

humanism An ethical doctrine that asserts the central importance of human life and experience on earth and the right and duty of each individual to explore and develop their potential. Humanism is, to some extent, in opposition to religious doctrines, like Christianity, that diminish the importance of earthly life and assert that human existence is merely a stage of preparation for heavenly life after death. In the social sciences, humanism is evident in those groups who argue that social theory must conceive of the human actor as a subject rather than an object.

hunter-gatherer society The earliest form of human society and still persisting to some extent in remote regions of the world. These societies have an economic base that rests on the use of the naturally occurring animal and plant resources of the environment. They do not practice agriculture or raise and herd animals. Social structure is usually egalitarian with little economic and gender inequality. Private property is minimal. In Canada, the Inuit and the First Nations communities were primarily hunter-gatherer societies prior to European contact. This aboriginal lifestyle had experienced major disruption by the second half of this century, but many communities are now attempting to recover traditional ways.

Hutterites An Anabaptist (opposed to infant baptism) group that emerged in central Europe in 1528 under the leadership of Joseph Hutter. The basic components of their religious beliefs are communal ownership of property, communal living, nonviolence, and commitment to adult baptism. A large number of Hutterites emigrated to Canada in 1918, and the majority now live in the prairie provinces and retain traditional styles of dress and custom. Mennonites originated at approximately the same time as the Hutterites, but arrived in Canada from the US in 1786. *See also* **sect**.

hybrid offence While offences in Canada are generally categorized as "summary" or "indictable," there are some offences for which the Crown prosecutor may select whether to have the offence treated as a summary offence or an indictable offence. Also known as *dual procedure offences. See also* **summary offence**; **indictable offence**.

hypothesis A testable statement (i.e., it may be true or false) of a specific relationship between or among variables. In the classic model of science, this testable statement is deduced from a theory. *See also* **hypothetico-deductive model of science**.

hypothetico-deductive model of science The classical or traditional model of how science operates: scientists are assumed to begin with a theory, deduce a hypothesis from the theory, and then gather evidence to test the hypothesis. If the hypothesis is confirmed, the theory is assumed to be correct or useful. *See also* **hypothesis; theory**.

I

I The term was introduced by George Herbert Mead (1863–1931) to refer to the aspect of identity, or self, that reacts in social interaction to the expectations of others. In social interaction, individuals are aware of the expectations of others, but they do not necessarily conform to these expectations in their reactions. This spontaneous, never entirely predictable element of individual personality makes each individual a unique social actor. *See also* **me**.

id Concept of Sigmund Freud (1856–1939), founder of psychoanalysis. The id is the unconscious drives and psychic energies of humans as biological organisms. As such, it is untouched by culture and social learning, and encompasses all that is primitive, natural, and pre-civilized in human passions and energies. Freud seems to have assumed that the human struggle to achieve self-consciousness against the ungoverned and unconstrained passions of the id remained deeply buried in the unconscious minds of all human beings. *See also* **ego; superego**.

ideal type An abstract model of a classic, pure, form of social phenomenon. It is a model concept and does not necessarily exist in exact form in reality. An example is Ferdinand Tonnies's dichotomy of *gemeinschaft* and *gesellschaft*. Tonnies described two opposite, or polar types, of social association: one personal and committed (community), and one impersonal and unemotional (society association). These two formal types then provide a benchmark for the analysis and comparison of actually existing societies. Max Weber also used this method of analysis with his ideal types of bureaucracy, authority, and social action.

idealism A perspective that asserts the independent causal influence of intellectual ideas on social organization and culture. It is contrasted to materialism, which focuses on concrete aspects of social organization as causative of particular intellectual ideas and values. Max Weber can be said to have given an idealistic explanation of the growth of capitalism by linking it to the emergence of a "Protestant ethic." *See also* **historical materialism**.

identity politics Thought to be a central aspect of postmodern politics and communities in which the legitimacy of a unitary public identity or an overarching sense of self has diminished, and in its place the previously private identities of citizens (based on their race, ethnicity, sexual preference, physical state, or victimization) compete for public recognition and legitimation. Some theorists fear that this will lead to private values and identities coming to take precedence over public involvement as citizens. *See also* **citizen**. Reference: Elshtain, J.B. (1993). *Democracy on Trial.* Toronto: Anansi Press.

identity theft Theft of one or more pieces of personal identification (e.g., social insurance number, passport, bank card, or birth certificate) for use as entry to that person's financial resources.

ideographic Explanations of specific events, phenomena, or behaviours that are sought in the careful examination of specific preceding events. For example, why did Mary murder the butler? Or, what caused World War I? For the most part, clinical psychologists and historians are interested in ideographic explanations. Other disciplines, like sociology, are interested in explanations of classes of events or behaviours and seek these in a careful examination of a few general categories or classes of preceding events. For example, why do men murder their partners? Or, what are the causes of international violence? These explanations are known as nomothetic explanations.

ideology A linked set of ideas and beliefs that act to uphold and justify an existing or desired arrangement of power, authority, wealth, and status in a society. For example, a socialist ideology advocates the transformation of society from capitalism to collective ownership and economic equality. In contrast, a liberal ideology associated with capitalist societies upholds that system as the best, most moral, most desirable form of social arrangement. Patriarchal ideology also has this characteristic of asserting claims and beliefs that justify a social arrangement: in this case, male social domination of women. Another example is a racist ideology claiming that people can be classified into distinct races and that some races are inferior to others. Racist ideologies are used as justifications for systems of slavery or colonial exploitation. Although there is often a dominant ideology in a society, there can also be counter-ideologies that advocate transformation of social relationships. *See also* **dominant ideology thesis**; **hegemony**.

Ignatieff, Michael Canadian historian Ignatieff in his 1978 publication, *A Just Measure of Pain*, provides a complex analysis of the rise of the penitentiary in which he claims that this development is the result of more complicated factors than the rational conspiracy of the ruling class. Subsequently, Ignatieff has become an important commentator on human rights, nationalism, and international conflict.

ignorance of the law is no excuse A fundamental principle of criminal law is that individuals may not offer the legal defence that they were unaware that their acts were designated as criminal under the law. All citizens are presumed to know the law.

immigration The movement of peoples into a country or territory (movement of people within countries is referred to as migration.) Immigration has played the central role in the development of Canada from the first permanent European settlements in the mid-1600s to the 1990s where 16 percent of Canadians were born outside Canada. The birth rate of Canada's population—the number of children born to a woman in her fertile years—is about 1.6, much lower than the 2.1 that would be needed to maintain a stable population. The prospect of a declining and aging population has led to some calls for increased immigration to Canada. Economic recession, the demands on public services resulting from the concentrated patterns of immigrant settlement, and concern about interethnic tensions have more recently led to controversy about levels of immigration. A special mention should be made of Quebec, where the population increased, until the 1960s, mostly through a high birth rate. In history, Quebec had one of the highest birth rates known in any world society. Although there has been immigration of francophones to Quebec, chiefly from old French colonial territories, the great majority of the francophone population has descended from the approximately 60 000 people who remained there when the French empire over Quebec was defeated in 1759. Reference: Avery, Donald. (1995). *Reluctant Host: Canada's Response to Immigrant Workers, 1896–1994.* Toronto: McClelland and Stewart.

imperialism Domination by one or more countries over others for political and economic objectives. It can be effected by force of arms or through the economic and political power exercised by state and corporate agencies. Imperialism is sometimes organized in a formal empire, with a ruling nation and colonized territories, but it can also exist where one nation or region exercises dominant influence over international trade and investment, patterns of economic development, and mass communication. See also **colonialism**; **metropolis-hinterland theory**.

incapacitation A philosophy of incarceration that argues that some offenders might have to be incarcerated not for what they have done but to prevent future harm to the community. This depends on the community's ability to identify those that might re-offend. Some also argue that it is unfair to punish people for what they might do, rather than for what they have done. Selective incapacitation is provided for under dangerous offender legislation.

incest Sexual intercourse between individuals who are culturally regarded as too closely related for sexual intimacy to be legitimate or moral. Incest rules vary cross-culturally, but generally all cultures forbid intercourse between parents and children, between siblings, and between grandparents and grandchildren. Rare historical exceptions to the rules include ancient Egypt and traditional Hawaii, where siblings were favoured marriage partners among the royal family and probably other members of the aristocracy and the wealthy. Many cultures have mythical or religious stories that warn of the terrible consequences of violating incest rules.

incidence A contrasting term to prevalence. Incidence tells us the frequency of occurrence of some event during a particular time period. For example there were 581 criminal homicides in 1997, or the rate of crime for one year is higher than for the previous year.

independent immigrant One of three classes of immigrants to Canada (the other two being family class and refugees). The independent class do not require sponsorship—they apply on their own—but they are rated on a point system, which tends to give points to education and training, labour market demands, age, and having family in Canada. *See also* **sponsored immigrant**.

independent variable Causal research examines the world in terms of variables (those things that reveal variation within a population). An independent variable is typically the cause, while a dependent variable is the effect. The independent variable is that variable assumed to be the causal variable. In experimental research, it is the variable the investigator manipulates. The effect (the dependent variable) is dependent on the causal variable. If unemployment is thought to cause crime rates to increase, unemployment is the independent variable (it can vary between high and low) and crime rates the dependent variable. Something that is an independent variable at one time can be a dependent variable at another.

indeterminate sentencing Sentencing, usually to prison, for an unspecified length of time. This practice is not followed in Canada, although the dangerous offenders provisions of the Criminal Code are the closest approximation. However, even here the offender is entitled to periodic reviews of the sentence length. Most other sentences are for a clearly specified length of time. Parole or reduction of prison time for good behaviour or for entering mandatory supervision in the community can still result in less time being served. A closer version of indeterminate sentencing is found in the United States where an offender may be sentenced to a flexible period of incarceration (e.g., for 10–20 years).

index Many of the concepts social scientists study are quite complex and cannot adequately be measured by a single indicator. In these cases, researchers develop several indicators and, in some cases, will give different weights to each indicator. This combination of indicators and weights is an index. Socio-economic status is difficult to measure; typically the indicators of income, occupation, and education are used. If occupation is seen as more central it may be given more weight. An index of socio-economic status is developed.

indexicality As used by ethnomethodologists, this refers to the contextual nature of behaviour and talk. Talk, for example, is indexical in the sense that it has no meaning without a context or can take on various meanings dependent on the context. As we construct talk or listen to talk, we all must engage in the interpretive process of constructing a context. With this context, we give the talk a sense of concreteness or definiteness. There is no way to avoid indexicality, however, nor a way to remove it, since talk about context itself is also indexical. For this reason, constructing a sense of reality is an ongoing accomplishment of social members.

Indian Act The British North America Act (1867), creating the nation of Canada, gave responsibility for the native peoples of the new nation to the federal government. Federal legislation governing native peoples was first passed in 1868, and in 1876 the first Indian Act was passed. This Act provides a legal definition of "Indian" and, for those covered by the designation, provides a framework in which their activities are governed. From the outset, the Act espoused the goal of assimilation and in the name of this end authorized many repressive actions by the state. The Inuit (until recently referred to as "Eskimo") of the north were not included in the Indian Act, and a court decision in 1939 was required to declare them a federal responsibility. The Act has been described as a "total institution" since the lives of native peoples covered by it are entirely lived out within its rule. The Act has been a powerful instrument for the colonization of native lands and peoples. Since 1970, there have been suggestions that the Indian Act be removed and native peoples become similar to other citizens in Canada. *See also* **institution, total**; **reserves**; **potlatch**.

indictable offence Generally speaking, more serious offences than summary offences and placing different limits on the police and the courts; once called *felonies*. *See also* **summary offence**; **hybrid offence**.

indigenous peoples Those people inhabiting a land prior to colonization by another nation. In Canada, this would include the Indians and Inuit, but would probably not include the Métis, who are of mixed European and aboriginal descent. *See also* **aboriginal peoples**.

individual pathology A term used to refer to biological or psychological explanations of criminal or deviant behaviour by individuals. The assumption is that the deviant behaviour of individuals can be at least partly explained by some physical or psychological trait that makes them different from normal law-abiding citizens.

individualism A value system, central to classical liberalism and capitalism, that upholds choice, personal freedom, and self-orientation. *See also* **classical liberalism**.

individualistic A theory that focuses on explaining the behaviour of individuals and using factors or features of the individual in explaining this behaviour. An alternative to this approach would be to explain the behaviour of a group (the crime rate of Canada) in terms of characteristics of this group.

individuation Unlike individualism, which refers to an individualistic value system, individuation refers to the process by which individualism is accomplished, the breaking down of obligatory ties and responsibilities to other people or institutions, so that the individual is freed from social bonds. Such a process must also lead to the adoption of the value of individualism. *See also* **individualism**.

inductive reasoning Developing a theory or reaching a conclusion after consideration of several empirical observations. *See also* **grounded theory**.

industrial relations A general term referring to workplace relationships between workers and management. Industrial relations has become an important professional and academic discipline, since successful management of industrial relations is closely linked to workplace productivity and product quality. There have been many different approaches to the management of industrial relations in modern capitalist societies, but they generally share the characteristic that they seek to discipline, motivate, and engage workers in processes of production or administration without making any fundamental change to the structure of ownership or direction of the workplace. At the end of the 19th century, scientific management became increasingly popular as a means of workplace direction, and this approach relied upon close and systematic control of the work process and of the methods of work employed. Beginning in the 1920s and 1930s, a new movement in industrial relations began to focus instead on the management of human relations in the workplace, after it was demonstrated that creation of a positive communicative atmosphere at work was capable of stimulating worker productivity. In more recent years, the idea of quality control circles, where workers take direct responsibility as work groups for productivity and work quality, has become popular following successful use of this approach in Japan. There have also been numerous schemes to increase worker participation in the workplace, either through enhanced workplace communication, consultation and co-operative worker–management planning, or through worker representation and participation directly in management. *See also* **scientific management**; **alienation**.

industrial revolution The production of goods for trade and profit using machines to enhance the productivity of labour. The term is used to describe the profound technological changes that began in England in the mid-18th century. Before the 18th century, there was very little power machinery except wind and water mills, and production was carried out with hand tools and hard human labour. The industrial revolution introduced technologies that could employ power from water, steam, gas, coal, electricity, and oil to replace or enhance human labour. This made possible a level of economic productivity that had never before been achieved, and it initiated a process of unending technological transformation and social change. Socially, the industrial revolution is associated with the rational organization of work, a transformation from a society of self-sufficient producers to a society of employed wage workers and the spread of a market-driven system of allocation of resources. In Canada, these changes occurred in the 19th century. Social scientists continue to be interested in how this technological transformation affected social relations, politics, community life, family structure, and women's role in society. Many people argue that the computerization of society is bringing with it a set of changes equal in importance to the industrial revolution. It is against the staggering changes brought about by the industrial revolution that sociology emerged, as well as an interest in social problems, including crime. Marx, Durkheim, and Weber, among other social scientists, were responding to these changes. In addition, the wealth from the industrial revolution made possible the building of asylums and prisons, and the new economy necessitated changes in policing and the administration of justice. Reference: Hobsbawm, E. (1969). *Industry and Empire*. London: Pelican Books.

industrialization The process of developing an economy founded on the mass-manufacturing of goods. Industrialization is associated with the urbanization of society, an extensive division of labour, a wage economy, differentiation of institutions, and growth of mass communication and mass markets. Many western societies are now described as post-industrial since much economic activity is based on the production of services, knowledge, or symbols.

inequality of condition Where individuals have very different amounts of wealth, status, and power. This is a characteristic of all complex modern societies; however, equality of condition is often present in small-scale, hunter-gatherer societies. *See also* **class.**

inequality of opportunity Where differences in individual possession of wealth, status, and power result in definite advantages and disadvantages in the pursuit of personal success.

infanticide An offence under the Criminal Code of Canada (introduced in 1948) involving the killing of a child under the age of one year by the mother who has not fully recovered from the effects of childbirth. A father committing such an act would be charged with murder. This is an unusual category of crime in that it appears to recognize that the psychological and physical condition of the offender may have contributed to the commission of the offence.

inference The logical process of moving from an indicator or observation to a conclusion or general rule.

inferential statistics Statistical tools or techniques used to draw inference about a population on the basis of research evidence from a sample. For example, estimating the frequency of value for a particular variable within a population. This is found commonly in reports of public opinion polls when it is noted that "a sample of this size is accurate to within +/− 3.2 percent [note, this number will vary], 19 times out of 20 (i.e., 95 percent)". *See also* **statistics; descriptive statistics.**

inferiorization Refers to the process of imposing a stigmatized or inferiorized identity on a group of people. The people stigmatized tend to adopt a sense of inferiority that leads to a sapping of confidence and ability, inhibits political organization, and results in a host of personal and collective social problems. This concept can be linked to the theory of a "culture of poverty."

informal economy Also known as the *underground economy*, or the *hidden economy*, refers to those economic activities that are carried on outside the institutionalized structures of the economy. For most purposes, this means they are transactions not reported to the taxation department, office of employment insurance, worker's compensation, or municipal governments. Usually these transactions are based on cash exchanges, but they may be bartered for goods or services.

infrastructure In Marxist theory or political economy theory, refers to the base or economic foundation of society upon which the culture and social institutions of society are built. The concept of infrastructure is similar to "mode of production" and would include the forces of production and the relations of production. *See also* **base (or infrastructure); mode of production.**

inherent right to self-government A right claimed particularly by native peoples in Canada. By declaring that this right is inherent, it rejects the notion that the right is bestowed by the government of Canada. Rather, the right existed prior to Canada becoming a nation and therefore acknowledges that native peoples were, and perhaps still are, nations with the right to fully make decisions for themselves. *See also* **nation.**

initial appearance The first appearance of an accused before a judge at which time the charge is read and bail set or pre-trail release arranged.

inquisitorial system A system of criminal procedure and trial in which judges actively cross-examine participants in the trial, including the defendant, witnesses, and lawyers for both the prosecution and the defence. This system is usually found in jurisdictions where the civil law system of continental Europe and one-time European colonies like Quebec has been adopted. (However, Quebec shares the same criminal law system as the rest of Canada and therefore does not have an inquisitorial system.) As in the adversarial system, associated with England and Wales (Scotland is inquisitorial and has the civil law system), English-speaking Canada and the United States, there is a presumption of the innocence of the defendant, and the involvement of judges in trials does not indicate that they are playing an accusatory role against the defendant; rather, they are seen as seekers of evidence upon which rational decisions can be based. *See also* **adversary system.**

insanity defence According to the Criminal Code of Canada, this is a defence available to a defendant who is "in a state of natural imbecility or has disease of the mind to an extent that renders him or her incapable of appreciating the nature or quality of an act or omission or of knowing that it is wrong." Since 1991, this defence has been known as the *mentally disordered defence.*

institution, social A pattern of social interaction, having a relatively stable structure, that persists over time. Institutions have structural properties—they are organized—and they are shaped by cultural values. Thus, for example, the "institution of marriage," in western societies, is structurally located in a cohabiting couple and regulated by norms about sexual exclusiveness, love, sharing, etc. There is not full agreement about the number or designation of social institutions in a society, but the following would typically be included: family, economy, politics, education, health care, and media.

institution, total A social institution that encompasses the individual, cutting them off from significant social interaction outside its bounds. These institutions are frequently involved in the process of resocialization whereby individuals are detached from their previous sense of identity and re-shaped to accept and absorb new values and behaviour. Examples include religious orders, prisons, and army training camps. Reference: Goffman, Erving. (1961). "On the Characteristics of Total Institutions." In Donald Cressey, (ed.). *The Prison.* New York: Holt, Rinehart and Winston.

institutional completeness The condition of a group within a larger society where the major institutions—economy, politics, family, and schooling—are reproduced, thus enabling the smaller group to have little social connection with the larger group.

institutionalization Where social interaction is predictably patterned within relatively stable structures regulated by norms. For example, seeking a diagnosis for a physical illness or obtaining advice or a cure is institutionalized within the "health care" institution; conflict over values or interests is institutionalized within the "political system;" sexual access and raising children is institutionalized within the "family."

instrumentalist Marxism A view of the role of the state from a conflict or Marxist perspective. The state is seen as an instrument of the dominant class of the society and is assumed to operate at its behest. This approach stresses the importance of the intimate connection of the capitalist class to the state power apparatus and argues that it is this interconnection that explains political and economic policies in capitalist societies. This view has now been largely displaced by a structurally focused analysis. *See also* **structuralist approach**; **relative autonomy**.

integration, social (1) The joining of different ethnic groups within a society into a common social life regulated by generally accepted norms and values. This process need not involve the obliteration of distinct ethnic identity, which would be assimilation, but it implies that ethnic identity does not limit or constrain commitment to the common activities, values, and goals of the society. Canada's official policy of multiculturalism assumes that social integration can be achieved without the elimination of the cultural distinctiveness of ethnic groups. (2) In the work of Émile Durkheim (1858–1917), the term refers to the density of connection between individuals and social institutions. He assumes that a society requires intense individual participation in a wide range of institutions for it to maintain social integration and provide individuals with a sense of meaning and belonging.

interest group A group of individuals and organizations linked together for the purpose of active promotion of particular values and objectives. Interest groups are usually associated with the political process through which they seek support and resources for their objectives. Interest groups encompass those with issue-specific goals (e.g., opposition to nuclear energy) as well as those seeking to regularly defend and advance their goals and objectives (e.g., the Canadian Federation of Independent Business, the Canadian Labour Congress). Pluralist theory upholds the view that political process and political decision-making is best thought of as consisting of open and competitive interest group interaction and advocacy within a framework of democracy.

intermittent sentence A sentence of 90 days imprisonment or less, which is served on a periodic basis. Offender may serve a sentence on the weekends to enable them to retain their employment.

internal validity A standard or criteria against which research results are judged. To be internally valid the results of an experiment or of a survey are considered to be accurate indications of the results of manipulating independent variables in experiments or to reliably reflect the attitudes or knowledge of respondents in the case of a survey. For example, if evaluation of a drug claimed to prevent colds was conducted by giving it to people unlikely to encounter other infected persons (e.g., lighthouse keepers), the results can be seen as produced by the way the experiment or survey was conducted, and then the results are internally invalid. Something internal to the research process produced the results, so researchers are no longer measuring what they claim to be measuring. Selection bias in the allocation of subjects to the experimental and control groups may contaminate the results as can questions in a survey that elicit socially desirable answers. Placebos and double blind procedures in experiments are used to enhance internal validity. The random assignment of subjects to the control and experimental groups is also essential for establishing internal validity. *See also* **double blind procedure**; **external validity**; **validity**.

International Criminal Court Established on July 1, 2002, when sufficient nations ratified the agreement to create the court. The court serves as an independent criminal court, overseen by the signatories, to which cases can be referred by the participating nations for violations of laws set out in the founding agreement.

International Criminal Tribunal for Former Yugoslavia Established by the United Nations in 1993 after reports of atrocities in the former nation of Yugoslavia. The tribunal was established to investigate charges of murder, torture, and "ethnic cleansing," and from 1996 to 1999 Canadian jurist Louise Arbor, who was later appointed to the Supreme Court of Canada, was its chief prosecutor. It was soon enmeshed in controversy when critics charged that its judges and prosecutors were suppressing evidence of war crimes by outside powers who intervened in the conflict.

International Criminal Tribunal for Rwanda Established by the United Nations in 1994 to investigate the murder of an estimated 600 000 people in Rwanda and to attempt to bring justice to the nation. *See also* **Rwandan genocide**; **war crimes**.

Internet luring The practice of communicating through the Internet with an underage person for the purpose of committing a sexual offence. Usually involves an adult "meeting" a child in a chat room and then encouraging the child over time to meet the adult in person. This offence was created through changes to the Criminal Code in 2002.

internment To segregate and confine those considered suspicious persons. Internment camps were used in Canada during both world wars. During World War I (1914–18), nationals of Germany and of the Austro-Hungarian (this includes Ukrainians) and Turkish empires were interned. During World War II, enemy nationals and Canadian citizens were interned, including Germans, Italians, and Japanese Canadians. A total of 720 Japanese-Canadian citizens were interned. Another 20 000 were removed from their homes and relocated away from the Pacific coast until 1949, when they were allowed to return. *See also* **War Measures Act**.

interpretive theory A general category of theory including symbolic interactionism, labelling, ethnomethodology, phenomenology, and social constructionism. The term is typically contrasted with structural theories, which claim to remove the subjectivity of the actor and the researcher and assume that human behaviour can best be understood as determined by the pushes and pulls of structural forces. Interpretive theory is more accepting of free will and sees human behaviour as the outcome of the subjective interpretation of the environment. Structural theory focuses on the situation in which people act while interpretive theory focuses on the actor's definition of the situation in which they act. *See also* **definition of the situation**.

intersubjectivity Sociologists who reject the assumption of the objective nature of social reality and focus on the subjective experience of actors have to avoid the fallacy of reducing the world only to personal experience. The concept of intersubjectivity achieves this: ordinary people as well as sociologists assume that if another stood in their shoes they would see the same things. We all constantly make our subjective experience available and understandable by others as well.

interval measures *See* **level of measurement**.

Inuit, first tried under Canadian criminal law *See* **Sinnisiak and Uluksuk**.

invisible hand of the market A phrase associated with the great classical economist Adam Smith (1723–90), referring to the self-regulating capacity of free markets. Free markets, through the mechanism of supply and demand, are assumed to provide the optimal allocation of scarce economic resources to alternate uses without the need for any conscious direction or control. *See also* **market economy**.

involvement The degree to which an individual is active in conventional activities. In Travis Hirschi's work, aspects of the *social bond*.

Ipperwash camp *See* **George, Dudley**.

iron cage A phrase associated with Max Weber, who wrote that the new emphasis on materialism and worldly success that arose with capitalism and Protestantism had imprisoned human society in an iron cage of self-perpetuating rationalization and depersonalization.

iron law of oligarchy First defined by German sociologist Robert Michels (1876–1936), this refers to the inherent tendency of all complex organizations, including radical or socialist political parties and labour unions, to develop a ruling clique of leaders with interests in the organization itself rather than in its official aims. These leaders, Michels argued, came to desire leadership and its status and rewards more than any commitment to goals. Inevitably, their influence was conservative, seeking to preserve and enhance the organization and not to endanger it by any radical action. Michels based his argument on the simple observation that day-to-day running of a complex organization by its mass membership was impossible. Therefore, professional full-time leadership and direction was required. In theory, the leaders of the organization were subject to control by the mass membership, through delegate conferences and membership voting, but, in reality, the leaders were in the dominant position. They possessed the experience and expertise in running the organization, they came to control the means of communication within the organization, and they monopolized the public status of representing the organization. It became difficult for the mass membership to provide any effective counterweight to this professional, entrenched leadership. Michels also argued that these inherent organizational tendencies were strengthened by a mass psychology of leadership dependency; he felt that people had a basic psychological need to be led. *See also* **oligarchy**.

J

Jekyll and Hyde The primary characters in the 1886 story by Robert Louis Stevenson (Dr. Jekyll and Mr. Hyde). Dr. Jekyll was the stereotypical member of the middle class—repressed and moralistic. Through the ingestion of a drug, Dr. Jekyll becomes his mirror opposite—vital, egocentric, a sexual predator, and ferocious. While expressing a Christian dichotomy between good and evil, the two characters are also seen as expressing the conflict within the self between "ego" and "id" as well as the conflict between "culture" and "nature."

Judeo-Christian ethic Refers to broad moral precepts associated with the Jewish and Christian religions. Among these are the idea of responsibility for one's own actions and of redemption of the criminal or sinner through just punishment and repentance.

judge-made law Another expression for "common law" where the cases decided by courts form the precedents on which subsequent decisions are based. It has also come to refer to the way that Canada's Charter of Rights and Freedoms has expanded the powers of judges to declare laws unconstitutional or to direct changes in the law and in government policies. While based in the Constitution, these decisions are often seen as undermining the role of electoral democracy and the sovereignty of Parliament.

Jukes and Kallikaks Two families whose offspring were traced by criminologists over many generations to determine the number of "social degenerates" in each family. The study of the Juke lineage was published in 1877 and of the Kallikaks in 1912. These studies were used to argue that criminal behaviour is inherited and that it begins with "bad genetic material." The Kallikak family, for example, had two branches: the first the result of a liaison with a feeble-minded barmaid (producing a large number of "degenerates"), and the second from a marriage to a virtuous Quaker girl, which produced only three "degenerates." These studies became part of a widespread eugenics movement and the forced sterilization of many individuals thought to have "bad genetic material." Reference: Gould, Stephen Jay. (1981). *The Mismeasure of Man.* New York: W.W. Norton.

Jung, Carl Originally associated with Freud, Carl Jung developed a distinctive tradition within psychoanalysis, known as analytical psychology, that focused on the idea that all humans share in a collective unconscious mind that is exhibited in the classic forms—or archetypes—of different cultures and in the thoughts, experiences, and behaviour of individuals.

jurisprudence This refers to the underlying philosophy or principles that shape legal decisions. Can be thought of as the collection of legal decisions.

Juristat The regular publication of the Canadian Centre for Justice Statistics, providing the most authoritative source of criminal justice statistics.

juristic person The legal concept that corporations are liable to the same laws as "natural persons." Treating corporations as individuals raises practical difficulties for legal enforcement and punishment.

just desert A philosophy of punishment usually contrasted with utilitarianism. Rather than justifying punishment in terms of its utility (the good it will produce), it justifies punishment solely in terms of what the offender did. The offender is thought to get what he or she deserves—his or her just deserts. An example of this type of reasoning would be as follows: if people are to be treated as rational and moral, they have a right to be punished when they have done wrong. To not punish would be to deny their moral agency. Reference: Von Hirsch, A. (1993). *Censure and Sanctions.* New York: Oxford University Press.

justice model When rehabilitation as a goal of punishment was under attack, a new model of sentencing and corrections arose, the justice model. This model tends to focus on the rights of the offender but also on proportionality in sentencing and the general goals of justice and fairness. *See also* **proportionality**.

justice of the peace Typically laypersons with no legal training who are available to the police to obtain warrants and lay charges, to conduct bail hearings, or even to conduct trials in minor matters.

Juvenile Delinquents Act (JDA) First enacted in 1908, and replaced by the Young Offenders Act in 1984, the JDA provided a welfare response to youthful delinquents. The Act was guided by the principle of attending to the best interests of the child and had the power to declare youths to be in a state of delinquency for violating the Criminal Code of Canada as well as a host of provincial or municipal statutes and bylaws. Certain behaviours such as incorrigibility, sexual promiscuity, and truancy could also be declared delinquent. Legal challenges to the Act in the 1960s questioned its constitutionality (asserting that it was welfare legislation rather than criminal legislation and thus touched on provincial jurisdictions) but these were unsuccessful, and the Act was declared to be criminal legislation. Changes to the Act were initiated in the 1960s, but a successful compromise was not found until 1984 after many of its provisions were found to be in violation of the Charter of Rights and Freedoms (introduced in 1982). *See also* **status offence**; ***ultra vires***; **Young Offenders Act**; **Youth Criminal Justice Act**.

K

Kansas city mobile patrol experiment An experiment conducted in 1974 to determine the effectiveness of mobile police patrol. The city was divided into three sections, one receiving the normal amount of police patrol, a second receiving double the normal amount of patrol, and the third receiving no patrol. The results were astonishing: no difference in the crime rate could be detected and citizens didn't seem to notice the changes in patrolling. In general, the experiment suggests that when it comes to crime prevention, random patrol work is not very effective. Reference: Kelling, G.L., T. Pate, D. Dieckman, and C. Brown (1974). *The Kansas City Preventive Patrol Experiment: A Summary Report.* Washington: Police Foundation Report.

Kent State killings Kent State University located in Kent, Ohio, gained international attention in 1970 when national guardsmen fired on an anti-war demonstration, killing four students.

Keynesian economics The economic theory of John Maynard Keynes (1883–1946) associated with a stress on the necessity of active government intervention in the direction and control of the economy. The most central idea is that the business cycle of capitalist economies, irregular alternations of boom and bust, can be smoothed out by government creation of credit, investment activity and income transfers during economic contraction, and the raising of revenue surplus during periods of expansion. This approach, in Keynes' theory, offered insurance against the human cost of mass unemployment and the wastage of productive capacity by economic instability. For several decades, beginning in the 1930s, this was the dominant model for the economic policies of western governments. Since the mid-1970s, monetarism has challenged and, to some extent, displaced Keynesian economics as the framework for public policy and academic work. Keynesian economics is linked to a strong public policy, the welfare state, and active state involvement in the economy, while monetarism supports a non-interventionist state, privatization, and reliance on the self-regulating forces of the market. *See also* **monetarism**.

killing fields (Cambodia) The recent history of Cambodia is complicated and tragic, involving the killing of approximately 1.5 million citizens of this small nation. Until 1954, Cambodia was under the influence of France, and when self-government was finally achieved, the government had to struggle to resist the growing communist influence penetrating the region. Cambodia entered an agreement with the United States to achieve military aid, but soon renounced this relationship, resulting in the US engaging in secret bombings of communist strongholds within Cambodia. As the situation deteriorated, many citizens became more sympathetic to communism and in 1970 American and South Vietnamese troops entered Cambodia. The Khmer Rouge (the communists) under Pol Pot eventually gained control of much of the country and massacred 1.5 million people.

Kingston penitentiary for men Built in Kingston, Ontario, in 1835 and modelled on the Auburn prison system established in the United States, it was the first penitentiary built in Canada. By the time of Confederation, there were three penitentiaries in Canada, and with the passage of the Penitentiary Act in 1868, the federal prison system was created. Kingston has been the scene of many serious disturbances and of many inquiries. It continues to operate, however, and is the institution used to house some of Canada's most notorious offenders.

Kinsey report Two volumes on the *Sexual Behavior of the Human Male* (1948) and the *Sexual Behavior of the Human Female* (1953) by researcher Alfred C. Kinsey (1894–1956). These two volumes stirred a storm of criticism as the results about the frequency of sexual activity such as premarital intercourse and masturbation were seen as alarming. Further, the report provided what was the first scientific enumeration of homosexual activity and suggested that this sexual preference was very common and must be regarded as normal.

kinship structure A term referring to the way social relationships between individuals related by blood, affinal ties, or socially defined (fictive) connection are organized and normatively regulated. Kinship is the central organizational principle of many traditional societies, since it is through the kinship structure that social placement, cultural transmission, and many functional necessities for life will be met. Extent of relevant kinship connection differs greatly from society to society. Kinship bonds are generally defined more broadly and extensively in traditional societies than in modern capitalist societies.

Kissinger, Henry Nobel Peace Prize winner, assistant for national security, and secretary of state under President Nixon, Kissinger remains an enigma. Is he the greatest diplomat of the modern age? Or, is he a war criminal? Kissinger, who was born of Jewish parents in Germany prior to World War II, published a book early in his career in which he advocated limited nuclear warfare and urged the building of bomb shelters in every house. He is alleged to have disrupted the peace process (to end the Vietnam war) taking place under the Johnston regime so that Nixon would be assured of victory. Kissinger then counselled President Nixon to engage in secret bombings of communist bases in Cambodia and subsequent massive bombings of civilian populations in Vietnam. He may have been involved in the overthrown of the Chilean government of Salvador Allende and its replacement by the military regime of General Pinochet, and he was knowledgeable of the Indonesia invasion of East Timor. Reference: Hitchens, Christopher. (2001). *The Trial of Henry Kissinger.* London: Verson.

kleptomania A compulsive disorder in which the person repeatedly steals things.

Komagata Maru The name of a ship chartered by a group of Sikhs and used to sail to Vancouver, Canada, in anticipation of immigration being granted. At the time of its sailing in 1914, Indians could only come to Canada if they sailed continuously (or directly) from India to Canada, although there were no such regular routes. All others were to be prohibited entry to Canada, a method to restrict immigration of people from the Indian sub-continent. The *Komagata Maru* sailed from Hong Kong with 376 Punjabis on board. On arrival at the port of Vancouver, they were denied entry and were kept on board for two months while negotiations proceeded. These negotiations eventually failed, and the ship returned to Calcutta where 20 of the passengers were killed in clashes with authorities who were suspicious of the politics of the travellers. Reference: Johnston, Harry. (1979) *The Voyage of the* Komagata Maru. India: Oxford University Press.

L

La Cosa Nostra More commonly known as the *mafia*, a criminal organization that grew in importance during the years of prohibition in the United States and are now involved in a wide range of criminal activity. Now consisting of approximately 24 families, many of Italian descent, the group has lost influence after hundreds of individuals were convicted in the United States.

labelling theory A theory that arose from the study of deviance in the late 1950s and early 1960s and was a rejection of consensus theory or structural functionalism. These approaches to deviance assumed that deviance could be understood as consisting of behaviour that violates social norms. Deviance is therefore something objective: it is a particular form of behaviour. Labelling theory rejected this approach and claimed that deviance is not a way of behaving, but is a name put on something: a label. Law is culturally and historically variable: what is crime today is not necessarily crime tomorrow. For example, in 1890 it was legal to possess marijuana, but illegal to attempt suicide. Today, the law is reversed. This shows that deviance is not something inherent in the behaviour, but is an outcome of how individuals and their behaviour are labelled. If deviance is therefore just a label, it makes sense to ask: Where does the label come from? How does the label come to be applied to specific behaviours and to particular individuals? The first question leads to a study of the social origins of law. The second question leads to an examination of the actions of labellers such as psychiatrists, police, coroners, probation officers, judges, and juries. *See also* **amplification of deviance**; **secondary deviance**; **moral entrepreneur**. Reference: Becker, Howard. (1963). *The Outsiders.* New York: Macmillan.

labour theory of value A fundamental component of the economic and social theories of Karl Marx (1818–83) and of his analysis of capitalist exploitation. Marx argues that the value of any commodity is determined by the socially necessary labour time that goes into its production. Marx uses the term *socially necessary labour time* because the labour time required to create a commodity depends on the society's levels of technology and craft. In Marx's theory, commodities should in principle be exchanged in the marketplace for prices that exactly correspond to the necessary labour time embodied in them. When a commodity is exchanged—or sold—for more than its labour value, a surplus value is realized. This theory of value provides the foundation of Marx's claim that labour is exploited in a capitalist society: the capitalist, through the power of capital ownership, is able to pay the worker less than the market value of the commodities produced, and the surplus value is captured by capital and largely re-invested to augment the means of production. *See also* **surplus value**.

laissez faire Literally, "to leave alone." This economic doctrine states that government should not interfere in the economic or social regulation of society unless absolutely necessary. It assumes that the competitive system of free markets is the best means of allocation of scarce resources between alternative uses. Government intervention in the marketplace to regulate economic activity is seen as illegitimate and inefficient. This doctrine lost popularity in the middle of the 20th century, with the rise of the "welfare state" and extensive public ownership of parts of the economy, but regained favour in the 1980s and 1990s. *See also* **classical economic theory; invisible hand of the market**.

land claims *See also* **comprehensive land claims; specific land claims; Calder case**.

Laporte, Pierre Laporte was a Cabinet minister in the Liberal government of Robert Bourassa when he was kidnapped by FLQ terrorists on October 10, 1970. He was killed by the terrorists on October 17. *See also* **October Crisis**; **FLQ**.

Latimer, Robert The Latimers had two children, one with major mental and physical disabilities that kept the child in constant pain. The family was much troubled by their inability to help their child and watching her suffer. On October 24, 1993, Robert Latimer placed his daughter in their truck, ran a hose from the tailpipe to the passenger compartment, and took his daughter's life. He was eventually convicted of second-degree murder. The community was greatly divided on the court's response and the Supreme Court eventually heard the case to determine if the fact that his daughter was severely disabled and in pain should be taken into account in sentencing. Some heard these arguments as supporting mercy killing. The Supreme Court upheld his life sentence with no parole for 10 years. Reference: Enns, R. (1999). *A Voice Unheard: The Latimer Case and People with Disabilities.* Halifax: Garamond.

Lavallée case On September 22, 1987, Angélique Lyn Lavallée was acquitted of the murder of her common-law husband. He was shot in the head while leaving the room. After much dispute, the judge allowed the jury to hear and use expert evidence of the abuse the defendant had endured at the hands of her common-law husband, and how this may have led to her murdering him in a form of "self-defence" arising from the "battered wife syndrome." This acquittal was accepted by the Supreme Court in a 1990 judgment and the criteria for using this defence were clarified. Reference: *R. v. Lavallée*, [1990] 1 S.C.R. 852.

law A body of rules or norms passed by a legislated authority and enforced by an authorized and specialized body. Law clearly identifies the defining characteristic of the state—the ability to establish and legitimately use coercion to enforce a framework of social regulation and direction. The state, by passing law and having the authority to force compliance, can coerce citizens to act in particular ways (or leave the country). Not all societies have law. While all large-scale, modern societies have law, it was not found among hunter-gatherer, pastoral, or horticultural societies. In these societies, social life was regulated primarily by custom and tradition.

Law Commission of Canada In 1997, the federal government established the Law Commission of Canada to act as an independent body to "rethink" the laws of Canada.

Law Reform Commission of Canada A creation of the federal government (1971–93) designed to study and make recommendations on the modernization of the law in Canada. It produced a great many reports and little legislative change. *See also* **Law Commission of Canada**.

LeDain commission Gerald LeDain was the chair of the 1969 Royal Commission on the Non-Medical Use of Drugs, investigating the role the government and courts should play in prohibiting and regulating drugs used largely for recreational purposes. The commission produced numerous published volumes, which rank among the most thorough and accurate assessments of drugs and drug policy in the world, but none of the recommendations were legislated. The commission stimulated the new sociology of deviance in Canada through its sponsorship of research. LeDain was later appointed to the Supreme Court of Canada.

left realism A criminological perspective emerging in Britain in response to the rise of neo-conservatism. The right-wing politics of Prime Minister Margaret Thatcher made it clear that left-leaning criminology had little impact on social policy and was going to have little significance in the future. Some critical criminologists struggled to make their work relevant and did so by focusing on the working class as victims of street crime, state, and corporate crime, and women as victims of male crime. They asserted that official studies of crime underestimated victimization of the working class and women, and supported community controlled research as a method of getting at the "reality" of their experience. Social policies to reduce victimization of marginal communities, involve communities in crime prevention, return political control to local communities, and increase police accountability follow from this beginning point. Left realism can be contrasted with left idealism, which, while also believing that the structure of capitalism is the culprit in crime, tended to see working class crime as acts of rebellion or political resistance. This can be seen as a somewhat romantic or idealistic view. Reference: Lea, John, and Jock Young. (1984). *What Is To Be Done about Law and Order?* London: Sage; MacLean, Brian. (1991). "The Origins of Left Realism," in B. MacLean and D. Milovanovic, (eds.), *New Directions in Critical Criminology*. Vancouver: Collective Press.

legal aid Subsidized legal services for those unable to pay for a lawyer in criminal and non-criminal cases. While free legal service is guaranteed to young offenders, such services for adults have been increasingly restricted. Provincial appeal courts have suggested that free legal service may be indirectly guaranteed by sections 7 and 11(d) of the Charter of Rights and Freedoms. The Supreme Court has not yet ruled on this, but in a 1994 decision it found that section 10(b) of the Charter of Rights and Freedoms did not impose an obligation on the provinces to provide free legal services. Legal aid services are funded in part by the federal government, but increasingly provincial governments pay most of the costs. Reference: National Council of Welfare. (2000). *Justice and the Poor*. Ottawa: Minister of Public Works and Government Services.

Legere, Allan Allan Legere escaped custody while serving a prison sentence for murder. He was free for some time, and fear ran through the communities of the Miramachi where he committed four killings between May and November of 1989. Legere's trial was the first to use DNA evidence. Reference: MacLean, Rick, and A. Veniot. (1985). *Terror: Murder and Panic in New Brunswick*. Toronto: McClelland and Stewart.

legitimation crisis A condition during which a political order, or government, is unable to evoke sufficient commitment or sense of authority to properly govern. The government, or those in authority, is no longer seen as legitimate. Low levels of voter turnout in the United States, for example, may be seen as an indicator of a legitimation crisis as may the massive rejection of the Charlottetown Agreement in Canada when acceptance was recommended by most of the established political leaders in the nation. From a political economy perspective, the major source of the legitimation crisis is the economic transformation of the world in conjunction with what is termed *globalization.* This transformation raises the possibility that citizens will see the economic system with its growing class-polarization and impoverishment as illegitimate as well as the governments that attempt to regulate this new world economic order. *See also* **globalization; exceptional state.**

Leninism Refers to the ideas of Vladimir Ilich Lenin (1870–1924), leader of the Russian Revolution (1917) and founder of the Soviet Union. Lenin's ideas were mainly derived from Marxism, but he had a distinctive view of the importance of leadership in creating a working-class revolution. He advocated the organization of the working class by a disciplined and centralized communist party, believing, unlike Marx, that class-consciousness could only develop under the guidance and direction of party leadership. Many historians have argued Lenin's focus on the dominant role of the party and of its central leadership led directly to the establishment of Stalin's dictatorship and to millions of deaths in the attempt to establish Soviet-style communism.

Lepine, Marc *See* **Montreal massacre.**

level of measurement In quantitative social science, concepts are measured in order to provide a frequency count for each value of a variable. Not all measurements have the same qualities, and some statistical tests require particular levels of measurement. There are four levels of measurement: nominal, ordinal, interval, and ratio. Nominal measures only allow for the placing of the subjects into categories; e.g., female and male. Ordinal levels of measurement allow the researcher to rank respondents; e.g., strongly agree and agree. Interval measurements allow the researcher to specify the distance between respondents; John has 10 fewer units of intelligence than does Mary. A ratio level of measurement allows the researcher to express various scores as ratios and this requires an absolute zero. For example, Mary has twice as many siblings as does John. Complex statistical tests require interval or ratio measurements.

lex talionis Refers to the law of retaliation. Similar to the concept of an "eye-for-an-eye," it results in a punitive system that attempts to match punishment to the original injury imposed on the victim.

liberal feminism A form of feminism that argues that the liberal principles of equality, freedom, and equality of opportunity must be fully extended to women. This form of feminism does not call for specific structural changes to society. Neither patriarchy nor capitalism are identified as the enemies of women, rather the restricted reach of liberalism is identified as the problem. *See also* **feminism; Status of Women report.**

Liberal Party of Canada Founded in the 1870s as Reform politicians from Ontario joined with those in Quebec to create a united federal party under a new name. In 1873, the first Liberal government was formed by Alexander Mackenzie. The Liberals have been Canada's most successful political party, occupying the middle ground between the more business-oriented Conservative party and the social democratic welfare-oriented policies of the NDP. Former leaders and prime ministers include Wilfrid Laurier, William Lyon Mackenzie King, Louis St. Laurent, Lester Pearson, Pierre Trudeau, and Jean Chrétien. Reference: McCall, Christina. (1982). *Grits: A Portrait of the Liberal Party.* Toronto: Macmillan Canada.

liberalism An ideology that upholds private property, individual rights, legal equality, freedom of choice, and democratic government. Liberalism suggests that the essence of freedom is to be free from constraint. Liberalism is an ideology that supports capitalism and advocates the principle of free markets, left largely undirected by governments. While liberalism upholds free markets, it also places great value on equal of opportunity and is strongly opposed to ascriptive processes in society, since they restrict individual choice and deny equal access to satisfaction. In the 20th century, a more active view of the state's role in creating improved equality of opportunity in society became important within liberalism. (This trend in liberalism was also a reaction to the development of trade unions and of socialist and populist movements.) There was a massive expansion in state-provided education, social programs etc. from the end of the 19th century until the 1960s and 1970s. In the 1980s and

1990s, a more classical view of liberalism has returned to prominence, one that advocates a much smaller role for the state and increased reliance on the workings of the free market. In making this argument, classical liberals claim that intervention in the market rarely, if ever, promotes choice, but frustrates the market adjustments that ultimately improve efficiency, the wealth of society, and the ability of individuals to make choices. *See also* **classical liberalism**; **neo-conservatism**.

liberation theology A mixture of Christian belief and political activism usually derived from a Marxist analysis of social inequality. Acceptance of this theology encourages priests to assume a political posture in the pulpit and in their activities with the community. This has led to many confrontations between churches and corporate interests, and the religious hierarchy has been urged to restrict the political activity of priests.

liberation thesis As the crime rates for women appeared to increase during the 1960s and 1970s, criminologists talked of the "new female criminal" and some argued that women's growing equality was resulting in a convergence of men's and women's crime rates. This was the liberation thesis and it was hotly contested. Reference: Adler, Freda. (1975). *Sisters in Crime.* New York: McGraw-Hill.

libertarianism A philosophy or belief system that gives priority to the liberty of the individual. May be associated with classical liberalism regarding economic matters or the protection of those negative liberties that declare the right of the individual to be free from interference by the state, or the community, unless the actions of the individual constitute harm to others. For example, the individual has the right to freedom of speech, freedom of association, freedom of religious expression, and freedom of contract. Libertarianism is related to individualism and contrasted with communitarianism. *See also* **communitarianism**.

lie detector Also known as a *polygraph*, this is a machine used to measure changes in the stress levels of individuals undergoing police questioning. Usually suspects submit to these tests voluntarily. The testing is based on the assumption that telling lies is stressful to individuals, and when heightened stress is noted, this suggests that the subject is telling lies. Tests measure rates of pulse and breathing and electrodermal activity of the skin in response to questions that vary from neutral topics to those central to the investigation. The tests are thought to be accurate in distinguishing truth from lies in the range of 80–90 percent. While sometimes a useful tool in police work, these tests are not admissible as evidence in the courts of most nations, including Canada.

life line concept A strategy used to help long-term inmates cope with the mental stress resulting from a sense of hopelessness arising from their distant release date. Programs using this concept attempt to break up the long sentence into manageable stages: adaptation to confinement, integration to the prison community, preparing for release, and reintegration to the community.

lifestyle/exposure theory A theory of victimization that acknowledges that not everyone has the same lifestyle and that some lifestyles expose people to more risks than do other lifestyles. If you go to bed early, you are less at risk than if you like to visit bars many nights a week.

Lilith According to Jewish religious tradition, Lilith was the first wife of Adam; she was replaced by Eve. Some of the writings describe Lilith as a wild creature, the mother of demons, and sexually insatiable. Was Lilith's displacement by Eve because she refused to accept a subordinate gender role as Adam's helpmate? Did she refuse Adam's authority? Was she lesbian? Whatever the answers, Lilith has become an increasingly important character in modern feminist myth. In Jewish tradition Lilith was a "night demon," but in modern mythology she stands for the independent woman. Canadian singer Sarah McLachlan has made the name popular through the many Lilith Fairs, featuring only female performers, that she has organized across North America.

living unit A program emerging in the 1960s that attempted to distinguish and separate the functions of security and correction (or rehabilitation). Living unit officers were those correctional staff who interacted with inmates on a daily basis, but were not to be seen as involved in security issues.

Lockerbie On December 21, 1988, a New York–bound airliner exploded and crashed near the town of Lockerbie, Scotland, killing all 259 passengers and 11 people on the ground. It was determined that the airliner had been bombed by Libyan terrorists. Years of negotiations were required to have the two suspects brought to trial. Reference: Johnston,

David. (1989). *Lockerbie: The Real Story*. New York: St. Martin's Press.

Lombroso, Cesare (1835–1909) His theory of crime proposed that criminals are biologically and developmentally distinct from law-abiding citizens. He identified various physical features or stigmata that allegedly distinguished criminals from non-criminals, such as distinct ear and finger shapes and slope of the forehead. *See also* **atavism; assumption of discriminating traits; Positivist school; stigmata.**

lone-parent family Used by Statistics Canada to refer to single-parent families.

longitudinal studies These measure relationships between variables over a period of time. For example, one might follow a group of males from birth to age 30 to measure their involvement with the criminal justice system over time and relate this information to their parents' socio-economic status. A series of cross-sectional investigations taken over time will provide a longitudinal study. Reference: West, D.J., and David Farrington. (1977). *The Delinquent Way of Life*. London: Heinemann.

looking-glass self Developed by C.H. Cooley (1864–1929) to describe the social nature of the self and the link between society and individual. In this formulation, social interaction is like a mirror; it allows us to see ourselves as others see us. This was an early formulation of symbolic interactionism, but less influential than that of George Herbert Mead.

Lorenz curve Developed by Max O. Lorenz (1880–1962) in order to describe the extent of inequality in a society. Imagine a graph in which the cumulated income (expressed as a percentage) is placed on the vertical axis and the cumulated number of households (expressed as a percentage) is placed on the horizontal axis. If there were perfect equality (so that the first 10 percent of the households received 10 percent of the income and 20 percent of the households received 20 percent of the income, etc.) a diagonal line would be drawn across the graph. When actual income distributions are depicted on this graph, the line (a curve) departs from the line of perfect equality. For example, the bottom 20 percent of households may receive only 4.5 percent of the total income. This line is the Lorenz curve and can be expressed mathematically. The Gini coefficient is an expression of the ratio of the amount of the graph located between the line of perfect inequality and the Lorenz curve to the total area of the graph below the line of equality. *See also* **Gini coefficient.**

Love Canal During the 1940s and 1950s, chemical companies were allowed to dispose of chemical waste in an empty canal in the city of Niagara Falls in New York. While the chemicals were sealed in drums, it was only a matter of time until chemicals seeped into the residential development built on top of the filled canal. Great human suffering resulted, and, in 1980, a national emergency was declared. A massive cleanup began and a process of compensation for residents begun. While there was industrial pollution prior to this date and certainly since, this site captured the public's imagination and a wariness of industry and its wastes emerged.

Lower Canada Established upon the division of the province of Quebec in 1791 as a result of the Constitutional Act, this territory was to eventually become the province of Quebec. *See also* **Constitutional Act, 1791.**

lower-class culture It has been argued by some that the lower class have developed and transmit to their children a different set of cultural values and expectations. They argue further that this culture is a barrier to their success in society. Used in this way it is associated with the "culture of poverty thesis". More recently, sociologists have rejected this emphasis on values and argue that structural barriers create the conditions that might generate these values and expectations. If this is so, the solution is to transform the structures and not to blame the poor.

lower court Courts that have jurisdiction over summary conviction offences.

LSD A powerful hallucinogen produced by transforming alkaloid compounds, which occur in nature or can be produced into D-lysergic acid diethylamide-25. This substance stimulates the sensory systems so as to produce visual hallucinations.

Luddites As technology began to transform the early 19th century workplace, workers in Britain initiated random attacks in which they destroyed the machinery of the developing industrial order and destroyed poorly manufactured and shoddy goods. The workers involved in these actions claimed to be led by Ned Ludd. It was said that Ned Ludd (like Robin Hood) lived in Sherwood Forest; historians assume the name was probably a pseudonym for an individual or group of leaders.

lumpenproletariat A term associated with Karl Marx and referring to the class of individuals in a capitalist society who do not regularly participate in wage labour, but subsist through occasional employment, begging, scavenging, or crime. This class is assumed to expand and contract in number in relation to levels of economic activity in the society.

M

MacGuigan report Also known as the Parliamentary Sub-Committee on the Penitentiary System in Canada, the MacGuigan committee delivered its report in 1977 and clearly stated that penal institutions should not be used for rehabilitation. Rather, offenders were sent to prison as punishment, and while in prison they may take advantage of opportunities to change their lives, improve their skills, seek help for addiction, and so on (known as the program opportunities model). This philosophy led to the expansion of probation, parole, community corrections, diversion programs and an array of programs aimed at reintegration of the offender. *See also* **Ouimet report**.

macho/machismo The public display of characteristically (and usually exaggerated) masculine behaviour. *See also* **doing gender**.

Mack case In *R. v. Mack* (1988), the Supreme Court of Canada established rules on the limits of undercover work. Specifically they determined that the police can only go so far as to provide the opportunity for a citizen to commit an offence and only if they have reasonable suspicion that the citizen is engaged in criminal activity. Otherwise, the police activity may be determined to amount to entrapment. Reference: *R. v. Mack* (1988) 44 C.C.C. (3rd) 513 (S.C.C.).

Maconochie, Alexander (1787–1860) Maconochie was warden of Norfolk Island prison, Australia, during the 1840s. While there, he demonstrated the importance of an indeterminate sentence by using a system of points for good behaviour that could be used by prisoners to "buy" their freedom. Prisoners of Norfolk Island were those offenders who had been transported from England to Australia and then had committed a further offence. In this early prison system, we see the beginnings of parole, "good time," behaviour modification, and the indeterminate sentence. While given the title of the "father of parole," once Maconochie returned to Britain, his policies were seen as too lenient, and his influence on the prison system came to an end. Reference: Morris, Norval. (2003). *Maconochie's Gentlemen: The Story of Norfolk Island and the Roots of Prison Reform.* New York: Oxford University Press.

macro-perspective The perspective, or the form of analysis, that focuses on the structure of society and provides a way of seeing society as a unified whole. In this perspective, minimal attention is given to the individual or the subjectivity of actors—the structures of society are thought to be primary and responsible for shaping the individual.

MADD *See* **Mothers Against Drunk Driving**.

mafia Originally used to identify a specific Sicilian crime group, it is now commonly used to identify any ethnic or regionally based crime organization.

magistrate A judge in the British court system, residing over a magistrates court. Typically, magistrates had no formal training in law and often sat with one or more magistrates to hear less serious charges. In some provinces, a Justice of the Peace has a somewhat similar role.

Magna Carta A document signed, under duress, by King John in 1215 and seen as the beginnings of English constitutional law since it redefined and greatly restricted the powers of the king.

majority In sociology, this term does not refer to a numerical majority. Rather, it refers to that group(s) that has power. In South Africa, the Blacks were the majority numerically, but a minority in terms of power. All this of course began to change with the inclusion of Blacks in the electoral process and the election of Nelson Mandela.

mal in se Something bad or evil in itself. An act that is evidently wrong or criminal because it is considered to be inherently unacceptable and immoral and damaging to other people and society as a whole. Crimes like murder, armed robbery, assault, fraud, and larceny have victims who are directly harmed. Law reform commissions have recommended that the criminal law be reserved only for these types of acts. Criminal law, however, still punishes a range of acts that are simply *mala prohibita*. *See also* ***mala prohibita***.

mala prohibita An act that is deemed to be wrong or even criminal only because it is prohibited. There is nothing inherent in the act that makes it criminal:

there is no victim and no obvious harm is done. Some would argue that this is the case with laws prohibiting the possession of marijuana; to possess marijuana is not evidently wrong in itself, but only because the law says it is wrong.

Malott case A Supreme Court decision clarifying the approach courts should take to cases that may involve "battered woman syndrome." The Court declared that the battered woman syndrome was not a defence in its own right, but only a psychiatric explanation of the mental state of a woman that might be relevant to understand a killing and to shape sentencing. Reference: *R. v. Malott* [1998] 1 S.C.R. 123.

Malthusian crisis Refers to the ideas of Thomas Malthus (1766–1834) who argued that while populations grow exponentially, the rate of increase in the food supply is much less. This creates a natural limit on populations and produces miserable conditions for society and inevitable mass starvation, unless of course individuals practise birth control. Malthus didn't advocate contraceptives, rather he advocated reducing sexual intercourse. *See also* **demographic transition**; **exponential growth**.

managerial revolution Traditionally, manufacturing enterprises had been owned and controlled by individuals or families. In the mid-19th century however, joint-stock companies began to emerge, and over time increasing numbers of investors held a share of ownership and received a portion of the profits. These companies no longer had a single owner, and managers emerged to control business operations. It was assumed that this new breed of salaried workers would transform the workplace: values other than profit would enter into business calculations, and there would be greater harmony between workers and executives. Since most managers have become large stock holders (and thus owners), the significance of the managerial revolution has been called into question.

mandatory minimum sentence *See* **minimum sentence, mandatory**.

mandatory sentence A sentence that a judge of the criminal court is required to impose. In these situations, the discretion of the judge is greatly reduced or removed. In Canada, for example, a person found guilty of first-degree murder receives a life sentence with no eligibility for parole for 25 years. The model of mandatory sentences is developed more fully in the United States where many states have created sentencing grids to be used by judges prescribing the sentence, with a small amount of discretionary room for which the judge must provide a rationale.

Mannheim, Hermann (1889–1974) Mannheim emigrated from Germany to England in 1934 where he was responsible for the introduction of criminology as an independent academic subject. Reference: Grygier, T. et al. (1965). *Criminology in Transition: Essays in Honour of Hermann Mannheim.* London: Tavistock Publications.

manslaughter Culpable homicide other than murder or infanticide. An offence that would otherwise be thought of as murder, except that the killing occurred in the heat of passion caused by sudden provocation or while intoxicated. In legal terms, there must have been no malice aforethought. *See also* **murder**.

market economy An economy in which goods and services are freely exchanged without obstruction or regulation, and where decisions about production and consumption are made by many separate individuals each seeking satisfaction of specific needs and desires. Sometimes used interchangeably with "capitalist economy," but this is an error since a cooperatively based economy could also be operated on market principles. See also **invisible hand of the market**.

Marsh report Published in 1943, the *Report on Social Security for Canada* was written by Leonard Marsh and resulted from his work as research adviser on the federal government Committee on Post-War Reconstruction. Although the Marsh report was largely ignored, it does provide the intellectual foundation for much of the welfare state, which was developed over the next 25 years. Marsh was born in London, England, and emigrated to Canada in 1930. After the war, he taught at the University of British Columbia. The Marsh report can be compared to the Beveridge report in Britain.

Marshall inquiry In 1971, Donald Marshall, a teenage Nova Scotia Micmac aboriginal, was convicted of a stabbing murder. He maintained his innocence, and after he had served 11 years of a life sentence, an official enquiry determined his innocence. In 1987, a Royal Commission of Inquiry examined the case and concluded that the criminal justice system had failed because of police and judicial prejudice and incompetence. Marshall was finally awarded almost a million dollars in compensation. His case, along with others in which justice miscarried, has served to increase Canadians' wariness of any return to a death penalty for murder. Reference: Nova Scotia. (1989). *Royal Commission into the Wrongful Conviction of Donald Marshall Jr.* Halifax: Queen's Printer; Harris, M. (1986). *Justice Denied: The Law versus Donald Marshall.* Toronto: Totem Books.

Martinson, Robert New York sociologist known for his meta-analysis of criminal rehabilitation programs which concluded that "nothing works." This finding has subsequently shaped American penal policy, yet in 1979, Martinson reported after further research that there was plentiful evidence of the effectiveness of some rehabilitation programs. This work was largely ignored, however, and his original conclusion continues to be influential. *See also* **nothing works**. Reference: Martinson, Robert. (1974). "What Works?—Questions and Answers About Prison Reform, New York." *The Public Interest* 35: 22–54; Martinson, Robert. (1979). "New Views: A Note of Caution Regarding Sentencing Reform," *Hofstra Law Review* 7: 243–58.

Marx, Karl (1818–83) German-born social philosopher, political economist, and sociologist. With his life-long collaborator, Friedrich Engels (1820–95), Marx was responsible for the development of the social and economic doctrines of communism. The core of Marxist theory is that each historical period has a distinct mode of production that rests upon particular forces—or technological organization—of production and distinct ways of organizing social relationships between people in the economy. This mode of production then exerts the primary influence in shaping social relations within the society in general as well as its politics, law, and intellectual ideas. This focus on the relationship of law, social control, ideology, and coercion and the economic and social organization of society lies at the heart of critical and left-leaning criminology. *See also* **alienation**; **class**; **contradictions of capitalism**; **historical materialism**; **Marxism**; **Marxist feminism**; **mode of production**; **reserve army of labour**; **superstructure**.

Marxism The body of philosophical, political, economic, and sociological ideas associated with Karl Marx and his life-long collaborator Frederick Engels. The term is also used more generally to refer to work in the social sciences and humanities that employs key ideas and concepts from Marx and Engels' original writings. *See also* **Marx, Karl**.

Marxist feminism A form of feminism that believes that women's oppression is a symptom of a more fundamental form of oppression. Women are not oppressed by men or by sexism, but by capitalism itself. If all women are to be liberated, capitalism must be replaced with socialism. In Frederick Engels' (1820–95) writing, women's oppression originated with the development of private property and of regulated family and marital relationships. Men's control of economic resources developed with settled society and the development of separate spheres of life for the two sexes. In capitalist societies, women become segregated into the domestic sphere and men into the outer world of paid work. Economic and social inequality between the sexes is increased and women's subordination in marriage, the family, and society in general is intensified. Engels assumed that socialist revolution, through which the means of production would become common property, would result in the development of equal access to paid work for both men and women and the consequent disappearance of gendered inequality between the sexes. *See also* **liberal feminism**; **radical feminism**.

masculine female By mixing the notions of gender and sex, this term identifies those of the female sex who demonstrate features of the masculine gender.

masculinization A term central to the critique of traditional academic discussions of the female offender and of popular depictions of female criminality. The term refers to the attribution of male characteristics to women in an attempt to understand their behaviour rather than locating women's behaviour in female experience or structural location. Freda Adler, for example, argued in 1975 that the women's liberation movement would lead to an increase in female crime because liberation would make women more like men. *See also* **liberation thesis**.

mass culture A set of cultural values and ideas that arise from common exposure of a population to the same cultural activities, communications media, music and art, etc. Mass culture becomes possible only with modern communications and electronic media. A mass culture is transmitted to individuals, rather than arising from people's daily interactions, and therefore lacks the distinctive content of cultures rooted in community and region. Mass culture tends to reproduce the liberal value of individualism and to foster a view of the citizen as consumer. *See also* **mass society**.

mass media Sociologically speaking, in modern times the "community" has been replaced by a "mass," a set of autonomous and disconnected individuals, with little sense of community. The mass media then is that media (radio, television, newspapers, etc.) that are targeted at the mass rather than at specific groups or communities.

mass murder Multiple murders which can be considered as a single event—for example, "shooting spree" murders.

mass society Refers to a society with a mass culture and large-scale, impersonal, social institutions. Even the most complex and modern societies have lively primary group social relationships, so the concept can be thought of as an "ideal type," since it does not exist in empirical reality. It is intended to draw attention to the way in which life in complex societies, with great specialization and rationalized institutions, can become too anonymous and impersonal and fail to support adequate bonds between the individual and the community. The concept reflects the same concern in sociology—loss of community—that Tonnies expressed in his idea of *gesellschaft*. *See also* **mass culture**.

master status A status that overrides all others in perceived importance. Whatever other personal or social qualities an individual possesses, he or she is judged primarily by this one attribute. "Criminal" is an example of a master status that determines the community's identification of an individual. A master status can also arise from other achieved or ascribed roles.

matriarchy A society or family in which women possess most of the power and authority. While there is some dispute among social scientists, there is no clear evidence of matriarchal societies existing in the world in either the past or the present. Individual families, however, have frequently exhibited matriarchal structure with women clearly possessing dominant authority and control. The term must be distinguished from *matrilineal*, which refers to the system of tracing descent through the bloodlines of women and which exists in a number of world societies. *See also* **matrilineal societies**.

matricide The killing of one's mother.

matrilineal societies Societies in which descent is traced through mothers rather than through fathers. In such societies, property is often passed from mothers to daughters and the custom of matrilocal residence may be practiced. In such systems, the descendants of men are their sister's children and not their own, who belong to their mother's matrilineage. Matrilineage is sometimes associated with polyandry or group marriage, where women have a variety of sexual partners and lines of male descent are uncertain.

maturational reform The observation that involvement in crime tends to decrease as people age. A visit to any prison confirms this, as would the tracking of 10-year-olds' crime involvements as they go through adolescence and into adulthood.

Matza, David (1930–) Professor of sociology at the University of California at Berkeley, he developed "neutralization" or "drift" theory to explain why many delinquents tend to drift into and away from deviant behaviour. The theory proposes that the attitudes, values, and norms of delinquents are similar to law-abiding citizens, but that delinquents develop techniques of neutralization that provide justification for acts they know to be delinquent. These techniques involve justifications that blame the victim, deny that significant injury was caused, deny responsibility, or claim that acts are justified by the behaviour of the victim. This approach rejects theories like differential association that locate causes of deviance in the individual's association with deviant subcultures. Reference: Matza, David. (1964). *Delinquency and Drift*. New York: Wiley.

maximum-security prison There are 10 prisons in Canada classified as maximum security and operated by the Correctional Service of Canada. These prisons house the most dangerous of offenders and place the most restrictions on inmates. Canada does not formally use the term "maximum security"; rather, there are six levels of security with number 6 indicating maximum security. Examples of this level of security are found in Dorchester, Archambault, Millhaven, Edmonton, and Kent.

McCarthyism Joseph McCarthy was elected Senator for Wisconsin and rose to public attention when in a 1950 speech he claimed to have in his hand the names of 205 individuals who were active members of the Communist Party, many within the government itself. From this point on, he campaigned against communists and others described as subversive to American interests. In 1953, he became chair of the Senate's permanent committee of investigation and turned the committee's attention to the pursuit of communists and subversives (including homosexuals). Although in control of this committee for only a short time, many people were named, many reputations damaged, and public expression of dissent was silenced for a decade. This movement also had an impact on Canada. In an effort to root out communists and potential security risks, tests were developed to identify homosexuals and at several times Minister of External Affairs Lester Pearson was pressured to fire Herbert Norman, an influential ambassador, but also a homosexual with communist associations in his past. When Pearson repeatedly refused to fire Norman, word was spread—probably by American sources—that Pearson himself may have been a communist sympathizer. Herbert Norman finally committed suicide while stationed as ambassador in Cairo when he realized that this harassment would never end. Reference: Scher, Len. (1992). *The Un-Canadians.* Toronto: Lester Publishing.

McDonald commission A 1981 report by Justice David McDonald, Commission of Inquiry Concerning Certain Activities of the RCMP, investigating allegations of wrongdoing by members of the RCMP. This inquiry investigated allegations that violations of the law were committed by the Security Service of the RCMP while gathering information in Quebec regarding the membership and financing of the separatist Parti Québeçois led by René Lévesque. The major outcome of this inquiry was the establishment in 1984 of the Canadian Security Intelligence Service (CSIS), thus reducing the mandate of the RCMP. Reference: Canada. (1981). *Commission of Inquiry Concerning Certain Activities of the R.C.M.P.* Ottawa: Queen's Printer.

McGee, Thomas D'Arcy McGee was elected to government in 1858 and became a supporter of Canadian federation. Of Irish birth, McGee spent many years defending Irish rights. He gradually alienated his Irish constituency, and when he was assassinated in Ottawa in 1868, it was believed he was the victim of a Fenian conspiracy. Patrick James Whelan was hanged for this assassination, although he proclaimed his innocence up until his public execution. Whelan, in fact, probably was not responsible for McGee's death, and his family continues to demand that the family name be cleared.

McGill school An approach to sociology begun at McGill University when Carl Dawson established the first department upon his return from the University of Chicago. Dawson initiated a version of the Chicago school with an interest in urban studies, the location of crime in the urban community, and social disorganization. *See also* **Chicago school**.

McJob A low-paying, low-status job usually performed on a part-time basis and having no career potential. In the past, these jobs were usually the first work experiences of new entrants to the labour market, but economic changes are now thought to have made them a long-term destination for growing numbers of workers.

McNaughten rule In 1843, Daniel McNaughten attempted to murder Robert Peel, the head of the Metropolitan Police Force of London, England. Mistaking his victim, he shot and killed Peel's male secretary. At trial, McNaughten successfully argued that while he knew what he was doing was wrong, he was unable to control his urges and should be found not guilty by reason of insanity. The outrage over his acquittal led legislators to establish new rules for determining insanity; these became the McNaughten rule. This rule states that an accused is not legally liable for wrongdoing if it can be proved that the accused did not know what he or she was doing or was otherwise insanely deluded. This rule has applied in Canada since that time.

me A concept of George Herbert Mead (1863–1921) referring to the aspect of personal identity or self that is aware of and has internalized the expectations of others. The "me" is guided and shaped by the culture of an individual's society or group, which is internalized and acts to direct and control behaviour. In social interaction, each individual's behaviour is shaped by the interaction of their socially shaped "me" and their more spontaneous and ego-focused "I". *See also* **I**.

mean A measure of central tendency for data at the interval or ratio level of measurement, commonly called an average. Determined by summing the values or scores in a distribution and dividing by the number of values or scores. *See also* **median**; **mode**.

means test A policy for the provision of social assistance or services that determines access by considering whether the applicant has the means to provide the service from their own resources. Legal aid in most provinces, for example, is means tested; legal aid is provided without charge to those unable to pay while others pay part or all of the cost of the service. A policy of universality is opposed to this and is one in which all citizens have a right to assistance or service without charge. In the past, for example, the "baby bonus" was offered to all mothers of children. Similarly, health care is now offered to all citizens without charge regardless of their income. There is a growing tendency towards means tests, however. Old age income support is now "clawed back" from seniors with incomes over a certain amount, for example, and in the future will only be given to those with income below a set amount. *See also* **universality**.

measure of crime All science at one point or another must deal with measurement. One can think of measuring the weight of a friend, measuring the height of all 3-year-olds, etc. The question is: what tool or method to use in the measurement? In the above examples, it seems obvious: use a bathroom or medical scale, or use a tape measure. It is much more difficult to decide how to measure crime. Do we rely on police records, do we find the number of people incarcerated, or do we use a victimization questionnaire? Whatever the tool or measurement one uses it must be asked: Is this measurement reliable? Is it valid?

mechanical solidarity A term used by Émile Durkheim (1858–1917) to refer to a state of community bonding or interdependency that rests on a similarity of beliefs and values, shared activities, and ties of kinship and cooperation. *See also* **organic solidarity; ideal type**.

median A measure of central tendency for data at the interval or ratio levels of measurement. When a set of values or scores are arranged in ascending order, it is the value that divides the sequence in half; half of the values or scores are greater than the median and half are less than the median. A median is frequently superior to a mean as a measure of central tendency when there are some scores or values that are significantly higher than all others in the distribution. The median gives these high scores the same emphasis as all other scores, while a mean gives them much greater weight or emphasis. *See also* **mean; mode**.

medical model A model of mental illness or other forms of deviance in which it is assumed that mental illness is a symptom of some underlying disturbance that can be identified and treated. There is also an assumption that the underlying disturbance is objective, so this model is associated with positivism.

medicalization The process of turning what were previously thought to be crimes or sinful behaviour into medical problems. Reference: Conrad, Peter. (1975). "The Discovery of Hyperkinesis: Notes on the Medicalization of Deviant Behaviour." *Social Problems* 23:12–21.

medium-security prison A term that is no longer used in Canada since there are six levels of security. Medium security would be found in those institutions classified as 3 or 4.

Meech Lake Accord An agreement by the prime minister of Canada and the 10 provincial premiers, signed June 3, 1987, to amend the Constitution of Canada to provide for the following: explicit recognition of Quebec as a "distinct society;" increased provincial power over immigration; limitation of federal government spending power; recognition of Quebec's right to veto further Constitutional change; and provincial participation over appointments of Supreme Court of Canada judges. The Accord required assent from Parliament and all 10 provincial legislatures, but did not receive final ratification in either Newfoundland or Manitoba before the June 23, 1990 deadline. Principal components of the Accord were later included in the Charlottetown Agreement (August 28, 1992), a further attempt to amend the Constitution of Canada, which was defeated in a national referendum. *See also* **Charlottetown Agreement**. Reference: Cairns, Alan. (1991). *Disruptions: Constitutional Struggles from the Charter to Meech Lake.* Toronto: McClelland and Stewart.

member A central term in ethnomethodological theory and replaces terms like "status position" or "role" in structural theories. From a structural perspective, an individual actor is examined according to their structural characteristics (gender, age, ethnicity, class) and is assumed to behave in accordance with these structural characteristics. The subjectivity of the actor is insignificant. Ethnomethodology, on the other hand, attempts to highlight the subjectivity of the individual actor and thus needs to identify the person in a way that acknowledges their knowledge, competence, engagement, commitment, or ability to make sense. The term *member* accomplishes this. Ethnomethodology also refers to membership categories (e.g., teacher, mother, employee) and identifies membership categorization devices and rules of application (e.g., the economy rule and the consistency rule) as a form of ethnomethodological analysis.

memory, recovered It is believed by some that memory has two important characteristics. First, memory records events in an accurate fashion, and second, that memories can be repressed and then regained at a much later date and recovered in an accurate state. This is a controversial concept that suggests that a person's memory of an earlier victimization may be completely blocked or lost, only to be recovered many years later, often through a process of therapy. This matter raises many questions about the nature of memory itself, and some suggest that memory is not a form of "photographic record," but is also a social construction. If this is so it may be possible to have "false memories." Recovered memories have been important in sexual abuse cases. *See also* **Ramona case**. Reference: Johnston, Moira. (1997). *Spectral Evidence: The Ramona Case: Incest, Memory and Truth on Trial in Napa Valley*. Boulder, CO: Westview Press.

mens rea Criminal intent. An act must be blameworthy. It must be done with criminal intent or be an act of gross negligence or recklessness. Canadian courts have traditionally favoured an objective definition of *mens rea* using the test of what a reasonable person would have thought and done in the situation. Recently, a more subjective view has been adopted.

mental disorder defence A legal defence known as *not criminally responsible on account of mental disorder* (NCRMD). Prior to 1992, a court could find an offender not guilty by reason of insanity; however, today, a mental disorder is not a true defence as a finding of mental disorder results in detention in a mental health facility for an indeterminate time.

mercantilism An economic theory that preceded the modern concept of a market economy regulated by the forces of supply and demand. Mercantilist ideas were quite varied, but a common theme is the importance to any nation of maintaining a favourable balance of international trade, ideally leading to net inflows of precious metals. To attain this end, it was appropriate for the state to intervene in the marketplace by vigorous economic regulation backed by state authority. Among classic mercantilist policies were laws requiring colonial territories to trade only with the imperial power, imposition of monopolies in merchant shipping and trading rights, and the establishment of physical quotas to manage and regulate trade. In Canada's early history, trading monopolies of both French and English origin—like the famous Hudson's Bay Company—were an expression of mercantilist policies, and they played a central role in the exploration and economic development of Canada.

mercy killing The taking of a person's life on the grounds that it is in that person's best interest. Such murders are against the Criminal Code of Canada and the Supreme Court case involving Robert Latimer did not accept mercy killing as a defence. *See also* **Latimer, Robert**; **Rodriguez, Sue**.

meritocracy Rule by those chosen on the principle of merit. The principle of merit is consistent with liberal theory and assumes equality of opportunity and occupational advancement based on achievement rather than ascription. Émile Durkheim's notion of the "spontaneous division of labour" and the argument of Kingsley Davis and Wilbert Moore (1945) on the function of inequality both depend on the belief that in a liberal society people will be rewarded on the basis of talent or merit and that the more talented and thus meritorious will come to occupy the more important positions in society. *See also* **autocracy**; **plutocracy**; **democracy**.

Merton, Robert (1910–2003) American sociologist instrumental in introducing the writings of Émile Durkhem to North America. Merton, writing during the Depression and an age of scarcity, develops the idea of "anomie" as an explanation for crime. Merton also introduced the concepts of the self-fulfilling prophecy and reference group to sociology. Reference: Merton, Robert. "Social Structure and Anomie." *American Sociological Review* 3: 672–82.

mescaline A common hallucinogen occurring naturally in the peyote cactus growing in Mexico and areas of the southern United States.

meta-analysis There has been so much research on specific topics (e.g., the effectiveness of corrections, the effects of divorce on children) that it is possible to do analyses of a collection of research results—this is meta-analysis. One of the more well-known examples of meta-analysis is that done by

R. Martinson, in which he concluded that "nothing works." Martinson did no original research on what works or doesn't work, but re-analyzed all of the available research on the topic.

meta-narrative A story, narrative, or theory that claims to be above the ordinary or local accounts of social life. Postmodernists claim that the majority of the writings of Marx, Durkheim, and Weber are offered as meta-narratives, presented as capturing universal properties of social life and thus superior to local or more grounded stories. Postmodernist social theorists argue for a return to the local, the rejection of grand theory, and a privileged position for science and its narratives, and an acknowledgment of the inherently political nature of all narratives.

methadone A synthesized narcotic used in the control of heroin addiction. It is believed to be less addictive than heroin.

methadrine A powerful amphetamine stimulating activity in the central nervous system. Also known as *speed* and *ice*.

method The tool or instrument one uses to measure crime (or height). One method might be to go to the police department and go through all of their files. Another might be to use the data provided by the Centre for Justice Statistics, and yet another might be to design a questionnaire to be given to people asking if they have ever committed a crime or been a victim of a crime. The method one might use to measure weight is to step on the bathroom scale. There are obviously other methods for measuring weight. There are many methods for measuring crime.

methodological holism An orientation in research and analysis where the aim is to understand the phenomenon under investigation in its totality as unique and apart from its component parts, rather than to seek to fragment it into known or familiar components. The key idea, in essence, is that the whole differs from the sum of the parts not only in quantity, but in quality.

methodological individualism The belief that all sociological explanations can be reduced to characteristics of individuals who make up the society. This position is also known as *psychologism*: explaining social phenomenon in terms of the psychological dispositions of members of society. This is a rejection of macro-structuralists working in the tradition of Émile Durkheim or Karl Marx who assumed that the characteristics of individuals need not be considered. They argued that social facts (society) had an existence of their own and that it was these that sociologists were interested in. *See also* **psychological reductionism**.

methodology The study or critique of methods. There are many philosophical issues around the use of a particular method or about positivism or measurement itself.

Métis Refers to people who have a mixed biological and cultural ancestry. These were usually mixtures of French and Indian or British/Scottish and Indian. Originally, the term referred to the French-Indian people who settled in the Red River area of Manitoba, a group who saw themselves as having a distinct cultural and political position in society, and their history is important in understanding Canada. This group is now represented by the Métis National Council. The Native Council of Canada acknowledges other people of mixed ancestry as being Métis. *See also* **Red River Rebellion**.

metropolis-hinterland theory A theory of social and economic development that examines how economically advanced societies, through trade and colonialism, distort and retard the economic development of less developed societies and regions. A metropolis is identified as the centre of political and economic power, as having a more advanced labour market, more skilled and educated workers, an abundance of value-added production, higher standard of living, etc. A hinterland would be less able to withstand the political and economic interference of the metropolis, would have an abundance of resource extraction industries, fewer skilled and educated workers, a lower standard of living, and in many ways would emulate the culture of the metropolis. For more than a century, Ontario, or even more narrowly the Toronto region, was seen as the metropolis to a vast Canadian hinterland, and the United States has been seen as the metropolis for a Canadian hinterland. *See also* **dependent development**; **world systems theory**. Reference: Davis, Arthur K. (1971). "Canadian Society as Hinterland Versus Metropolis," in R. Ossenberg (ed.), *Canadian Society: Pluralism Change and Conflict*. Scarborough: Prentice Hall.

micro-perspective A perspective, or form of analysis, that focuses on the individual and his or her subjectivity, rather than focusing on the structures of society thought to be external and constraining on the individual. This perspective is found in symbolic interactionism, ethnomethodology, labelling theory, and interpretive theory.

middle class There have been several different approaches to defining this term. (1) In Karl Marx's (1818–83) analysis of class, the middle class is the "petite bourgeoisie" who are in small scale independent businesses or crafts or who have special skills that provide an income outside the wage system of employed labour. Marx assumed that this class would diminish in number as capitalist enterprises developed, consolidated into larger units and eliminated small-scale competition. (2) The term can also be used statistically to define a group of individuals who occupy an intermediate position in a society's income strata: for example, those who earn between 66 percent and 133 percent of a society's average family incomes. These are attempts to define the "middle class" objectively, by some standard of measurement, but a more subjective view is possible: the middle class are those individuals who orient themselves to the values and expectations that they consider normative for average members of their society. This approach is useful for understanding why most Canadians irrespective of occupation, wealth, or income identify themselves as middle class.

middle-class measuring rod A phrase suggesting that children and young people from the lower class often find themselves in situations in which they are measured against middle-class standards. The school, for example, rests on the middle-class values of reading and writing, and the teachers are primarily middle-class. Lower-class children often realize they are never going to "measure up" and so anticipate failure, become frustrated, or drop out of school. They may also begin to move toward other marginal students in the school and become engaged in deviant or criminal activity. Reference: Cohen, Albert. (1955). *Delinquent Boys.* New York: Free Press.

Milgaard, David Milgaard was convicted of the 1969 murder of a young woman in Saskatoon. He spent 23 years in prison before the Supreme Court set his conviction aside in 1992. Milgaard was subsequently acquitted on the basis of DNA evidence. Reference: Karp, Carl, and C. Rosner. (1991). *When Justice Fails: The David Milgaard Story.* Toronto: McClelland and Stewart.

Mills, C. Wright (1916–62) Mills was an American sociologist critical of the prevailing paradigm of sociology of his day, functionalism. In his 1956 book, *The Power Elite*, he draws attention to the linkages among power groups in America and uses the phrase the "military industrial complex." In more recent years, this phrase has been changed to discuss what many see as the "prison industrial complex," a powerful group of corporations with self-interest in maintaining and expanding prisons and privatizing the vast array of services required for prisons to function.

minimum-security prisons Those institutions with a security level of 1 or 2 and offering the most open prisons. These institutions may allow inmates to live in dormitories or group living situations, seldom have guards, and may not even have locked doors. Those in minimum security are those not deemed to be a danger to the community.

minimum sentence, mandatory There are only a few instances in the Criminal Code of Canada where a court is required to impose a minimum sentence regardless of the circumstances surrounding the crime. For example, on a second conviction for driving while impaired the court must impose at least a 14-day sentence and 90 days for each additional conviction. Mandatory minimums are also established for high treason, first-and second-degree murder, use of a firearm during an offence, and for a few others. A mandatory minimum sentence of seven years upon conviction for importing or exporting a narcotic was struck down by the Supreme Court in 1987. Reference: *R. v. Smith* [1987] 1 S.C.R. 1045.

ministerial responsibility Associated with parliamentary systems of government, this is the convention that a minister is answerable to Parliament for the conduct and actions of his or her ministry's personnel. Originally, the responsibility was quite strictly imposed on a minister and resignation might be demanded even where the minister did not have, and could not reasonably have been expected to have, knowledge of improper or negligent acts or omissions by officials. In recent times, this idea has been abandoned, and it is rare for a minister to accept responsibility and resign.

Minneapolis domestic violence experiment Conducted in 1984, this was the first scientific study to investigate the effect of police responses on domestic violence. Police officers were randomly assigned one of three ways to deal with an incident: arrest the suspect, counsel the couple, or remove one member from the home. The results showed that those offenders who were arrested showed a marked reduction in recidivism. Reference: Sherman, Lawrence, and Richard Berk. (April 1984). "Minneapolis Domestic Violence Experiment," *Police Foundation Reports* 1.

minority group A group distinguished by being on the margins of power, status, or the allocation of resources within the society. "Visible minority" refers to those racial or ethnic groups in a society that are marginal from the power and economic structure of society, not to those that are few in number. In South Africa, Blacks are the statistical majority, but were for countless decades a social minority. Women can also be identified as a social minority group.

miscegenation Sexual intercourse between individuals of differing racial groups. At various times and places (including the American south and South Africa under apartheid), there have been laws prohibiting both sexual intercourse and marriage between racially mixed couples. The Supreme Court of the United States struck down miscegenation laws in 1967.

misdemeanor Those offences of a less serious nature and thus contrasted to felonies. This term has little use in Canada but corresponds somewhat to the notion of summary offence. *See also* **felony**.

misandry The hatred of men.

misogyny The hatred of women.

missing women case Over the course of about 10 years, approximately 60 women sex-trade workers disappeared from the streets of Vancouver. It appeared to take a long time for the police to realize that something out of the ordinary was going on, but finally a major investigation was undertaken. Eventually, clues led to a farm in a nearby suburb where prostitutes and drug addicts had been lured with the promise of alcohol and drugs. One of the owners of the farm (Robert Pickton) was charged with the deaths of many of the missing women as a result of the largest forensic investigation ever undertaken in Canada.

mitigating factor Factors associated with the offence or the offender that reduce the seriousness of the offence or the level of culpability of the offender, and which accordingly result in a more lenient sentence. For example, first offenders are punished less severely than repeat offenders.

mobility, social The movement of an individual or group from one class or social status to another. Usually, the point of reference is an individual's class or status of social origin, and social mobility occurs when later class or status positions differ from those of origin. Social mobility would be high where individuals have equal opportunity to achieve new statuses and low where there are inequalities of opportunity and processes of status ascription. *See also* **demand mobility**; **open class ideology**.

mode A measure of central tendency useful for data at any level of measurement. The most frequently occurring number in a set of scores or values. In a series of numbers, there is frequently more than one mode. Other measures of central tendency are the median and the mean. *See also* **mean**; **median**.

mode of production The dominant form of social and technical organization of economic production in a society. Historically, a variety of modes of production can be distinguished based on both technology and the structure of social relationships. Historical modes of production include hunter-gatherer, with very simple technology and common ownership; ancient, with more advanced technology and slavery; feudal, with simple technology and landowning lords and bonded serfs; and capitalist, with sophisticated technology, private ownership of capital and a wage system. *See also* **state capitalism**.

modelling A form of learning that occurs as a result of watching and imitating others.

modernization theory A theory of social and economic development, following functionalist or consensus assumptions that societies need to have harmony among their component parts. This assumption leads to the belief that modern economies (capitalist) demand special characteristics in their culture and the structure of social relationships. For example, family systems are assumed to change towards a narrow conjugal form, and away from an extended structure, in order to accommodate the individualism and occupational flexibility that is demanded by a modern complex economy undergoing continual transformation.

monarchy, constitutional A system of government in which the head of state is an individual usually acquiring the position by hereditary descent. In earlier times in history, monarchs were often absolute in their effective power and were unconstrained by either legal or political limitations. Britain's system of monarchy, from which Canada's is derived, has been subjected to formal constitutional limitation since the Magna Carta issued in 1215 by King John of England. The Magna Carta was demanded from the king by England's landowning aristocracy who wanted definite and permanent legal limitations on royal power. Over the centuries, England's monarchical system became gradually transformed to the modern constitutional structure where the monarch possesses only formal legal power that must, by political convention, be exercised only with the advice and agreement of the monarch's ministers. These ministers are chosen by a prime minister who the monarch appoints, but who, by political convention, must be the party leader whose party commands majority support, or the most support, in the elected House of Commons. The convention that the monarch will act only with the advice and consent of the prime minister and the Cabinet makes monarchy compatible with a system of parliamentary democracy. Canada's monarchy is similarly structured. The Governor General represents the queen (or king) in Canada, possesses the formal legal powers of the monarch, but by political convention exercises them subject to the advice of the prime minister and other federal ministers. Since 1926, the autonomy of Canada from Britain has been recognized by the requirement that the Governor General of Canada be appointed by the monarch only on the advice of the prime minister of Canada. The system of monarchy contrasts with republics, where the head of state is an individual either directly elected by the people (e.g., the United States, France, Mexico) or appointed by an elected state parliament (e.g., Germany, Israel).

monetarism An economic theory advocating that governments use interest rates and control of the supply of money for the purpose of economic regulation. This is in contrast to Keynesian economics, which advocates taxation and budgetary ("fiscal") policy. Use of monetary instruments for economic regulation is said to provide a lever to influence macro-economic cycles in the economy, while avoiding bureaucratic regulation or distortions of market forces. Monetarism has become the dominant framework of theory in both academic economics and public policy. It is closely associated with neo-conservatism, a version of liberalism that stresses free markets and individualism rather than the "welfare state" vision that had become dominant in most western societies. There is controversy over the role of monetarist policies in the current deficit problems of most of the worlds' largest economies. *See also* **fiscal crisis**; **Keynesian economics**.

monetary policy The use of monetary levers—interest rates, money supply, foreign exchange rate—by governments to achieve some control over the performance of the economy. *See also* **fiscal policy**.

monopoly A situation in which one company has gained control of the market for a particular good or service. This is in direct conflict with the values of liberalism, which emphasize competition among numerous producers.

monozygotic twins Commonly known as *identical twins*, they are from a single egg that has divided after fertilization to create two embryos; consequently, they share exactly the same genetic material and are of the same sex. Monozygotic twins who have been separated in earliest infancy and raised apart have provided a classic research situation for social scientists because their genetic identity, yet different social experience, makes it possible to disentangle the separate effects of heredity and social environment. *See also* **dizygotic twins**. Reference: Bock, G.R., and J.A. Gode. (1996). *Genetics of Criminal and Antisocial Behaviour*. Chichester: John Wiley and Sons.

Monster of the Miramachi *See* **Legere, Allan**.

Montreal, Criminology at the University of Denis Szabo, the father of Canadian criminology, established a criminology program at the University of Montreal in 1960.

Montreal Forum riot On March 17, 1955, riots erupted in Montreal as hockey fans both inside and outside the Montreal Forum showed their displeasure with National Hockey League President Clarence Campbell. Four days before Campbell suspended Montreal Canadiens star Rocket Richard for the rest of the season for fighting. Richard was the best hockey player of his generation and many others. He was a hero for Montreal fans, and at the first game back at home their outrage led to street rioting outside the Forum, which was then carried inside, leading to an attack on Campbell who was watching Montreal play Detroit. (The game is forfeited to Detroit who were leading 4–1 when it is abandoned.) The Montreal hockey team was perhaps the most successful team in the league, and during the 1950s and 1960s, the team carried the nationalist emotions of the Québeçois. When the Parti Québeçois was created and won the 1976 election, new political avenues for national expression emerged, and hockey lost its national symbolism. In 1967, too, the league was expanded and the number of games against its major rival, the Toronto Maple Leafs, was reduced. The team lost much of its drive and became much more ordinary.

Montreal massacre On December 6, 1989, Marc Lepine entered the École Polytechnique in Montreal and killed 14 women students before taking his own life. This event has been a rallying point for women's groups who see the killings as reflective of generalized devaluation and violence against women in society. December 6 has become a National Day of Remembrance and Action on Violence Against Women. Reference: Rathjen, H., and C. Monpetit. (1999). *December 6: From the Montreal Massacre to Gun Control.* Toronto: McClelland and Stewart.

moral development theory Refers generally to theories of individual psychology that investigate how moral reasoning emerges and develops as the individual matures. Jean Piaget (1896–1980) is acknowledged as the founder of this approach to human development. Reference: Duska, Ronald. (1975). *Moral Development: A Guide to Piaget and Kohlberg.* New York: Paulist Press.

moral economy The central characteristic of economic activity in a tribal society. Rather than economic exchanges being motivated by self-interest, greed, or profit, exchanges are driven by moral obligations created by kinship relations, gift giving, and rituals. A hunter or food gatherer may by obliged to give much of the food to a network of relations, thus accounting for the distribution of food within the community. It was the final collapse of economic exchange as moral obligation that Karl Marx (1818–83) bemoaned when he described the "cash nexus" that has become the central medium and motivator of exchange in a capitalist society. *See also* **potlatch**.

moral entrepreneur To be in the business of persuading the society to make policy from particular moral viewpoints. In symbolic interactionism (or labelling theory), social policy is not seen as the implementation of a shared consensus about what is best. Rather, the society is viewed as consisting of a plurality of understandings of what is best. In order for social policy to arise, some individual or group has to initiate a social movement whose task is to articulate a definition of a social problem such that a desired social policy is consistent with this definition of the problem. These individuals or groups are referred to as moral entrepreneurs. MADD (Mothers Against Drunk Driving), the pro-life movement, the gun lobby, anti-pornography groups, Emily Murphy, and the anti-tobacco lobby would all be examples of moral entrepreneurs. Reference: Becker, H. (1963). *Outsiders: Studies in the Sociology of Deviance.* New York: Free Press.

moral panic A term, coined by sociologist Stanley Cohen in 1972, that suggests a panic or overreaction to forms of deviance or wrongdoing believed to be threats to the moral order. Moral panics are usually fanned by the media and led by community leaders or groups intent on changing laws or practices. Sociologists are less interested in the validity of the claims made during moral panics than they are with the dynamics of social change and the organizational strategies of moral entrepreneurs. Moral panics gather converts because they touch on people's fears and because they also use specific events or problems as symbols of what many feel to represent "all that is wrong with the nation." The moral panic over youth violence, for example, presents this violence as a symbol of all that is wrong with Canada—it is claimed that the Charter of Rights and Freedoms has undermined authority; the family has fallen apart; immigration has brought many disreputable groups into the country; governments and their agents have become self-serving and out of touch with the reality of social life; and economic transformation has marginalized and demoralized young people. Reference: Cohen, Stanley. (2002). *Folk Devils and Moral Panics.* 3rd ed. London: Routledge.

moral rhetoric In the study of crime, this is the set of claims and assertions that deviants make to normalize and rationalize deviant behaviour. Individuals, businesses, and public institutions may be blamed for unfairness, exploitation, or some moral or biological failing, thus justifying them as targets of crime. The moral rhetoric of a group is an important component of socialization into a deviant identity.

Morgentaler, Henry Born in Lodz, Poland, 1923, he was Jewish but survived the war-time Nazi death camps and came to Canada, where he trained as a physician, in 1950. He began general practice in Montreal in 1955. He soon became interested in family planning and by 1967 appeared before a House of Commons Committee to urge repeal of the criminal law against abortion. In 1973, he publicly announced that therapeutic abortion was safe and socially necessary and that he had successfully carried out 5000 operations. These operations were illegal, since he had not followed the procedures for approval set out in an abortion law amendment in 1969. He was soon prosecuted, but in November 1973 found not guilty by a Quebec jury despite conclusive evidence that he had broken the law. Then, in a highly controversial decision in February 1974, the Quebec Court of Appeal set aside the jury verdict and imposed its own verdict of guilty, sentencing Morgentaler to 18 months in prison. The Supreme Court upheld the decision. In 1975, while still in jail, Morgentaler was prosecuted again for additional offences and again found not guilty by a Quebec jury. Parliament then passed an amendment to the Criminal Code, proposed by the minister of justice, which eliminated the power of appellate courts to set aside acquittals and order imprisonment. The minister of justice also ordered a new trial for Morgentaler on the original charges. In September 1976, the new trial resulted in another acquittal by a Quebec jury. In November 1976, the newly elected Parti Québeçois government of René Lévesque announced that there would no longer be prosecutions of doctors who perform abortions in Quebec. Having made abortion more freely available in Quebec, Morgentaler turned his attention to Ontario and opened a clinic there. He was soon charged and prosecuted for performance of illegal abortions and in November 1984 was tried and acquitted by an Ontario jury. The Ontario government appealed this acquittal to the Supreme Court and, as a result, brought the story to a conclusion. With the Charter of Rights and Freedoms now in place, the Supreme Court in 1988 ruled on appeal that the abortion law be struck down as offending the Charter's section 15, Equality Rights, guarantee of sexual equality. Since then abortion has been legal in Canada. Reference: Dunphy, Catherine. (1996). *Morgentaler: A Difficult Hero.* Toronto: Random House of Canada.

Morin, Guy Paul Morin was convicted in 1992 of the murder of 9-year-old Christine Jessop. After many bizarre twists and turns, the Ontario Court of Appeal acquitted Morin on the basis of DNA evidence in January 1995. Morin joined a growing list of the wrongfully convicted, and his acquittal led to a lengthy investigation of the justice system. *See also* **DNA matching**. Reference: Makin, K. (1993). *Redrum the Innocent.* Toronto: Penguin.

morphine A narcotic derived from opium, but much stronger than opium. The term comes from Morpheus, the Greek god of dreams.

Mothers Against Drunk Driving (MADD) A successful lobby group since its founding in the US in 1980 by Candy Lightner.

motivated offenders To be motivated is to be ready to engage in a particular experience or action. You may have been motivated to attend college by your upbringing or by a particular role model. Others are motivated to offend, perhaps because they have a drug dependency, are poor, lack self-control, or any number of other reasons. It is argued that something has to happen to turn this motivation into action. Perhaps you had to get a scholarship or the offender has to see a car with the keys in it.

Mount Cashel orphanage *See* **Cashel, Mount.**

multiculturalism A term having two distinct but related meanings. On the one hand, it refers to a condition of cultural pluralism and the attitudes of tolerance that make this possible. On the other hand, it refers to a set of federal government policies designed to "assist all Canadian cultural groups ... to grow and contribute to Canada" as well as to assist members of all cultural groups "to overcome cultural barriers to full participation in Canadian society." While there is little debate about the first of these meanings, there is great debate about the implications of the second. Reference: Kymlicka, Will. (1995). *Multicultural Citizenship.* New York: Oxford University Press.

multinational corporation A company that has operations in more than one nation. The development of these corporations has challenged the belief of liberal ideology that economic power can be counterbalanced by political power. As corporations have less dependence on a national market and can adopt practices that minimize the effect of national policies, they move outside the reach of any political system.

multivariate analysis A form of quantitative analysis that examines three or more variables at the same time, in order to understand the relationships among them. The simplest form of this analysis is one in which the researcher, interested in the relationship between an independent variable and a dependent variable (e.g., gender and political attitudes), introduces an extraneous variable (e.g., age) to ensure that a correlation between the two main variables is not spurious. Presented in tabular form, this analysis divides the age variable into its constituent values (e.g., young and old) and then subdivides each of these values into the values of female and male. Having done this, it is possible to determine whether there is a correlation, among young people, between the variables of gender and political attitudes. Other forms of multivariate analysis are examined in methodology texts under the heading of the elaboration model, and here one finds conditional variables, intervening variables, and extraneous variables.

mundane reasoning *See* **commonsense reasoning**.

Munsinger affair In 1958, Pierre Sevigny, the minister of defence in the fresh-faced Conservative federal government, began an affair with Gerda Munsinger, a German immigrant known to the RCMP as a security risk with communist affiliations. By December 1960, the RCMP uncovered rumours of the defence minister's affair, and placed Munsinger's apartment under surveillance. Sevigny was seen to call—and stay overnight. The RCMP reported to Canada's justice minister, David Fulton. He passed the news to the prime minister. Diefenbaker called Sevigny to his office to confront him with the allegations. The minister confessed, but denied any breach of security. The prime minister insisted that the affair be stopped immediately, demanding that Munsinger be vigorously encouraged to return to Germany. He also decided to retain Sevigny in the Cabinet and to take no further action. The incident remained the secret of a very small circle. But in December 1964, it became obvious that the circle has widened when the new prime minister, Lester Pearson, whose government was under fire for scandals involving Liberal Cabinet ministers, wrote to Diefenbaker to express his concern about the handling of the Munsinger case by the previous Conservative government. Perceiving it as a threat, Diefenbaker met Pearson to threaten him in turn with revelations of "his days as a communist." It was not until March 4, 1966, when Diefenbaker, speaking in the House of Commons, attacked the Liberal's handling of a security case involving a Vancouver postal clerk, George Spencer, that the public began to find out about the affair. Spencer had been dismissed from the post office on suspicion of spying for the Soviet Union. Charges were not laid, but the government directed that he be deprived of his pension and placed under permanent RCMP surveillance. To add pathos to the story, Spencer was dying of cancer. Lester Pearson reviewed the case and upheld the actions taken, but Diefenbaker, incensed by the arbitrary denial of due legal process, implied that it is a way to look tough on communism and distract attention from allegations of communist affiliation that had been made about Prime Minister Lester Pearson himself. Responding in kind, Justice Minister Lucienne Cardin divulged to the House that there were badly handled "security cases" during Diefenbaker's government, particularly the Monseignor (sic) case. The press seized upon this hint of wrongdoing, and within days the *Toronto Star* discovered the story and located Munsinger in Munich. She named not only Sevigny, but also George Hees, minister of transport in Diefenbaker's government, as her intimates. A public inquiry was established to investigate. The inquiry reported there was no breach of security, but criticized Diefenbaker for retaining Sevigny in the Cabinet and censured the behaviour of David Fulton and George Hees. While the press and the public were riveted by this affair of sex, spying, and political blackmail, there was worry that the Liberal government used its access to security information to damage its Conservative opponents. The handling of the affair seems more sordid than the affair itself.

murder To kill a human being willfully, deliberately, and unlawfully.

murder, first-degree An offence under the Criminal Code of Canada. To be charged with this offence, one of four conditions must be met: (1) The killing is planned and deliberate. (2) The killing is of an on-duty police officer or prison personnel. (3) The killing is committed during the commission of certain other criminal offences. (4) The killing is by someone previously convicted of first-degree or second-degree murder. The idea of distinguishing types of murder was first introduced to Canada in

1961 with two categories: capital murder and non-capital murder. *See also* **Coffin, Wilbert**; **mass murder**; **serial murder**; **manslaughter**. Reference: Boyd, N. (1988). *The Last Dance: Murder in Canada*. Scarborough: Prentice-Hall.

murder, second-degree Those killings which, while deliberate, do not meet one of the four conditions required to be charged with first-degree murder. The distinction between first and second-degree murder is often disputable. *See also* **murder, first-degree**.

Murdoch case A very controversial decision by the Supreme Court of Canada (1975) in deciding the property entitlement of a farm wife upon her divorce. Mrs. Murdoch claimed an equal share of the family property and produced evidence that she had contributed money to the downpayment on the farm, had carried out farm work and housework for more than 25 years, and had been actively involved in running and administering farm business. The Supreme Court decided that Mrs. Murdoch's work had been no more than typical for a farm wife and did not establish any special entitlement to a share in the farm itself. In so deciding, the court upheld traditional views of the property rights of women—for a wife to own property it must be bought in her name or she must make a direct contribution to its purchase. While the court agreed that Mrs. Murdoch was entitled to an equal share of the farmhouse and the land on which it was immediately situated, they ruled that this entitlement did not extend to the farmland and equipment. The resulting controversy, led by Canadian women's groups, resulted in an overhaul of statute law, first in Ontario and then in other provinces, to redefine "family assets"—property divisible between the partners—to include all property used by the partners to the marriage during the course of their relationship. Reference: *Murdoch v. Murdoch* [1975] 1 S.C.R. 423.

mutual conversion A phrase suggesting that conversion to deviance (and perhaps to other lifestyles) is not a solitary activity but is achieved interactively. Someone might encourage you and in accepting and perhaps by redefining or justifying the activity you further convert the first person.

My Lai massacre A story of bureaucratic intrigue and mass murder dating from the Vietnam War involving a March 16, 1968 incident when an American fighting unit entered the village of My Lai and killed 400 unarmed women, children, and old men. Four soldiers were eventually brought to trial and one convicted. Reference: Bilton, M. and K. Sim. (1992). *Four Hours in My Lai*. New York: Penguin Books.

mystification The process of masking or covering up central aspects of society or of social relationships. Conflict or critical theorists are interested in the ways in which forms of social domination based on sex, class, or colonialism are camouflaged so that these social structures, and the state which assists in their reproduction, are seen as legitimate. Mystification allows for domination that is not based on evident coercion or force, but is maintained by a wide variety of social institutions and cultural values. *See also* **legitimation crisis**; **hegemony**.

myth Often used incorrectly to refer to a claim considered to be untrue. More correctly, myth refers to a narrative account or story that contains the collective wisdom of a society and articulates beliefs concerning key aspects of individual identity or collective life. All societies, for example, have myths about the origin of human life, some have myths about their origin as a society, and others have myths about the shaping of national identity or the evolution of love. Social scientists are interested in the role these myths play in society and what they might say about the nature of the human mind.

myth of mental illness A term coined by Thomas Szasz intended to challenge the medical model of mental disorders. Szasz argued that mental disorders unlike physical diseases typically have no objective problems that can be identified: there are no broken bones or infections. If mental illness has no objective signs, then mental illness is just a label typically applied to behaviours that arise from what Szasz calls ordinary "problems of living." Reference: Szasz, Thomas. (1974). *The Myth of Mental Illness*. New York: Harper and Row.

N

NAC *See* **National Action Committee on the Status of Women**.

NAFTA *See* **free trade**.

nation A word somewhat similar to society in that it includes all those persons who share common descent, language, and history and close association with each other. For Canadians, the term reflects a major debate about the nature of Canada. In

English, the term nation implies a community of people who have political autonomy and who occupy a distinct territory. In French, in contrast, the term is closer in meaning to a community of people sharing common origins and ties of interrelationship. Thus when French speakers refer to Quebec as a "nation," they tend to mean Quebec as an historic community of people, rather than necessarily implying that Quebec is, or ought to be, completely politically autonomous and detached from Canada. It is noteworthy that Quebec refers to its legislative house as the *national assembly*, while other provinces use the term *legislature*. There are approximately 170 nation states in the world, but there are 15 000 nations in the second sense of the word.

National Action Committee on the Status of Women This committee, founded in April 1972, is an umbrella organization of women's groups in Canada dedicated to lobbying the federal government to adopt changes to enhance the position and life chances of Canadian women. NAC replaced the National Ad Hoc Committee on the Status of Women, organized in 1971, to pressure for implementation of the recommendations of the Royal Commission on the Status of Women.

National Anti-poverty Organization Founded in 1971, this national organization conducts research and engages in advocacy on matters of concern to low-income Canadians.

national assembly (*assemblée national*) The title national assembly was adopted by Quebec's legislature in 1968 after the abolition of its legislative council, which had formed a second chamber alongside the legislative assembly. The new name was symbolic, while the rest of Canada's provinces had mere legislatures, Quebec now had an assembly expressing its status and dignity as a distinct culture and a founding nation of Canada.

national deviancy conference Formed in Britain in 1968, this group reflected the changing mood of criminology. They were critical of the positivism practised in criminology departments and were critical of the close relationship between criminology and the state and its apparatus of social control. NDC tended to focus on symbolic interactionism rather than Marxist theory.

National Firearms Association (NFA) Founded in Canada in 1985, the NFA is a lobby group for firearms owners and users.

National Parole Board (NPB) The NPB is a division within the federal ministry of the Solicitor General and is responsible for decisions on the early release of federal inmates into the community. Members of the board are order-in-council appointments and serve fixed terms. NPB also makes release decisions for those provinces without their own parole board. Members of the parole board travel to institutions and hear the offender's arguments for early release. Due to growing criticism of these decisions, the parole board now has a restrictive list of the types of factors they can consider in their decisions.

National Party A short-lived Canadian federal political party started by Nationalist publisher Mel Hurtig in 1993. The party advocated repeal of the free trade agreement with the United States, increased public involvement in political decision-making, and major reforms to fiscal and taxation policy. In the 1993 federal general election, the party received almost 200 000 votes, but failed to win any parliamentary seats. After the election, the party was weakened by internal controversy, and it ceased to be an active political force.

National Rifle Association of America Formed in 1871, this organization has become a powerful lobby against gun control legislation in the United States.

nationalism The concept of nationalism, like the concept of nation, has two quite distinct meanings. Common to both definitions is the idea that it is the nation that provides people with their primary form of belonging and that these nations should be self-governing. People of the world are thus located within nations, identify with these nation states, and political activity is organized around these nation states. Michael Ignatieff distinguishes two forms of nationalism. First, "civic nationalism," meaning that all citizens within a nation state are treated as equal and share political values. Within this sense of nationalism, one would find pluralistic communities acting as one and treating citizens with equality. It is this sense of nationalism that many thought was emerging after narrow religious and ethnic struggles of the 19th and early 20th century. The second sense of nationalism revolves around the equation of "people" with the nation state. In this formulation, the nation or the people exists prior to the state and in a sense creates the state. In these communities then, the nation and sense of national identification flows from a common characteristic (usually ethnic heritage) and thus excludes others. This form of nationalism may be less tolerant of difference and can be found in the German nation state where citizenship continues to be defined in terms of ethnicity. The concern that nation states and thus nationalism are increasingly being organized around ethnic (or other) characteristics is frequently described as the tribalization of the modern world. Tension between the two meanings of nationalism can be found in discussions around Quebec's right to self-determination; is civic nationalism at work or is it "people" nationalism? *See also* **tribalism**; **identity politics**; **postmodernism**. Reference: Ignatieff, Michael. (1993). *Blood and Belonging: Journeys into the New Nationalism.* Toronto: Viking.

nationalization The collective or public ownership or management of economic resources; in contrast to privatization. Canada has long relied on public (or state) ownership of economic resources. In 1962, the Liberal government of Jean Lesage nationalized the hydroelectric industry in Quebec, and this was an important component of the rapid economic growth and emerging sense of self-confidence that has come to be referred to as the "Quiet Revolution" in the province. *See also* **privatization**.

Natuashih *See* **Davis Inlet**.

natural attitude As used by Alfred Schutz (1899–1959), it refers to characteristics of the world as it is encountered by people living in it. Some of the properties of this attitude are the world is experienced as being historically organized prior to their arrival; it is intersubjective—experienced similarly by others; people accept the world as it is given through experience; people address the world pragmatically.

Nazism The political doctrine of the National Socialist Party of Germany led by Adolf Hitler, who became Chancellor of Germany in 1933 and who assumed absolute dictatorial power until the defeat of Germany in 1945 at the end of World War II. Nazism is chiefly remembered for its ideology of racial purity and of the superiority of the so-called Aryan race. This ideology resulted in the conquest and destruction of much of Europe and its peoples, and the mass murder of political opponents and those judged inferior or deviant. The greatest Nazi crimes were committed against the Jews of Europe on whom the Nazis unleashed a Holocaust of systematic mass killing, claiming six million victims, in the name of "racial purification."

NDP *See* **New Democratic Party**.

necessary condition In thinking about or looking for a causal relationship, researchers have to decide if they are dealing with a necessary condition. A necessary condition (or variable) is that which must be present for the effect to occur. To put it another way, if B appears then A must have been present. Social sciences seldom deal with necessary conditions (other than logical ones); rather, they are happy to find sufficient conditions.

necrophilia A form of sexual disorder in which the person has a strong desire to have sex with a corpse.

necrophobia A form of anxiety disorder in which the person has exaggerated fears of dead bodies.

needle exchange A program that allows drug addicts to exchange a used needle for a new one, with the intent of containing the spread of disease among the drug-user community. These programs are usually controversial but are one part of a "harm reduction" program in urban areas.

negotiation of criminal status Refers to the fact that authorities and offenders against the law are involved in an interactive process of defining criminality. Police or judges may ask: Was the offence intentional? Is the person who committed it someone who requires control from the criminal justice system? Is it important to deter them from further potential crime or is repetition unlikely? The behaviour of the offender in interaction with police and judges will shape what label, if any, will be applied to the situation. Thus defining criminal status is an interactive process involving participants in interpretation and negotiation.

neighbourhood watch A program usually organized by the police of a local area to get the residents of a neighbourhood to work together to prevent crime. Activities may include marking household property, calling neighbours to report a crime in the area, keeping a watch on unusual activity, and getting to know other residents.

neo-conservatism A resurgence of economic and political beliefs associated with classical liberalism of the early 19th century; should correctly be called neo-liberalism. Aspects of this philosophy include an acceptance of an unregulated market economy; a minimal role for government; a suspicion toward the welfare state; a view of citizens as motivated only by self-interest; and a commitment to the central value of individualism. *See also* **classical liberalism**.

neo-liberalism *See* **neo-conservatism**.

net widening Within critical criminology, this term is used to describe the effects of providing alternatives to incarceration or diversion programs to direct offenders away from court. While all of these programs developed since the late 1960s were intended to reduce the numbers of offenders in prison or reduce the numbers going to court, it has been found instead that the total numbers of offenders under the control of the state have increased while the population targeted for reduction has not been reduced. In short, the net of social control has been thrown more widely (or some might say the mesh has been made smaller). *See also* **crime net**. Reference: Roach, Kent. (2000). "Changing Punishment at the Turn of the Century: Restorative Justice on the Rise," *Canadian Journal of Criminology* 42(3): 249.

Nettler, Gwynne Moved from the United States to the University of Alberta in 1963 and established a significant criminology program within the sociology department.

neutralization techniques A set of linguistic techniques that an otherwise conventional person uses to neutralize the guilt they feel from engaging in deviant behaviour. These techniques allow the conventional person to drift further into deviance. Reference: Matza, David. (1964). *Delinquency and Drift.* New York: John Wiley.

Neve, Lisa In 1994, she became one of the few Canadian women to be declared a dangerous offender. This designation was removed in 1999, and the case has become illustrative of the way women are perceived in the criminal justice system.

new criminology The title of an influential book and a general term for criminology as it emerged from the attack on positivist criminology during the 1960s and 1970s. This new approach reintroduced symbolic interactionism to criminology as well as Marxist theory. Reference: Taylor, Ian, Paul Walton, and Jock Young. (1973). *New Criminology.* London: Routledge and Kegan Paul.

New Democratic Party Successor to the CCF, the New Democratic Party was formed in 1961 to widen the appeal and broaden the organization of Canadian social democracy. It combined the old CCF with Canada's labour union movement and various social democratic organizations. Like its predecessor, the new party has had limited success in federal politics, although it has exercised considerable influence, especially over the policies of the Liberal party. The party had its greatest impact on federal politics in the years 1972–74 when the minority Liberal government was dependent on it for parliamentary support. In provincial politics, the party has been much more successful and has formed governments in Saskatchewan, Manitoba, British Columbia, and Ontario.

nolle prosqui No prosecution. The term to describe a prosecutor's decision to not prosecute a case or to stop a case after a formal charge has been made. Reasons for this decision may be the reluctance of witnesses, police error, and so on.

nolo contendere No contest. An admission of guilt in a criminal case without contest, usually on the condition that this admission cannot be used against the person in a civil case.

nominal measures *See* **level of measurement**.

nomothetic *See* **ideographic**.

Norfolk Island prison *See* **Maconochie, Alexander**.

norm A culturally established rule prescribing appropriate social behaviour. Norms are relatively specific, precise, and elaborate the detailed behavioural requirements that flow from more general and overarching social values. For example, it is a value in western society that one should respect the dead; it is a norm that one should dress in dark colours for a funeral. *See also* **values**.

normal crime This term has two distinct meanings. (1) Émile Durkheim used the concept to refer to what he took to be an average or acceptable amount of crime in society. Part of his argument that crime (normal crime) is both inevitable and functionally useful for society. (2) David Sudnow uses the term to refer to how prosecutors typify individual crimes as fitting into a normal pattern for that category of crime. He refers to normal burglaries, normal pedophilia. A normal crime is more likely to result in a plea bargain in order to speed up the court process. Reference: Sudnow, David. (1976). "Normal Crimes: Sociological Features of the Penal Code in a Public Defender's Office," *Social Problems* 12: 255–76.

normal curve *See* **bell curve**.

North American Free Trade Agreement (NAFTA) *See* **free trade**.

Northwest Rebellion of 1885 Like the Red River Rebellion of 1869–70, the Northwest Rebellion was led by Louis Riel and the grievances of the settlers and Métis (of what is now Saskatchewan) were much the same. Demands were for democratic control of the region and for the protection of land, religious, and language rights. The decade between the two rebellions, however, saw the English of Ontario transform the image of Riel into that of a traitor and stiffened their resolve to ensure that the west not become an extension of the French-speaking province of Quebec. Military and police strength had also been established and the railroad provided transportation for this colonial enforcement arm. The Métis were quickly suppressed and Riel was hanged in Regina on November 16, 1885. The Métis people prefer to refer to this incident as an act of resistance rather than a rebellion. *See also* **Métis**; **Red River Rebellion**. Reference: Woodcock, George. (1975). *Gabriel Dumont: The Métis Chief and His Lost World.* Edmonton: Hurtig Press.

nothing works In 1974 authors D. Lipton, Robert Martinson, and J. Wilks, using "meta-analysis," assessed all the evaluations of criminal rehabilitation programs between 1945 and 1967. They reached the following conclusion: "With few and isolated exceptions, the rehabilitative efforts that have been reported so far have had no appreciable effect on recidivism." The results of this assessment convinced them that not much seemed to work, and one program did not seem more effective than another. Robert Martinson made this conclusion available much more widely when he published a short piece in the *Public Interest* (a liberal magazine begun in New York in 1965), asserting that "nothing works"; the phrase has been associated with his name since. In a 1978 publication, he admitted that they had left out of their study some pieces of research that may have shown rehabilitation to be more effective than they had publicly stated. This phrase "nothing works," however, became the mantra of those opposed to rehabilitation and had some influence in moving the public away from liberal programs of rehabilitation and towards retribution or deterrence as justifications for punishment. *See also* **meta-analysis**. Reference: Martinson, Robert. (1974). "What Works? – Questions and Answers About Prison Reform," *Public Interest* 35: 22–54.

nuclear family *See* **family, nuclear**.

null hypothesis When testing a research hypothesis, which the researcher has good reason to believe is true, it is customary to use a null hypothesis. This is typically a hypothesis of no difference or of no association between variables. If the research hypothesis is that men have a higher rate of suicide than do women, the null hypothesis would be that there is no difference in suicide rates between men and women. Researchers then try to disprove the null hypothesis and if they fail to reject it, they accept the research hypothesis. *See also* **falsifiability (or refutability)**.

numbered treaties Treaties had been signed with many native groups in eastern Canada prior to Confederation. With Confederation in 1867 and the purchase of lands from the Hudson Bay Company, Canada assumed responsibility for the native peoples of western Canada. Beginning in the 1870s, negotiations were begun with native groups. These negotiations resulted in treaties that were numbered, and are still known by those numbers. The total number eventually reached 11.

Nuremberg trials A tribunal established in the German city of Nuremberg in 1945 by Great Britain, France, the Soviet Union, and the United States, to bring to trial those war criminals whose actions during World War II were deemed to be international crimes against humanity. Many were brought to trial and some sentenced to death. Another tribunal was established in Japan to try Japanese war criminals. Other nations brought to trial those thought to be guilty of war crimes against citizens of one nation. Israel, for example, brought Adolf Eichmann, a major figure in the organization of the Holocaust, to trial in 1960, found him guilty, and he was hanged. *See also* **International Criminal Court**; **war crimes**.

O

objectivity This term is used in two distinct but related ways. The first refers to the actions of a social scientist: assuming a position of disinterestedness or impartiality, or being open-minded in the assessment of evidence. Objectivity is thought to be central to the procedures of the scientific method. The second meaning refers to the nature of the statements people make: a statement can be objective as opposed to the scientist being objective. An objective statement is one that can be agreed upon by others regardless of their backgrounds or biases.

obscenity *See* **pornography; Butler case**.

obsessive A form of mental disorder in which the person has recurrent and unwanted thoughts they cannot get out of their mind.

occupational crime White-collar crime committed by an individual or group of individuals exclusively for personal gain. The distinction between this crime and organizational crime is difficult to maintain.

occupational distance This is the distance between one occupation and another where occupations are ranked on a hierarchy of status. The concept is central to studies of social mobility because it permits some measurement of the extent of mobility. For example, to change one's occupation from unskilled labour to semi-skilled labour involves less occupational distance than to move from unskilled labour to professional accountant. Occupational distance is therefore an important measurement in determining the relevance of social mobility. *See also* **social mobility**; **demand mobility**.

Ocean Ranger An off-shore oil rig which sank off the coast of Newfoundland in 1982, killing 84 workers. Investigation determined that inadequate safety equipment was in place to respond to emergencies. Reference: (1984–85). *Royal Commission on the Ocean Ranger Marine Disaster*. Ottawa.

October Crisis On October 5, 1970, the Front de Libération du Québec (FLQ) kidnapped James Cross, the British Trade Commissioner in Montreal, and on October 10, kidnapped Pierre Laporte, minister of labour in the government of Quebec. The federal government, led by Pierre Trudeau, invoked the War Measures Act, and armed soldiers entered the province of Quebec. Laporte was murdered the next day. Over 450 persons were detained in Quebec, few of whom were charged. Cross was released in exchange for safe passage to Cuba for the kidnappers. The government's handling of the kidnapping and subsequent events were extremely controversial.

Oedipus complex A concept of Sigmund Freud (1856–1939) that infants become erotically fixated on their mothers and must be psychologically conditioned, by fear of punishment and disapproval, into diverting or suppressing their sexual energies.

Oka On July 11,1990, a dispute over land in the Quebec town of Oka erupted in violence between Mohawk residents of the Kanesatake reserve outside Montreal and the provincial police. During a brief gun battle, a police officer was killed. A prolonged standoff and road blockade led the province to request that the military be brought in to bring the confrontation to an end. This is one of the few occasions in Canadian history when the army was used against Canadian citizens. An inquiry failed to determine who killed the police officer, and although the prime minister branded the native residents as "criminals," many Canadians sided with them. Reference: York, Geoffrey, and Loreen Pindera. (1991). *People of the Pines: The Warriors and the Legacy of Oka*. Toronto: Little Brown and Co.

Oklahoma City bombing On April 19, 1995, shortly after the start of the workday, a powerful blast shattered a government building in Oklahoma City, killing 168 people and injuring many more. While the first reaction was to blame "foreigners" and more specifically Muslims, Timothy McVeigh was eventually charged and convicted of the bombing. McVeigh had been part of an anti-government group in the United States.

Old Bailey Central criminal court of London, England, which also hears serious cases sent forward from other parts of England and Wales (Scotland has an entirely separate civil law system of criminal trial). Originally founded as a Sessions House for court proceedings in 1539 and located on Old Bailey Street next to the infamous Newgate Prison. In 1673, the court was rebuilt but with the courtroom itself situated in the open air in the courtyard of the building. This was intended to reduce the risk of spectators and court personnel being infected with "jail fever" or typhus, which was endemic among prisoners. In 1737, possibly to reduce the unruly throngs of the public who attended proceedings, the court was enclosed, and in 1750, as feared, typhus did indeed strike and killed 60 people including two judges. In 1774, there was further rebuilding; in 1834, the location became known as the Central Criminal Court for England and Wales.

oligarchy A society or social system ruled by a few people. As societies or organizations become large, it is thought that political power becomes concentrated in the hand of a few individuals. *See also* **iron law of oligarchy**; **plutocracy**.

oligopoly The situation where a small number of companies own or control the production of a particular good or provision of services within a market economy. This situation typically arises from the concentration of ownership and provides a challenge to liberal theory that claims benefit from a plurality of producers operating in a very competitive market. *See also* **monopoly**.

Olson, Clifford Clifford Olson is the most notorious of serial killers in Canada (perhaps to be surpassed by Robert Pickton), and for many has come to represent the essence of evil. Between the years of 1980 and 1981, Olson murdered at least 11 children and young people in the lower mainland of British Columbia. He was eventually identified and convicted. Prior to conviction, however, he struck a deal with RCMP involving payment of $100 000 to disclose the location of all the bodies of the missing persons. These monies went to his wife and child. In addition to this controversy, there was worry about the failure to identify Olson early on. Two weeks after the first murder, the father of a friend of the murdered girl heard a broadcast stating that Olson was being charged with a rape. He called the police and asked if Olson could also be responsible for the missing child. He was told that the rape victim was a prostitute and her testimony would not be considered reliable. In addition, they had already checked out Olson and did not think he was the offender. Ten more young people were to die before Olson was caught. Reference: Mulgrew, Ian. (1990). *Final Payoff: The True Cost of Convicting Clifford Olson.* Toronto: Seal Books.

one-percenter A term coined after a gathering of the American Motorcycle "Gypsy Tour" on July 4, 1947. The 3000 riders descended on Hollister, California, which was sponsoring a "dirt hill climb." When violence broke out, the Motorcycle Association issued a statement saying that 99 percent of riders were respectable pleasure riders and the other 1 percent were troublemakers. Since that date, groups like the Hells Angels have referred to themselves as the "one-percenter." This event was depicted in the Hollywood movie *The Wild One.*

online pornography Given the speed of the Internet and the anonymity of the users, it is not surprising that the Internet has become a major distribution site for pornography. Changes to the Criminal Code in 2002 gave the courts powers to delete child pornography posted on the Internet and to seize materials used in a child pornography offence.

open class ideology This is a component part of liberal ideology: the key claim is that an individual has meaningful opportunity to rise (or fall) in social class and status as a result of personal ability, hard work, and individual merit. The concept therefore claims that society's status system is based on achievement and not on ascription. *See also* **social mobility**; **liberalism**.

open custody A disposition of the youth court where the young offender is sentenced to a form of custody in an institution without locks. The young person may go out to school or to recreational activities and the inside environment is a little less secure and demanding. There is, however, wide variation in the nature of this form of custody from province to province. Approximately 18 percent of young offenders found guilty are given this disposition. The Youth Criminal Justice Act no longer uses the terms *closed custody* and *open custody,* but it does require each province to maintain two levels of custody and further mandates the courts to use the least restrictive form of custody unless certain requirements are met. It is anticipated that the rate of incarceration will decline under the new Act. *See also* **closed custody**; **Young Offenders Act**; **Youth Criminal Justice Act**.

operant conditioning The basic process by which an individual's behaviour is shaped by reinforcement or by punishment.

operationalization In quantitative research, the act of specifying exactly how a concept will be measured. Before measuring the concept of "violent crime," a researcher must decide what are indictors of violent crime and then specify how these indicators will be counted. One might, for example, decide to use official reports of crimes known to the police and count all instances of homicide; manslaughter; attempted murder; assault levels 1, 2, and 3; and sexual assault levels 1, 2, and 3. Examining how a researcher has operationalized a concept is the first place to look for weakness in the research design. In the above example, for instance, many would argue that assaults level 1 (the lowest level of assault) contain many acts which many would not really see as indicators of the concept of "violence." The United States government, for example, does not include this kind of assault in their measures of violent crime.

operationally defined To define some concept of study in such a way that it can be observed and measured. For example, "well-being" might be measured by asking people to rate their overall satisfaction with their lifestyle, or "anti-social behaviour" might be measured by frequency of arrest or criminal prosecution.

opium A narcotic drug derived from the juice of the opium poppy flower. Both morphine and heroin are derived from opium.

Opium Act With the passage of the Opium Act in 1908 Canada became the first western nation to prohibit, under criminal law, the import, manufacture, and sale of opium. Opium was manufactured and used primarily by the Chinese at this time, which raises the question: Why was there a need for a criminal law? While there is some dispute about the origins of the Act, it can be noted that British Columbia was experiencing increased labour tension due to the rapid process of deskilling labour that was occurring. The craft organization of work was breaking down as management gained control of the work process and began to hire cheap unskilled labour to do much of the work. The Chinese provided a great deal of this cheap labour and some members of the labour movement saw them as the source of their problems. Others, of course, saw the problem in terms traditional labour–management conflict and argued for a socialist response (reducing private ownership of the means of production). It is clear that there was anti-Asian sentiment in the province, and federal legislation had attempted to restrict Chinese immigration. When Mackenzie King, the labour minister, was sent to Vancouver to investigate the 1907 riot, he saw that Chinese businessmen involved in manufacturing opium made claims for compensation; he perhaps also saw the solution to his labour problem: scapegoat the Chinese and turn what was really a labour problem into a racial problem.

Opium War Fought between England and China from 1839 to 1842 over China's refusal to continue importing opium. England had forced China to import opium so English boats would not have to arrive in China for tea with no cargo. Much of early English capitalism was thus built on a foundation of opium. China lost the war and ceded Hong Kong to Britain as payment. Hong Kong was returned to China in 1996. Reference: Travis, W., and F. Sanello. (2002). *The Opium Wars: The Addiction of One Empire and the Corruption of Another.* Naperville, IL: Sourcebooks.

opportunity structure A shortened phrase referring to the notion that opportunity, the chance to gain certain rewards or goals, is shaped by the way the society or an institution is organized (or structured). The opportunity for girls to succeed in mathematics may be structured by the fact that most of the mathematics teachers are men, and that perhaps all teachers tend to discourage such an endeavour or suggest that girls are not good at this subject. There may be a sexist structure in the school that shapes opportunity. Reference: Cloward, Richard, and Lloyd Ohlin. (1960). *Delinquency and Opportunity.* New York: Free Press.

order-in-council In the British constitutional system, inherited by Canada, the monarch is Head of State, must approve all laws for them to be valid, and is advised by a Privy Council of Ministers. By constitutional convention, the monarch accepts only the advice of members of the Privy Council who are also Cabinet ministers and who have the support of the House of Commons. Most legislation passed by the House of Commons outlines only the broad principles of law and legal regulation and the law usually provides for the bureaucracy to develop detailed provisions that are then given legal status by being approved by the Governor General (representing the monarch) in council.

ordinal measures *See* **level of measurement**.

organic mental disorders Those forms of mental disorder that have organic or anatomical causes; for example, brain injury or degenerative brain tissue. This is found in senility and in Alzheimer's disease.

organic solidarity A term used by Émile Durkheim (1858–1917) to refer to a state of interdependency created by the specialization of roles and in which individuals and institutions become acutely dependent on others in a complex division of labour. The basis of solidarity is abstract and may be weakened by anomie when people fail to comprehend the ties that bind them to others. *See also* **mechanical solidarity**; **ideal type**.

organizational crime White-collar crime committed with the support and encouragement of a formal organization and intended at least in part to advance the goals of that organization. Usually distinguished from white-collar crime.

organized crime The operation of illegal business entities whose members are bound together because of their group interest and their desire to profit from illegal activity.

Osborne, Helen Betty A 19-year-old aboriginal student living in La Pas, Manitoba, who was murdered on November 13, 1971. She had been stopped on the street by four men who wanted to engage her in sex. When she refused, she was abducted, then raped and brutally murdered. While the whole town seemed to be aware of the men involved in the murder, it was several months before the RCMP concluded that the four men in question had been involved. It was not until December 1987 that one man was convicted of murder. A Commission of Inquiry reported on these events in 1991 and outlined the many ways in which racism had affected the investigation, charges, and trial.

Ottawa University, criminology at A criminology program was established at the bilingual Ottawa university in 1967 under the leadership of Tadeusz Grygier. Grygier (1913–) was born in Poland and in 1939 was exiled to Siberia. This experience shaped his life as well as his interest in the social sciences. He taught in the school of social work at the University of Toronto before moving to Ottawa.

Ouimet report Set up to study the broad field of corrections in its widest sense, the Ouimet commission reported in 1969. It is noteworthy for acknowledging that there was no longer (if ever) a consensus about the purpose of imprisonment and for recognizing that the public was not entirely in favour of supporting rehabilitation for offenders. Ouimet, however, continues to talk as though rehabilitation is, and should be, one of the desirable ways to protect society. It was not until 1977 and the MacGuigan report, however, that it is stated that rehabilitation must not be a purpose of incarceration. *See also* **MacGuigan report**.

overrepresentation A group that has a number of its members in some condition in greater numbers than their population would suggest. If a group makes up 20 percent of the population, then a researcher might for example predict, other things being equal, that they would represent 20 percent of offenders, victims, and those in prison. For example, men are overrepresented in prisons, as are Aboriginal people. Aboriginal people constitute between 3–5 percent of the Canadian population, but represent approximately 19 percent of admission to provincial and territorial custody facilities and 17 percent of federal custody. Aboriginal people also represent approximately 24 percent of homicide suspects. Women are overrepresented as victims in sexual assault offences. *See also* **Gladue case**. Reference: Hendrick, D., and L. Farmer. (2002). "Adult Correctional Services in Canada, 2000–2001." *Juristat* 22(10): 1–24.

P

P4W *See* **Prison for Women**.

padlock laws May 2, 1951: In an event that says much about the political style of "Le Chef" Maurice Duplessis, premier of Quebec, the Quebec Superior Court (all courts in Quebec at this time had a large crucifix placed behind the judge) ordered him to pay damages of $8000 to a Jehovah's Witness, Frank Roncarelli, whose licence to sell liquor was cancelled by the Quebec Liquor Commission in 1946, on the express order of the premier. The premier's displeasure had been incurred because Roncarelli had stood bail for Jehovah's Witnesses harassed and charged for distributing their religious literature. Roncarelli's business had been essentially "padlocked" (because with no liquor licence he could do little business) under provisions of a law passed by the Quebec legislature giving the state and the premier wide powers. This law came into effect after the federal government removed section 98 of the Criminal Code, a provision first introduced in 1917 to control those seen as troublemakers during the Winnipeg General Strike. The court ruled that the premier's actions were motivated by religious hostility, had amounted to political interference with an independent commission, and that he must be held personally liable for the financial damages Roncarelli had experienced. This decision was appealed, however, and went to the Supreme Court where Constitutional lawyer (and faculty member at McGill University) Scott argued the case against Duplessis. On January 27, 1959, the Supreme Court decided against Duplessis and awarded Roncarelli $33 000 plus interest from the 1951 decision, and awarded him another $20 000 to $30 000 in costs. This was the end of the infamous "padlock laws" in Quebec. This and other victories soon made it necessary to appoint Scott dean of the law faculty, a position he had been denied in the past due to his radical and outspoken ideas. Issues like the Roncarelli case renewed the interest of Scott and others in the need for a Bill of Rights of sufficient strength to control the abuse of power against citizens. His wish came true in 1982, with the introduction of the Charter of Rights and Freedoms.

pains of re-entry It is known that inmates, particularly long-term inmates, suffer a number of difficulties on their re-entry to the community and readjusting to the demands of non-institutional life.

pains of imprisonment A term used by Sykes (1965) to explain the emergence of the prison subculture. Sykes argues that it arises from the pains of imprisonment: the deprivation of liberty; deprivations of goods and services necessary to maintain an earlier sense of identity; deprivation of heterosexual relationships; the deprivation of autonomy; and the deprivation of security. The convict subculture provides solutions to problems caused by many of the deprivations. Reference: Sykes, G.M. (1958). *The Society of Captives.* Princeton University Press.

panel study A form of longitudinal research in which a panel of respondents or subjects is selected and then followed or interviewed over time. If a panel of first-year university students is selected, the researcher would, for example, be able to learn what their routes are toward an undergraduate degree. Drawing a sample of undergraduates at year one, year two, and year three would not provide the same degree of detail.

panhandling With the rise in homelessness and increasing poverty, there has been growing public concern about the number of people begging for money on the streets. Many people report being frightened or intimidated by aggressive panhandling. Politicians have attempted to respond to this in several ways, including the passing of the Safe Streets Act in Ontario in 1999. Many argue that legislation of this type interferes with basic civil liberties of citizens.

pan-Indianism This term has been applied to social movements among both Asian Indians and North American First Nations peoples. In both contexts it refers to a social movement and a political philosophy that asserts a people's common identity and unity across political or state boundaries and tribal divisions.

Panopticon The plans for a prison design set out by English theorist Jeremy Bentham (1748–1833) in a series of letters between 1787 and 1791. This design provided for a circular structure in which guards could see prisoners at all times and yet prisoners could not see the guards. For this reason the design became known as the "all seeing eye." Bentham was paid for his design after much lobbying, but few institutions were built. An example can be found in Stateville penitentiary near Chicago, built in 1916.

Papon, Maurice Papon was a senior bureaucrat and a politician in France. During the German occupation of France, a puppet government was established with headquarters in the town of Vichy (known as the Vichy government). Maurice Papon, a senior bureaucrat in this government from 1942 to 1944, signed the papers sending about 1500 French Jews to their deaths in German concentration camps. The Jews of France were probably the most assimilated of Europe and could well have remained undetected, but the Vichy government was a right-wing government and passed anti-Jewish laws without being asked by Germany. By 1943, Papon was cooperating with the French resistance movement and became somewhat of a hero. His complicity in the deaths of Jews eventually came to light and in 1998 he was brought to trial. Found guilty, he was sentenced to 10 years in prison.

paradigm A framework used in thinking about and organizing an understanding of natural or social phenomena. All societies, and the individuals within them, tend to have relatively fixed assumptions about how to understand and interpret the world, but there is great variation in these assumptions from place to place and from time to time. For many centuries, for example, natural phenomena like the eclipse of the sun, thunder, lightning, or floods were explained within a paradigm of religious belief and myth; today, they fall within the paradigm of science. This process of sets of assumptions changing over time can be referred to as a paradigm shift: there emerges a new way of looking at the world. The term came into social science vocabulary from the writings of Thomas Kuhn (1970), a historian of science. He challenged the conventional wisdom of history that claimed that science was a long, slow process of building on previous knowledge. Rejecting this view, Kuhn argued that the history of science can be seen rather as a history of dominant paradigms and paradigm shifts. A paradigm in his presentation was a set of assumptions about the kinds of questions to ask in science and how to go about looking for answers. As a particular body of knowledge builds up, there are a growing number of anomalies that can only be forced with difficulty into the dominant theory. At some point people begin to see things differently and to ask different questions in an attempt to explain their observations, and they eventually arrive at a new theory that better accounts for the anomalies.

paraphilia Sexual urges directed towards non-human objects or sexual arousal from the giving or receiving of pain or sexual urges directed to those unable to grant consent.

pardon Since a criminal record may be a barrier to foreign travel, adoption, career advancement, bonding, and many other things, the National Parole Board of Canada, acting under the Criminal Records Act, can shield a person from disclosure of their record, although this does not erase the fact of conviction. A pardon normally means that your criminal record will not be given out without the approval of the Solicitor General of Canada. The shielding is less thorough for some sexual offences where public safety may be at issue. Normally a person can apply for a pardon after three years for a summary conviction and five years for an indictable offence.

parental responsibility Legislators have been under pressure to make parents more responsible for the wrongdoings of their children. Manitoba (1997) and Ontario (2000) have passed Parental Responsibility Acts allowing victims of youth crime to sue the parents of the offender.

parliament The highest legislative assembly in many countries including Canada. Canada's Parliament consists of the House of Commons, the Senate, and the Crown (represented by the Governor General). Members of the House Commons are elected by constituencies across Canada. The maximum term of the House of Commons between elections is five years, though elections may be held at any time prior to that if called by the Governor General acting on the prime minister's advice. The Senate is not elected; its members are appointed until age 75 by the Governor General on the advice of the prime minister. Seats in the Senate are regionally distributed as set out in the 1867 Constitution Act.

parole The conditional early release (on day parole or full parole) of a person from incarceration. The decision to release is made by the National Parole Board of Canada and the prisoner is typically placed under some form of supervision. Eligibility for parole varies depending on the sentence. Normally an inmate can apply for parole after serving the first one-third of a sentence. For offenders convicted of violent crimes or serious drug offences, the judge may change this to one-half of the sentence. Normally a person serving a life sentence can apply for parole after seven years. However, many sentences for murder now stipulate a much longer waiting period prior to eligibility. There is no parole for young offenders, although there is a period of mandatory supervision.

parricide The killing of a near relative, more usually a parent. Not to be confused with patricide. *See also* **patricide**.

Parti Québeçois Founded in 1968 under the leadership of René Lévesque, the party had the main aim of achieving political sovereignty for Quebec within the framework of a continued association with Canada. It first came to power in 1976 and began to prepare a political strategy leading to a referendum vote on "sovereignty-association" in 1980. The referendum proposal was defeated by a majority of 60 percent to 40 percent, but under its immensely popular leader, the party was able to comfortably win the 1981 provincial election. After losing the subsequent election under new leadership, the party returned to power in 1994 and immediately prepared for a new referendum on sovereignty-association. The proposal was brought to a referendum in 1995, defeated once more, but by a very narrow margin, ensuring that the issue of Quebec's relationship with Canada will remain at the centre of Canadian political life in the coming years.

participatory management *See* **industrial relations**.

participatory research Distinguished from other research techniques in that the subjects, usually oppressed or exploited groups, are fully involved in the research, from the designing of topics to the analysis of data. While the findings of such research may be useful and indeed emancipatory, the process of community or neighbourhood-building during the carrying out of the research is of equal importance.

patriarchy Literally "rule by the father," but more generally it refers to a social situation where men are dominant over women in wealth, status, and power. Patriarchy is associated with a set of ideas, a "patriarchal ideology" that acts to explain and justify this dominance and attributes it to inherent natural differences between men and women. Sociologists tend to see patriarchy as a social product and not as an outcome of innate differences between the sexes; they focus attention on the way that gender roles in a society affect power differentials between men and women. *See also* **ideology**; **hegemony**. Reference: Smith, Michael. (1990). "Patriarchal

Ideology and Wife Beating: A Test of a Feminist Hypothesis." *Violence and Victims* 5(4): 257–73.

patriation of the constitution The "bringing home" of all legal authority over the laws and Constitution of Canada. The Constitution Act, 1867 (formerly the BNA Act) was British legislation, and it could be changed only by Britain's Parliament (although this was done only on the request of Canada's Parliament). In the Constitution Act, 1982, a new exclusively Canadian amending procedure was established and the parliament of Great Britain no longer holds any legal authority regarding Canada. Reference: Russell, Peter H. (1993). *Constitutional Odyssey: Can Canadians Become a Sovereign People?* Toronto: University of Toronto Press.

patricide The killing of one's father. In the psychology of Sigmund Freud, the urge to patricide is present in the infant male whose intense erotic attachment to his mother creates the desire to kill the father in order to take possession of her. In his speculations about the origins of the incest taboo, Freud imagines that in the earliest times of human groups (the "primal horde"), the sons did in fact kill their father to gain possession of their mother and this led to subsequent quarrelling and murder between the sons. These terrible consequences were then averted by the cultural development of the incest taboo and of the castration complex which created infantile fear of the father and forced the turning away of erotic attention from the mother to permitted sexual partners.

patrimony A right, a status, or tangible asset inherited from a father or other ancestor. In principle, a patrimony may be inherited by either sex although the term is generally associated with patrilineal transmission of status, property, and wealth.

pattern variables These are five dichotomies, developed by Talcott Parsons (1902–79), to draw out the contrasting values to which individuals orient themselves in social interaction. One side of the dichotomies reflects the value patterns dominant in traditional society (*gemeinschaft*); the other reflects the dominant values of modern society (*gesellschaft*). The variables, listed with the traditional side of the dichotomy first, are: affectivity–affective neutrality; diffuseness–specificity; particularism–universalism; ascription–achievement; collectivity orientation–self orientation. Social scientists, using the tradition of pattern variables, have argued that signs of Canada being a more traditional society are the lower crime rates and greater deference to authority.

pay equity Generally refers to laws and public and corporate policies that have as their objective the elimination of pay differentials linked to gender, ethnic identity, or particular minority status. Pay equity is usually concerned with correcting gender-based labour market inequality experienced by women. (In principle, such policies could apply also to men, but there is little evidence of gendered disadvantage for men in the labour market.) Two issues are addressed. First is the problem of relatively direct discrimination: women being paid less than men for the same or essentially similar work. This practice is now illegal in Canada: the law requires *equal pay for equal work.* Second is a more complex problem of identifying and correcting wage inequality that results from historical undervaluation of the types of work that are dominated by women. For example, day care workers are among the worst paid in Canada, but day care work is crucial to the working of Canada's economy. Policy makers have concluded that such examples indicate a need for an active principle of establishment of pay equity: *equal pay for work of equal value.* This principle allows comparison of pay rates between different types of work that are evaluated and weighted according to criteria such as skill, education, effort, and working conditions. There are federal and some provincial laws mandating this form of pay equity, but there has been cautious application of them.

peace bond Any person who fears they are likely to be victimized by a specific person can seek to have some restraint placed on that person. There are three ways to do this; all three are generally referred to as peace bonds. Literally this means that the potential offender is required to keep the peace and failure to do so is itself a criminal offence. The most common peace bond is a restraining order provided for by section 810 of the Criminal Code. *See also* **restraining order**.

pedophilia A form of sexual disorder in which the person is sexually aroused by children. *See also* **child sex tourism**; **Internet luring**; **Badgley report**; **online pornography**; **Sharpe decision**.

Peel, Robert (1788–1850) The first commander of the Metropolitan Police Force of London, England, formed in 1829. Playing on the name of their founder, the police became known as "Bobbies."

Peel developed an organizational structure for the police and a set of principles that provided a model for modern police forces throughout the western world. Peel was to become prime minister of England.

penitentiary Prisons built in the early part of the 19th century and embodying the principle of solitary confinement as punishment for a criminal offence. The first penitentiary in North America was at Auburn, New York, built in 1816–25, and came to be known as the silent system. Offenders were confined in solitary cells at night and worked in congregate (and silence) during the day. Eastern State Penitentiary, built at Cherry Hill, Pennsylvania, in 1829, embodied the solitary system, as offenders were confined to solitary cells for the entire period of confinement. Canada's Kingston penitentiary was opened in 1835, modelled after the Auburn penitentiary. As suggested by the name, penitentiaries had a strong Christian influence. A penitent is one who repents of sins, or feels pain or sorrow for offences. Also one who is admitted to penance, which is the sacrament consisting in repentance or contrition for sins. Early advocates of the penitentiary, such as John Howard, were influenced by their Christian faith and equated crime with sin. This model provided a philosophy of punishment and also shaped Anglo-European penology by assuming that criminal offenders would be reformed or rehabilitated. Reference: Ignatieff, Michael. (1978). *A Just Measure of Pain: The Penitentiary in the Industrial Revolution, 1750–1850.* New York: Pantheon.

Pennsylvania system A type of penitentiary first opened in Pennsylvania in 1826, involving a massive building constructed to house inmates in solitary confinement. Silence was imposed and inmates lived in enforced idleness. This method of incarceration results in high rates of suicide and demoralization. While the principles of solitary confinement and silence were maintained, later versions of this system allowed inmates to work in their cells or to work sitting at the door to their cell. Very few North American prisons were built on this model. Rather, a competitor model, the Auburn system, won more approval in North America. *See also* **Walnut Street Jail**; **Auburn system**.

penology The study of the treatment and punishment of criminal offenders. Penology is now included within criminology.

per capita *Capita* comes from a Latin term referring to head. Criminologists and sociologists refer to crimes (or divorce rates, etc.) per capita. For example, if there are only 0.01 crimes per capita, this would mean you have a risk of being victimized 1 percent. Criminologists usually use the idea of a rate per 100 000 rather than the idea of per capita.

peremptory challenge A challenge (and thus removal) to any potential jury member without having to show cause. A peremptory challenge can be made by either the defence counsel or the prosecutor.

persons case An important Canadian case that determined that women were indeed "persons" under the Constitution Act, 1867 (formerly the BNA Act). Following women's federal enfranchisement, a debate arose over the eligibility of women to be appointed to the Senate. Requests to the government to make an appointment (the name of Judge Emily Murphy was offered) were rejected in 1919 on the grounds that a reading of the Constitution meant that "persons" referred only to men. In 1927, Emily Murphy was able to use a provision of the Supreme Court Act of 1875 to request a constitutional interpretation of the BNA Act: all five judges who heard the case agreed that "Women are not 'qualified persons' within the meaning of Section 24 of the BNA Act, 1867." Judge Murphy took her case to the Privy Council in London, and on October 18, 1929, the Privy Council announced that women were indeed persons. Reference: Baines, Beverly. (1993). "Law, Gender, Equality." In Sandra Burt et al. (eds.), *Changing Patterns.* Toronto: McClelland and Stewart.

petite bourgeoisie A middle class of professionals and small-business people who work for themselves or own small productive facilities. Marx predicted that this class would be gradually eliminated by the consolidation of large capital under competitive forces.

phenomenological sociology Defined as the study of phenomenon, phenomenology has had its primary influence on ethnomethodology. In the early development of phenomenology, a distinction was drawn between *phenomena* (things as they appear in our experience) and *noumena* (things as they are in themselves). Immanuel Kant (1724–1804) believed that all we can ever know are the former. Edmund Husserl (1859–1938) argued that natural and social environments differ in that social objects appear only as perceived objects (i.e., there is no *noumena*); they depend on human recognition for their existence, and, because of this, social reality is in constant flux and ambiguity. Social reality is only an experienced reality rather than a natural reality. The *experience* of objects, events, activities, etc. is all there is. By accepting this claim, ethnomethodology has emerged as the study of the creation of social reality through mundane reasoning, account giving, or the use of documentary method. The concreteness or factuality of the social world is seen to be an accomplishment of members of society and the methods of this accomplishment are the topic of investigation.

phrenology A biological theory of criminality developed by Franz Gall (1758–1828) and Johan Spurzheim (1776–1832) built on the assumption that segments of the brain are linked to particular emotions and characteristics. This being so, an examination of the skull shows which of these areas is overdeveloped or underdeveloped. It was believed that criminality could be identified in this way. Although later proved to be without empirical support, for a time, every prisoner had a phrenology chart on file.

Pickton, Robert William By January 2004, he had been charged with the deaths of 15 women, making him the most notorious serial killer in Canada. Forensic investigation at the pig farm owned by his family had, by 2004, discovered the remains of 31 women and the police continue to investigate and lay new charges. *See also* **missing women case**; **serial murder**.

pillory A wooden framework with holes for legs and arms in which an offender could be imprisoned in a public place, allowing the public to humiliate the offender. Also known as a *stock*.

pink collar A term that denotes jobs and employment sectors dominated by women workers.

pink-collar ghetto Expanding the dichotomy between blue-collar and white-collar occupations, this phrase captures the particular concentration of women in jobs traditionally thought to be "women's work." In 1991, for example, 57 percent of female workers (and only 26 percent of men) were in the three occupational categories of clerical, sales, and service; 13.5 percent of women were in the specific occupations of stenographers, secretaries, and sales clerks. Interestingly, 88 percent of cashiers were women, as were 98 percent of secretaries, 93 percent of receptionists, and 81 percent of elementary and kindergarten teachers.

Pinto, Ford *See* **Ford Pinto**.

Pitre, Marguerite The last woman ever to be executed in Canada. Pitre was hanged in Montreal, January 9, 1953.

plaintiff The person who initiates a civil case believing that he or she or his or her interests have been harmed by the defendant.

plea In criminal court, the accused's formal response to the charge(s). Normally a plea is either guilty as charged or not guilty as charged.

plea bargaining Negotiation between the Crown prosecutor, defence counsel, and the accused to determine which charge will be laid or what sentence will be recommended. Typically this negotiation is undertaken in an effort to have the accused plead guilty and avoid the need for a trial.

pluralism Has three principal meanings in the social sciences. First, it is a model of politics where power is assumed to be widely dispersed to different individuals and interest groups within a society, thus ensuring that political processes will be relatively open and democratic, and will reflect a spectrum of social interests rather than the domination of particular groups. Second, it describes a society where individual and group differences are present and are celebrated as enriching the social fabric. Canada's policy of multiculturalism reflects pluralist values. Third, it is a view of the causation of social phenomena, especially of social change, that examines the interaction of a variety of factors rather than relying on a single explanatory cause. For example, Max Weber, in stressing the importance of cultural as well as material forces in creating change within a society, offers a more pluralistic framework for explanation than the more exclusively materialist approach of Marx. *See also* **Protestant ethic**; **Marxism**; **historical materialism**.

plutocracy Literally "rule by the rich," the term is used to denote a wide range of situations where a group of individuals are able to exert disproportionate power and influence in society and social institutions because of their wealth.

polarization of classes In Marxian analysis, the inevitable historical process of the class structure becoming increasingly polarized. Over time, it is argued, the secondary classes of capitalism (the self-employed, the residual aristocracy, etc.) will disappear and be absorbed into either the bourgeoisie class or the proletariat. The class structure will come to consist only of these two classes. *See also* **class.**

police caution The Youth Criminal Justice Act allows the police to issue a formal caution to a young offender and thus avoid prosecution.

police culture An example of an occupational culture to which new recruits become socialized. It is thought that police culture is one of several demand characteristics that shape routine decision-making by the police. *See also* **demand characteristic**.

police personality Social scientists believe that a police personality emerges from certain aspects of police work (danger and isolation) rather than from pre-existing traits of the individual. Reference: Skolnick, J. (1966). *Justice Without Trial.* New York: Wiley.

political assassinations Politics is a hazardous occupation and many politicians throughout history have paid with their lives for their involvements. William Shakespeare's play *Julius Caesar* commemorates one of the most famous: the murder of Julius Caesar in the Roman Senate on March 15, 44 B.C. Many other celebrated political figures have also died at the hands of assassins. These include American presidents Abraham Lincoln (April 14, 1865) and John F. Kennedy (November 22, 1963); Tsar Alexander II of Russia (March 1, 1881); Archduke Franz Ferdinand (June 28, 1914), an event which contributed to precipitating World War I; Dr. Martin Luther King (April 4, 1968), and Swedish prime minister Olof Palme (February 28, 1986).

political economy theory A major tradition in Canadian history and the social sciences. This is not a specific theory, but a general approach to social analysis that stresses the interconnection of social, political, and economic processes in society. Classic writers within this tradition include Harold Innis (1894–1952) and C. B. Macpherson (1911–1987). It remains central to contemporary Canadian social analysis and academic discourse.

political policing The way in which the process of policing the community acts to maintain and reinforce deference to authority. By living within a system of social order, people are socialized to accept order, justified by legitimating ideas, like tradition, inspired leadership, or representative democracy. It can also mean, more narrowly, the way in which police activity, while superficially about maintenance of the criminal law, can be about the control or surveillance of particular groups and communities.

political socialization The component of the process of individuals coming to learn and internalize the culture of their society or group that is directly related to the transmission of political values and behaviours.

politics This can be narrowly defined as all that relates to the way a society is governed. Politics is the process by which the community makes decisions and establishes values that are binding upon its members. This definition comes from the original Greek meaning of *politics*, the government of the city state. In general speech, politics refers much more widely to processes that involve the exercise of power, status, or influence in making decisions or establishing social relationships. This latter meaning is implied by the idea of "office politics" or "sexual politics" (as used by Kate Millett) or the claim that "the personal is political."

polity An umbrella term used to refer to the roles and institutions of a society that directly shape the way the society is governed. There is debate about what institutions should be included in a description of the polity. It involves state institutions of government, the political parties, and interest and advocacy groups. It will also include the media and other institutions directly affecting political values, opinions, and behaviour.

polygamy A marriage structure in which there is more than one spouse at a time: the term covers both polygyny and polyandry. While polygamy is a violation of the criminal law, there is at least one polygamous colony in Canada, the colony of Bountiful in British Columbia. Male residents of this colony follow the traditional Mormon practice of having more than one wife. The Attorney General has decided not to enforce the law in this case, although a civil suit is being initiated by women who have been able to leave the colony.

polygraph tests Also known as a *lie detector test*, this psychological technique based on physiological responses to lying is not allowed in Canadian courts.

popular culture Intellectual opinions of popular culture, the culture of the masses, have been deeply shaped by critical theory. Since the Frankfurt school, which identified with the "high culture" of the intellectual classes, popular culture has been seen as trivial, demeaning, and commercialized, serving the interests of the capitalist system. Postmodernist theorists, however, no longer accept the belief that there is some objectively superior high culture setting a standard from which to make evaluations of others. They have been more interested in popular culture as representing the voices of the previously silent, and by adopting the methods of film analysis or literary criticism, they examine the way popular culture is produced and the underlying assumptions upon which its meaning rests. *See also* **critical theory**; **consumer culture**; **postmodernism**.

population All elements that a researcher wishes to generalize to. Or, all members of a given class or set. For example, adult Canadians, teenagers, Canadian inmates, and criminal offenders can each be thought of as populations. Populations are difficult to study because we cannot find all of the members (heroin addicts or male prostitutes) or because of the expense (surveying all teenagers). Social scientists avoid this problem by gathering a sample from the population and then generalizing from the sample to the population.

pornography Literally, "to write about the harlot." The terms pornography and obscenity are often used interchangeably and the law itself is stated in terms of obscenity. Control of sexual expression has a very long history and it is only recently that a woman's point of view has shaped the way this regulation is discussed. See the Butler case for the recent Canadian development. *See also* **Butler case**; **Sharpe decision**.

positivism One way to think about the relationship between science and society, found in the early writings of Auguste Comte (1798–1857). All of the assumptions that Comte makes are now rejected by postmodernists. Comte begins by imposing meaning on history, arguing that societies evolve through three stages: the theological stage, the metaphysical stage, and the positive (or scientific) stage. Each of these stages is reproduced in the evolution of the human mind. The human mind, and the most privileged among these was the sociologist's, would use the scientific method to arrive at an understanding of the universal laws of social development. Comte argues against democratic discourse in the belief that parties involved in the political process are always committed to a particular viewpoint. Only science can rise above the local and particular and understand impartially. The application of this knowledge to society would enable the liberation of individuals. Positivism, therefore, places science in a privileged position; assumes the possibility of a scientific understanding of human and social behaviour; assumes the separation of knowledge and power; and assumes the possibility of objectivity and impartiality. Positivism shaped sociology for the next 100 years. *See also* **postmodernism**.

Positivist school In criminology, this refers to the first scientific school consisting of the Italian criminologists Cesare Lombroso (1836–1909), Raffaelo Garofalo (1852–1934), and Enrico Ferri (1856–1928). They supported the assumptions of positivism and argued that criminality is determined—the effect in a cause–effect sequence—and that the mandate of criminology should be to search for these causes. It was believed that with the exception of those deemed to be "born criminals," the discovery of the causes of crime would allow for effective treatment. This school therefore adopts a medical model (crime as sickness) and advocates rehabilitation of offenders, indeterminate sentences, and the dominance of professionals in correctional decision-making. See also **positivism**; **classical criminology**; **critical criminology**. Reference: Ferri, Enrico. (1913). *The Positive School of Criminology*. Chicago: Charles H. Kerr and Com.

post-critical (criminology) The term denotes a time following the period in which a critical or conflict perspective was dominant. This perspective would accept the assumptions central to postmodernism or deconstructionism. *See also* **postmodernism**. Reference: O'Reilly-Fleming, T. (1996). *Post-Critical Criminology*. Toronto: Prentice-Hall.

post-industrial thesis The theory that modern economies in the western world have moved from a focus on goods production (an industrial base) to a new foundation of knowledge and sophisticated services. This new economy is assumed to demand different kinds of workers, to allow for more job satisfaction, and to foster less labour conflict.

postmodernism A difficult term to grasp and having somewhat different significance in architecture, literary criticism, and art than in the social sciences. In social theory, it is best seen as a rejection of central assumptions of the modern world or of what has been described as the "enlightenment project." This project has had at least two core beliefs. First is the assumption that modern society will become more democratic and just, because of our growing ability to rationally and objectively understand the community's best interests. Second is the assumption that scientists and social theorists hold a privileged viewpoint since they are taken to operate outside of local interests or bias. Each of these assumptions suggests the possibility of disinterested knowledge, universal truths, and social progress. The late 20th century writings of Michel Foucault (1926–84) and Jean Francois Lyotard called these assumptions into question. Foucault's work has argued that knowledge and power are always intertwined and that the social sciences, rather than empowering human actors, have made humans into objects of inquiry and have subjected them to knowledge legitimated by the claims of science. Similarly, Lyotard has argued that social theory has always imposed meaning on historical events (think of the writings of Marx) rather than providing for the understanding of the empirical significance of events. This rejection of the idea of social and intellectual progress implies that people must accept the possibility of history having no meaning or purpose, abandon the idea that we can know what is or is not true, and accept that science can never create and test theories according to universal scientific principles because there is no unitary reality from which such principles can be established. We are left living in a fragmented world with multiple realities, a suspicion of science or authoritative claims, and many groups involved in identity politics in order to impose their reality on others. The clearest signs of a postmodern approach to sociology can be found in social constructionism, ethnomethodology, and labelling theory. *See also* **positivism**; **meta-narrative**.

potlatch A custom of the First Nations peoples of the Pacific northwest coast, where a ceremonial period of feasting was accompanied by lavish giving away, and sometimes destruction, of goods and property. Those who gave away or destroyed the most property earned the greatest social prestige. Anthropologists have described the ceremonies as a form of "war with property." The potlatch also had important elements of economic distribution, social bonding, and political processes, all central to the maintenance of a society. The Canadian government considered the practice to be destructive of the stability and felt it established a hierarchy of native communities; it was outlawed (from 1884 until 1951) and rigorously suppressed. *See also* **cultural genocide**.

poverty line That division, arbitrarily arrived at and usually based on income, which divides the poor from the non-poor. There is considerable controversy about how this line should be determined, and Statistics Canada uses the term low income rather than poverty and calculates low-income cutoffs. This line or cutoff can be determined in a variety of ways. One method is to determine the minimum income required to purchase a basket of goods and services thought to be necessary to maintain a minimum standard of living. Another alternative is to look at expenditures on the basic necessities of food, shelter, and clothing. Poverty or a low income may be determined when a family spend 20 percent more of their income on these necessities than does the average family. This method has been used by Statistics Canada. A third method would be to assert that a family is in poverty if its income is less than 50 percent of the median family income, adjusted for family size. Changes to Statistics Canada policy in the late 1990s reduced the extent of poverty considerably by redefining the concept.

power The capacity of individuals or institutions to achieve goals even if opposed by others. Sociologists and political scientists, among others, have examined the way power is exercised through political parties and institutions of the state or the way that men exercise power within the family or the workplace. Since the work of Michel Foucault (1926–84), however, there has been an interest in the way that "knowledge" itself is an instrument of power. Postmodernists such as Foucault adopt a position of "incredulity towards metanarratives" so they no longer assume the validity of particular ways to look at the world or the truth or objectivity of specific perspectives (such as social science theory). Rather, Foucault draws attention to the ways in which the theories of the human sciences, including sociology and political science, are themselves the outcome of struggle between different competing perspectives in which one becomes temporarily victorious and then becomes a source of repression and constraint. This perspective has roots in the traditional concerns of the sociology of knowledge.

power-control theory An explanation for differences in criminality building on the idea that social control is stratified within the family. Traditionally, for example, girls have been subjected to more social control than have boys. Further, mothers have traditionally been responsible for exercising social control and their increasing involvement in the workplace may enhance their power within the home, decrease their social control activity, and affect the willingness of girls to violate norms. Reference: Hagan, John. (1985). "The Class Structure and Delinquency: Toward a Power-Control Theory of Common Delinquent Behaviour." *American Journal of Sociology*, 90: 1151–78.

practical reasoning *See* **commonsense reasoning**.

pre-experimental design A research design that does not fit the standards of an authentic experiment; usually undertaken for exploratory purposes. Typical of this design is the elimination of a control group, thus it is often called a single-group experiment. This design will not allow definitive conclusions about the causes of the effect observed.

prejudice To make a judgment about an individual or group of individuals on the basis of their social, physical, or cultural characteristics. Such judgments are usually negative, but prejudice can also be exercised to give undue favour and advantage to members of particular groups. Prejudice is often seen as the attitudinal component of discrimination.

preliminary inquiry A preliminary inquiry is not a trial but is called to establish if there is sufficient evidence, if believed by the judge or jury, to convict a person. At the end of such an inquiry, the judge may order the accused to stand trial or discharge the accused. The preliminary inquiry has become the place at which the defence counsel is able to learn the evidence to be called by the prosecutor. There is typically a ban on publication of information from a preliminary inquiry so as to ensure that the accused has a fair trial.

premeditation To think out or plan an action beforehand. Premeditation is required for a first-degree murder charge to be laid.

preponderance of evidence The standard of evidence used in civil cases. *See also* **standard of proof**.

presentation of self As used by Erving Goffman (1922–82), it refers to the methodical as well as the unintentional practices of presenting or displaying one's "self" in ways that create a particular definition of the situation. This presentation may include verbal messages as well as gestures, clothing style, hair style, posture, etc. People may try to present themselves in a particular way by "dressing up" to go to court or may find themselves the victim of a jury's definition of the situation derived from the accused's appearance. The presentation of self is usually done front stage, while in the back stage the actors can let their guard down and "act themselves". Reference: Goffman, Erving. (1959). *The Presentation of Self in Everyday Life.* New York: Doubleday & Co.

pre-sentence report A report prepared for the court and read after a conviction has been obtained in order to receive guidance on sentencing. Usually prepared by a probation officer, these reports will provide a brief background on the offender, including the likelihood of rehabilitation, support networks, and emotional or physical needs. The court may or may not take this information into account.

presentism A term referring to an error in reasoning when someone uses the standard of present social and moral values to judge events and persons of the past. This label is often applied to the claims of those who want apologies from governments and other institutions for historical wrongs.

prevalence This term tells us about the number of particular events in the community. AIDS, for example, may be very prevalent (the total number with this syndrome), but the incidence (new cases) is going down each year.

price fixing Corporate interference in the marketplace by conspiring with others to not compete by setting a fixed price for goods or services.

primary group *See* **group, primary**.

primary labour market All research on labour markets has shown them to be divided or fragmented. The term used today is *segmented labour market*, suggesting there are many components to the market. Earlier, it was thought the market was divided into a primary labour market and a secondary labour market. This was interesting because men dominated the primary market, while women and minorities dominated the secondary market. Primary labour markets tend to offer high salaries or wages, better working conditions, and more job stability. This market tends to be found in those sectors of business that are capital intensive. The labour that is required tends to be more skilled and the high costs of labour can often be covered by the profit generated from an efficient plant. Workers are more apt to be unionized and to be able to make greater wage demands than workers in a secondary labour market. *See also* **secondary labour market**.

primitive communism An imagined first society in which all resources were owned in common. Has a close correspondence with some actual hunting and gathering societies.

primitive society A term used to denote simple human societies that are assumed to represent how human beings lived in communities in the earliest times of history. The dictionary defines the word as "belonging to the beginning or to the first times." The term is now out of favour in both sociology and anthropology because it appears to denigrate these simple societies by suggesting they are less civilized than modern societies. While "primitive" can be used in its formal sense to describe simple societies, the favoured term today is "hunter-gatherer society." *See also* **hunter-gatherer society**.

Prison for Women (P4W) Opened in 1934, in Kingston, Ontario, P4W was a source of regular controversy. As the only federal institution for women inmates, women from all across Canada were housed here, leaving many far away from family and support systems. Given the small number of inmates, there were also charges of inequality, since women received fewer program services than did men. Almost from its opening there were calls for its closure. Modelled on a 19th century maximum security prison for men, the institution never met the needs of women. After a controversial incident in the 1990s, a Commission of Inquiry led by Louise Arbour recommended the institution be closed; by the end of the century, the P4W was closed.

prison subculture The culture of prison society and thought by some to arise from the "pains of imprisonment," while others believe it is imported to the prison. Also known as the *convict code*, some of the features of prison subculture are: do not inform on your fellow prisoners, do not trust staff, help other residents, show your loyalty to other residents, and share what you have. Reference: Wieder, D.L. (1974). *Language and Social Reality: The Case of Telling the Convict Code.* The Hague: Mouton.

prisonization The process of being socialized into the culture and social life of prison society to the extent that adjusting to the outside society becomes difficult.

private domain (sphere) The distinction between the public domain (or sphere) and the private domain became an important tool of early feminist analysis as it helped in describing and understanding women's location in society. The parts of society consisting of politics and paid work are seen as the public domain, and family life as the private domain.

private sector That part of the economy which is controlled or owned by private individuals, either directly or through stock ownership. There has been a proliferation of private police in Canada and this has raised several questions about training and citizen rights. *See also* **public sector**. Reference: Swol, K. (1998). *Private Security and Public Policing in Canada.* Ottawa: Canadian Centre for Justice Statistics.

privatization (1) The process of moving economic resources from the public sector to the private sector. Publicly owned transportation resources, natural resources, hospitals, etc., may be sold to private individuals or to privately owned corporations. Canada has been unusual in having a large public sector. Classical liberal theory, however, is opposed to government involvement and interference in economic activity and the recent resurgence of interest in classical liberalism (*see also* **neo-conservatism**) has led to pressure to privatize government-owned resources and services. *See also* **classical economic theory**. (2) The term has also been applied to the growth in modern societies of a family life separated from the outer community. In traditional societies, there is little separation of private and public spheres, but privatization appears to take place with urbanization and industrialization. *See also* **family, bourgeois**.

pro bono From the Latin phrase meaning "for the public good." In regard to legal work, it is work done without charge.

probability sample In social science research, a sample drawn from a population using methods to ensure random selection; each member of the population must have an equal probability of being drawn.

probable cause The standard that must be met in order to arrest a person or for a judge to issue a warrant for the arrest of a person or a warrant to search a premise. Generally speaking, a "reasonable person" must be convinced that the facts suggest that a named person likely committed an offence or a premise contains evidence linked to an offence.

Without "probable cause," an arrest may be determined to be illegal.

probation In Canada, the court is enabled to suspend a sentence. This means that the court actually suspends the process of sentencing, rather than passing a sentence and then suspending it. Typically if the court chooses this option, a probation order is also made. If the probation order is not satisfied by the offender, he or she may be returned to court to have the sentence that would have been given for the original offences effected. Probation orders must contain the following: "that the accused shall keep the peace and be of good behaviour and shall appear before the court when required to do so by the court." In addition, the court may impose a wide range of other conditions and many of these are designed to meet the particular needs of the individual. A probation order cannot be issued in situations where the offence carries a mandatory minimum sentence.

problem-oriented policing A form of policing associated with community policing in which the police engage in efforts to solve community or neighborhood problems which produce criminal activity, rather than simply responding to the criminal activity itself.

problem population As capitalism matures and more investment is made in technology than in labour, workers become increasingly surplus to the economic engine. Some of these people become problems to the stability of the society and require increasing social control. Reference: Spitzer, S. (1975). "Toward a Marxian Theory of Deviance." *Social Problems* 22: 638–51.

procedural law Procedural law lays out the rules which agents of the state must follow in investigating crimes and convicting offenders. For example, rules around search and seizure, rights to counsel, bail procedures, etc. These rules are what is meant by "due process." Procedural law originates in common law (the civil law in Quebec), and court judgments based on equity, natural justice, and statute. Procedural rules are often the target of dissent among the socially conservative in Canada who believe that they obstruct the work of the justice system in pursuing offenders.

profession The sociology of work sees a number of occupations evolving over time and becoming professions. All professions are thus occupations, but not all occupations are professions. A profession is an occupational group that is largely self-regulating. Such a group has the legitimate authority (usually delegated from government) to set its own standards for entrance, to admit new members, to establish a code of conduct, to discipline members, and it claims to have a body of knowledge (achieved through education) which legitimizes its autonomy and distinctiveness. Examples of professions include physicians, lawyers, clinical psychologists, and real estate agents. Other groups, such as nurses, police officers, etc. can be seen as having some of these attributes and can be described as "professionalizing"—in the process of becoming a profession.

professional style of policing A model of policing in which constables are to leave their personal philosophies at home and to enforce the law by following the book. This reduces the amount of discretion a constable may have and increases the reporting of crime, particularly less serious forms of crime.

Progressive-Conservative Party of Canada Canada's longest established political party until its merger with the Canadian Alliance Party in 2003. Originally the party developed from the Liberal-Conservative coalition that took office in the Province of Canada in 1854. Conservative John A. MacDonald (later Sir John) was a member of the coalition and it was he who led the Liberal-Conservatives at the time of confederation in 1867. After MacDonald's government fell in 1873, as a result of a financial scandal, the party name Liberal-Conservative was replaced by Conservative and a separate Liberal Party also emerged. In 1942, Manitoba Premier John Braken, who had led a Progressive Party government, won the leadership of the federal Conservative Party, which then changed its name to Progressive-Conservative. The Liberals are the only other party to have formed Canada's governments since Confederation. *See also* **Conservative Party of Canada; Liberal Party of Canada.**

Progressive Party A party formed in the early part of the 20th century and coming to prominence in the federal election of 1922 and in several provincial governments. The party was a broad coalition of social reform groups including farmers and some women's groups. In 1942, the federal Conservative Party changed its name to the Progressive Conservative Party, in order to attract Premier

Bracken, leader of a Progressive government in Manitoba.

progressive taxation A taxation structure that progressively increases the percentage of a citizen's income (or wealth) which is paid in tax as income (or wealth) increases. The consequence should be that the more well off are taxed at a higher rate than are the less well off. Canadian income tax is of this form, although recent changes in taxation regulations have made it somewhat less progressive than before. *See also* **regressive taxation**; **flat tax**.

progressivism A political philosophy characterizing American society from approximately 1890 to 1920. Set against decades of expansion and growth, progressives became acutely aware of the price paid for this development in terms of inequality and social problems. To address these, they called for policy committed to social justice and social democracy. They found new sympathy for the poor, for minorities, and for women and children. To address the needs of these peoples, it saw a need for a strong central government and increasing regulation of many segments of the business world. These attitudes about the role of the state are sometimes referred to as "progressive liberalism" (in contrast to classical liberalism). *See also* **classical economic theory**; **classical liberalism**.

proletariat A term associated with Karl Marx and referring to the class of individuals in a capitalist society who have no means of production of their own and must subsist economically by selling wage labour to owners of capital. In Marxist sociology, it is assumed that this working class will engage in economic and political struggles with owners of capital and eventually develop class solidarity and revolutionary class consciousness.

proof beyond reasonable doubt The standard of proof required in criminal cases. The judge or jury must be sure before conviction that there is no reasonable doubt that the accused did not commit the crime. If there is a reasonable doubt, the accused must be acquitted. *See also* **standard of proof**.

prosecutor *See* **crown counsel**.

prostitution The regulation of the market exchange of sexual services has long been achieved through criminal law. In Canada prior to 1985, the Criminal Code made soliciting illegal and the prohibition was more specifically aimed at "persistent" behaviour. That is, prostitutes had to make a nuisance of themselves (not taking no for an answer) before law enforcement could be invoked. After 1985, the Canadian law prohibited communicating in a public place for the purposes of prostitution. This infringement of free speech was upheld by the Supreme Court in 1990, and many believe has forced prostitutes into more dangerous parts of the community in order to seek clients. In British Columbia, for example, there were one or two murders of prostitutes a year prior to 1985 and as many as five a year after implementation of the new law. *See also* **vagrancy**. Reference: Boritch, H. (1997). *Fallen Women: Female Crime and Justice in Canada.* Toronto: Nelson.

protective custody A section of a prison or penitentiary used exclusively for housing those inmates who are thought to be in danger of harm from other inmates. Typically those housed in this section are police informants, sexual offenders, and child molesters.

Protestant ethic This ethic, or set of ideas, emerging in the 16th century, was cited by Max Weber (1864–1920) as an important influence in encouraging the development of capitalist society. For Protestants, particularly those influenced by the ideas of John Calvin, obedience to God's will demanded energetic and enterprising work in one's occupation or "calling." Profits were morally justified as the reward for this hard work and, so long as they were not casually squandered on luxuries, the making of profit and the achievement of wealth was a just reward for dutiful and energetic work. Max Weber argued that the "Protestant ethic" was so strongly supportive of capitalist development that countries where Protestantism became dominant quickly moved ahead of Catholic countries in their level of economic development. Weber claimed that the Catholic church, in contrast, promoted ideas and attitudes that tended to obstruct economic development. Catholic doctrine stressed the importance of humility and acceptance of one's position in life, it discouraged pursuit of achievement by suggesting that seeking self-advancement was a distraction from the pursuit of a good and moral life in preparation for eternal life after death. Reference: Weber, M. (1904). *The Protestant Ethic and the Spirit of Capitalism.* New York: Charles Scribner and Sons [1958].

provincial police While all provinces have municipal police forces, only Ontario and Quebec have provincial police forces responsible for policing those areas without police forces. In the other provinces, the RCMP are contracted to police areas without municipal policing. In the past, other provinces (for example, British Columbia) had their own police forces.

provincial prison Normally called prisons, rather than penitentiaries, these are institutions operated by the provinces and house inmates sentenced to terms of less than two years. There are some exceptions to this last rule regarding women offenders and young offenders.

psychiatric unit Each region of Canada has a penitentiary designated as a psychiatric centre or unit. Inmates in the penitentiary system may be ordered to attend such a unit or may volunteer to attend if they wish to deal with serious psychiatric problems. Those participating in such programs are typically removed from the general population of inmates and housed in a separate unit to avoid the peer pressure and the stigma of seeking help for a psychiatric problem.

psychoanalytic theory Associated with its founder Sigmund Freud, it is essentially the concept that many illnesses and neurotic fixations in adults are caused by traumatic infantile experiences in emotional and sexual development. By using means such as dream analysis and free association of words and symbols to help recall earliest memories and emotions, the process of psychoanalysis takes the adult back in time to confront and hopefully resolve the effects of these early negative experiences.

psychological reductionism The process of reducing all social activity and behaviour to the psychological characteristics of the human actors involved. Such reduction eliminates the possibility of sociology since it denies that there is anything greater than the individual. Society is simply an aggregation of individuals. Émile Durkheim (1858–1917) argued against this in his study of suicide by arguing, and demonstrating, that even after providing a psychological explanation for individual acts of suicide there was something still to account for: the difference in suicide rates between societies. This, he showed, was derived from characteristics of the society and could not be explained as dependent on individual psychological characteristics.

proportionality A term used to refer to the practice of selecting a punishment that is proportional to the harm done by the original crime. This does not mean that the punishment should be the same as the original crime, but that it be selected from the range of possible punishment that is proportional to the severity of the crime. Proportionality can be argued from a retributivist viewpoint as well as from utilitarian theory.

psychologism *See* **methodological individualism; psychological reductionism.**

psychopaths Although there is dispute about whether "psychopath" is an authentic psychiatric condition, it is typically classified under "personality disorder." Psychopaths tend to be lacking in what is considered conscience, are unable to form emotional attachments (even to friends or family), are quite impulsive, and are only self-interested. There is also considerable debate about whether this group can be changed.

psychotherapy A treatment technique for mental disorders or other problems which involves the verbalization of the patient's problem. A form of treatment that centres on getting the patient to talk about their lives, their childhood, etc. This form of treatment works best with those with good verbal skills and thus is used quite frequently with middle-class patients.

public execution *See* **execution, public.**

public health model Unlike a "crime control model" which focuses on punishment or moralizing with the offender, a public health model looks at particular kinds of crime (often drug abuse, prostitution, and youth violence) as public health issues. A public health officer takes a very different view of crime than does a police constable. The public health model encourages us to think of ways to stop the spread of drug abuse or violence, for example, or how to prevent drug abusers from harming themselves or spreading infection to the community, or on initiating education programs in schools to teach young people how to recognize the possible onset of violence, how to prevent it, who to call if violence is experienced, etc.

public images of crime The perception of crime and the threat of crime generally held by members of the community. Their perceptions may be manipulated by authorities and the media to focus on some types of crime and criminal behaviour and divert attention from others. Public perceptions of crime have typically been quite separate from an objective account of the amount of crime or its distribution.

public sector That part of the economy which is owned or controlled by the public, usually through government agencies. Most schooling is part of the public sector as are hospitals, provision of social services, and some transit services. The more substantial portion of the economy consists of the private sector, those economic activities controlled or owned by private individuals, either directly or through stock ownership. *See also* **private sector**; **privatization**.

punishment A negative sanction imposed on the violator of a system of rules and imposed by an authorized agent of that system of rules. The criminal courts can punish people for their violations of criminal law, the referee can punish those who violate the rules of a game of hockey, and the principal can punish students who violate rules of the school. Reference: Garland, David. (1990). *Punishment and Modern Society: A Study in Social Theory*. Chicago: University of Chicago Press.

pyromania A form of compulsive disorder in which the person repeatedly sets fires.

Q

Quakers A Christian group, also known as the Society of Friends, which forbids formal doctrine and ministers. Their commitment to peaceful principles has put them at the forefront of peace movements and the search for punitive measures based on Christian ideas rather than torture or coercion. These ideals placed them at the centre of the development of the penitentiary, and then when its harm-producing structures became evident, at the centre of criticisms of the penitentiary.

qualitative research Research using methods, such as participant observation or case studies, that result in a narrative, descriptive account of a setting or practice. Sociologists using these methods typically reject positivism and adopt a form of interpretive sociology. *See also* **quantitative research**; **ethnographic research**. Reference: Palys, Ted. (1997). *Research Decisions: Quantitative and Qualitative Perspectives*. Toronto: Harcourt.

quantitative research Research using methods allowing for the measurement of variables within a collection of people or groups and resulting in numerical data subjected to statistical analysis. By its very nature this is a form of positivism. *See also* **qualitative research**; **variables**. Reference: Palys, Ted. (1997). *Research Decisions: Quantitative and Qualitative Perspectives*. Toronto: Harcourt.

quasi-experiment A research design having some but not all of the characteristics of a true experiment. The element most frequently missing is random assignment of subjects to the control and experimental conditions. Examples of this research design are the natural experiment (where nature has assigned subjects to the two conditions) or trend analysis.

queer culture The word *queer* was a derogatory term for many years, but has now been appropriated by a radical section (the "in your face" section) of the gay and lesbian community to identify gay and lesbian culture or studies. Gay and lesbian studies are becoming as legitimate in the academic community as women's studies or Black studies. Cultural studies is interested in examining gay and lesbian culture as depicted in the writings, films, or art work of the community, and in analyzing the public identity of this cultural community. *See also* **cultural studies**; **identity politics**.

Quetelet, Adolphe (1796–1874) Major figure in the statistical school of social research. He worked in many areas of statistical research, including meteorology and geophysics. He developed the still-used Body Mass Index, which relates height to weight to define measures of obesity. In criminology, he is linked to the study of the numerical patterns and consistencies of crime using statistics and probability theory. His most well known work is *A Treatise on Man* written in 1835.

Quiet Revolution A period of rapid social change in Quebec symbolized by the 1960 election defeat of the conservative rural-dominated Union Nationale by Jean Lesage and the Liberals on a policy of modernization and nationalism. This resulted in the unleashing of modern liberal ideas and the transformation of social institutions such as schooling the family, politics, and government to reflect those values. These changes led to a decline in influence for the church, an increased divorce rate and a decreased birth rate, the creation of modern universities and schools, and expansion of the role of government in society. The dynamic new role of government became a focus for the nationalist aspirations of the Quebec people. In 1976, the Parti Québeçois was elected, leading to a 1980 referendum on the issue of changing Quebec's position within Canada from that of a province like others to some form of sovereignty-association. This referendum was defeated; a second, conducted in 1995 on a question of separation with some form of continued economic association, was also defeated, but by a margin of less than 1 percent.

Quinney, Richard Social philosopher associated with critical criminology and the movement for restorative justice and healing rather than coercion and retribution. Like other critical theorists, he located the genesis of law and the mode of its administration in the conflict of group interests in society. The groups that are socially dominant are then able to use their power to impose their own concepts of law and of crime upon others. In this perspective, harsh criminal penalties for property offences and lenient penalties for corporate crime are explained as state coercion to maintain the domination of some social groups and classes over others. Thus law is about political relations rather than consensual social regulation, and law violation is often best viewed as a political act. Reference: Quinney, Richard. (1977). *Class, State and Crime: On the Theory and Practice of Criminal Justice.* New York: D. McKay Co.; Quinney, Richard, R. Pepinsky, and E. Harold (eds.). (1991). *Criminology as Peacemaking.* Bloomington: Indiana University Press.

R

race A classification of humans beings into different categories on the basis of their biological characteristics. There have been a variety of schemes for race classification based on physical characteristics such as skin colour, head shape, eye colour and shape, nose size and shape, etc. A common classification system uses four major groups: Caucasoid, Mongoloid, Negroid, and Australoid. The term was once popular in anthropology, but has now fallen into disrepute, because the idea of racial classification has become associated with racism—the claim that there is a hierarchy of races. The idea of race categories also appears to be unscientific, since humans are able to mate across all "races" and have done so throughout history, creating an enormous variety of human genetic inheritance. In addition, the defining characteristics of "race" do not appear in all members of each so-called race, but merely occur with some degree of statistical frequency. If the defining characteristic of each "race" does not appear in all members of each "race," then the whole definition is clearly inadequate.

racial profiling Using race as a search characteristic when looking for offenders. The police, for example, may believe that Blacks are more likely to commit crimes than are whites and thus stop more Blacks while driving or on the street in the hopes of catching criminals. Research by the University of Toronto has revealed that this is what in fact happens. "Bad " Black kids and "bad" white kids were equally likely to be stopped by the police; however, "good" Black kids were much more likely to be stopped than were "good" white kids. Racial profiling is a very controversial practice, and police usually deny that they engage in it. Reference: Ontario Human Rights Commission. (1993). *Paying the Price: The Human Cost of Racial Profiling.* Toronto: Queen's Printer.

racism An ideology based on the idea that humans can be separated into distinct racial groups, and that these groups can be ranked on a hierarchy of intelligence, ability, morality, etc. *See also* **ethnocentrism**; **race**.

radical feminism This form of feminism is relatively recent and differs from traditional Marxism in arguing that women's oppression is historically primary, harder to transform, causes more harm, and is more widespread than class oppression. Similarly it is argued that women's oppression provides a model for understanding other forms of oppression, such as racism and class domination. Some radical feminists claim that women's oppression is rooted in biology, and its elimination will require a biological revolution, transforming women's relation to reproduction. Within criminology, they focus on documenting and analyzing ways in which the content of law and practices of law enforcement have served to entrench and strengthen male dominance in society. *See also* **feminism**; **liberal feminism**.

Ramona case Gary Ramona, living in Napa Valley, California, charged with sexual abuse of his daughter, who recovered her memory of these events through therapy, won the opportunity to sue the therapist in 1994 for the harm done to him. For the first time the issue of "recovered memory" went to be on trial. After a bitter court battle, Gary Ramona won, and the recovered memory movement suffered a serious setback. Hundred of cases have gone before the courts based on recovered memory, but in general terms, the courts have not been very sympathetic to these claims. Reference: Johnston, Moira. (1997). *Spectral Evidence: The Ramona Case: Incest, Memory and Truth on Trial in Napa Valley*. Boulder, CO: Westview Press.

rape The original meaning of the term *rape* was to steal or carry off the belongings of another. As women were considered the property of men (their fathers or their husbands) and virginity was all important prior to marriage, sexual assault or even sex outside of marriage could be considered a violation of the man's property. The Statute of Westminster (1275) formalized this offence and laid the foundation which carried forward into modern times. It made rape an offence against the state, introduced the notion of statutory rape (sexual intercourse with a child with or without consent), declared that unless a woman resisted the attack she was partially responsible, and proclaimed that a husband could not be charged with rape of his wife. Until 1982, rape was a criminal offence in Canada and was defined as the offence of forcible sexual intercourse, involving penetration, with someone who has withheld consent, or, in the case of consent, with someone whose consent has been obtained by threat, impersonation, or misrepresentation of the nature of the act. Feminist critiques of this law and the coming of the Charter of Rights and Freedoms produced changes; the offence of rape was replaced with three offences of sexual assault.

rape shield laws Legal prohibitions that restrict the ability of the defence to explore the sexual past of the victim (usually a woman) during a rape or sexual assault trial. This provision entered Canadian law as section 276 of the Criminal Code of Canada in 1983. The provision was struck down by a 1991 Supreme Court decision ruling that the prohibition could deny an accused a fair trial. In 1992, a new law was passed by Parliament also restricting exploration of the sexual past of rape victims, but more limited in its scope and allowing more discretion for judges in determining the admissibility of evidence. This new law was unanimously upheld by the Supreme Court in October, 2000.

rate When studying crime, if a researcher wishes to compare the amount of crime over time or between communities of different sizes, it is not adequate to do a gross count of the amount of crime because the population bases may be different. To get around the problems involved with this, criminologists calculate crime rates (or incarceration rates, conviction rates, and recidivism rates). This is done by dividing the amount of crime by the population size and multiplying by 100 000. This produces a rate per 100 000, but occasionally it is useful to calculate a rate per million or some other figure.

ratio decidendi The essential and relevant reasons for a judge's decision.

ratio measures *See* **level of measurement**.

rational choice theory A theory of criminal behaviour found in the Classical school of criminology and widely accepted during the last quarter of the twentieth century. Rather than seeing some abnormality in the offender that distinguishes them from other citizens, rational choice theory argues that offenders are making rational choice to commit crime after having examined the likelihood of being caught or convicted. These assumptions about behaviour are the foundation on which deterrence as a philosophy of punishment is built. *See also* **classical criminology**; **deterrence**.

rationalization This term has two specific meanings in sociology. (1) The concept was developed by German sociologist Max Weber (1864–1920) who used it in two ways. First, it was the process through which magical, supernatural, and religious ideas lose cultural importance in a society, and ideas based on science and practical calculation become dominant. For example, in modern societies, science has rationalized our understanding of weather patterns. Science explains weather patterns as a result of interaction between physical elements like wind speed and direction, air and water temperatures, humidity, etc. In some other cultures, weather is thought to express the pleasure or displeasure of gods or spirits of ancestors. One explanation is rationalized and scientific, the other mysterious and magical. Rationalization also involves the development of forms of social organization devoted to the achievement of precise goals by efficient means. It is this type of rationalization that we see in the development of modern business corporations and of bureaucracy. These are organizations dedicated to the pursuit of defined goals by calculated, systematically administered means. (2) Within symbolic interactionism, rationalization is used more in the everyday sense of the word to refer to providing justifications or excuses for one's actions. *See also* **accounts**.

RCMP *See* **Royal Canadian Mounted Police.**

reaction formation A psychological mechanism that emerges when failure is imminent. Albert Cohen, for example, found that lower-class boys often turned middle-class values, the very values causing them to fail, on their head. There was a certain degree of nihilism; rather than taking money to purchase things they needed, they may throw the money away, give it to others, or purchase useless articles. Or, rather than valuing the middle-class sofa, they might defecate on it.

reasonable doubt In criminal cases, the standard of proof needed to convict a person is "proof beyond a reasonable doubt." This standard does not demand absolute certainty, only that there should be no reasonable doubt that the person committed the offence.

reasonable person A hypothetical manifestation of the legal standard of intelligence and care expected of a member of society. Judges or lawyers often refer to this hypothetical person to mean reference to the above standards.

Rebellion (of 1837–38) in Lower Canada Rebellions occurred in both Upper and Lower Canada (and in many other parts of the world) in 1837–38 with the main issue being the rejection of colonial rule and demand for local, responsible government. In Lower Canada, an additional objective of rebellion was the desire to establish primacy for the Québeçois nation within Canada. British troops put down the rebellion, often rather brutally, and this event is seen by many as the reconquest of the Québeçois (a repeat of the battle of the Plains of Abraham, 1759), which stimulated the growth of Quebec nationalism.

recidivism (criminal) Repetition of criminal behaviour by an offender previously convicted and punished for an offence. Recidivism is a measure of the effectiveness of rehabilitation programs or the deterrent effect of punishment. While an important concept in evaluation research, criminologists have great difficulty in defining and measuring recidivism. For example, is it recidivism to commit a less serious offence than the previous offence? Is it recidivism to be returned to prison for a violation of the terms of parole (i.e., a new criminal offence has not been committed)?

recovered memory *See* **memory, recovered.**

Red River Rebellion A revolt during 1869–70 of the settlers and Métis of what is now Manitoba. In 1867–68, the government of Canada negotiated the purchase of the lands owned by the Hudson Bay Company without consulting with the residents of the territories involved (the largest group were French-speaking Métis). This annexation led to fears, particularly among the French-speaking and Catholic Métis, that language, religious, and education rights would be lost. The residents declared a provisional government in direct opposition to the federal government's wishes, leading to negotiations that resulted in the creation of the province of Manitoba and established French language rights, acknowledgment of the tenure of existing farms, and the promise of millions of acres of land to settle Métis land claims. Métis peoples prefer to refer to these events as acts of resistance rather than a rebellion. *See also* **Métis; Northwest Rebellion of 1885.**

reefer madness A film made in 1937 depicting marijuana as a drug-producing madness and thus to be avoided and banned. While the film is humourous in hindsight, it was a powerful piece of propaganda at the time.

reference group A term from social psychology identifying that group to which people refer or make reference in evaluating themselves. One may make reference to "social science students" when contemplating what political party to vote for or one might refer to "feminists" when deciding to change or not to change one's name after marriage.

referendum To refer a political question to an electorate for direct decision. Referendums do not fit well with a parliamentary system of government; Canada has used them infrequently. The first was in 1898 on a question of prohibition, and the next in 1942 on the matter of conscription. English-speaking Canada voted in support of allowing the government to use conscription, while French-speaking Canada voted against it, thus creating a crisis for government. A federal referendum was also held in 1992 to seek support for a constitutional change (the Charlottetown Agreement); this was soundly defeated. Provincial governments have relied on referendums somewhat more often. Newfoundland, for example, held a referendum in 1948 on the question of entry to Canada (it took two votes to win agreement, and then by only 52.3 percent); in 1988, the province of Prince Edward Island held a referendum on the question of whether a fixed link with mainland Canada should be established; in 1980, Quebec held a referendum on permission to negotiate sovereignty-association with the rest of Canada (this was defeated by 60 percent of voters), and a second referendum was held in Quebec in 1995 on a more direct question of separating from Canada (this was rejected by 51 percent of the voters).

reflexivity As used by ethnomethodologists, the term means that an object or behaviour and its description cannot be separated one from the other; rather, they have a mirror-like relationship. Reflexivity and indexicality are properties of behaviour, settings, and talk that make the ongoing construction of social reality necessary. Both of these properties question the objectivity of accounts, descriptions, explanations, etc. An ethnographic description of a setting is reflexive in that the description seeks to explain features of a particular setting (e.g., village life), but the setting itself is what is employed to make sense of the description. *See also* **indexicality**.

Regina Manifesto The founding political program of the Co-operative Commonwealth Federation, adopted at a convention in Regina in 1933. The Manifesto was strongly socialist and called for extensive nationalization and radical measures to promote equalization of wealth and incomes. In subsequent years, the party retreated from the radical goals of the Manifesto and, in 1956, this change of policy was made explicit in the Winnipeg Declaration and became embodied in the policies followed by the New Democratic Party which succeeded the CCF in 1961.

Regina riot During the depression, the federal government established work camps for unemployed men in a hope of containing anger and frustration. Early in 1935, relief workers in British Columbia staged a strike in support of better living conditions and higher wages. In an attempt to force the government to take action, union organizers planned an "On-To-Ottawa" march. Prime Minister Bennett ordered the march be brought to and end when it reached Regina. This resulted in a riot on July 1, 1935, in which one policeman was killed and at least 100 people were injured.

regression (analysis or line) A measure of association between two quantitative variables. This form of statistical test is only possible with interval or ratio data. If an independent variable and a dependent variable are placed on the two axes of a graph with the actual data then scattered on the graph, it is possible to draw a line through the resulting points in a way that minimizes the distance between the points. The resulting line (which may be straight or curved) is a regression line. Any particular value for the dependent variable can then be predicted by multiplying the value of the independent variable by the regression coefficient (a number that determines the slope of the line).

regressive taxation A tax structure that requires the more well-off to pay a lower percentage of their income (or wealth) in tax than a less well-off citizen. Sales tax and the federal goods and services tax (GST) are of this type, as these taxes remain constant regardless of one's income. The consequence is that the more well-off citizen pays a smaller percentage of their income to cover the tax on a new refrigerator than does a less well-off person. *See also* **progressive taxation**; **flat tax**.

rehabilitative ideal As defined by F. Allen (1981), this refers to the belief that a primary purpose of punishment is to effect a change in the character, attitudes, and behaviour of convicted offenders, so as to strengthen the communities social defence, but also to contribute to the welfare of the individual. This belief can be traced back to the 18th century work of John Howard, and its influence is seen again in an American Congress of corrections held in 1870 and put into place in the Elmira Reformatory (opening in 1877). In Canada, these ideas shape the discussions of the "new penology" through the 1920s and 1930s, but they were not firmly implemented until the early 1950s; they are perhaps best demonstrated by the 1957 Haney Correctional Institution located in British Columbia. *See also* **nothing works**. Reference: Cullen, F.T., and K. Gilbert. (1982). *Reaffirming Rehabilitation.* Cincinnati: Anderson.

reification To treat as though real that which is just an abstraction or a conceptualization. Sociologists since Durkheim have been accused of reifying society, which critics say is just an abstract concept and does not exist. To act as though society exists and thus can act or make decisions or coerce people is to reify society.

reinforcement A process in which a behaviour is strengthened; increasing the probability that a response will occur by either presenting a contingent positive event or removing a negative event.

reintegration The process of reintroducing a released inmate into the community. *See also* **pains of re-entry**.

relations of production *See* **social relations of production**.

relative autonomy A theory of state power based on Marxist ideas. This perspective assumes that the state can and does play a limited independent role in the maintenance and stabilization of capitalist society. It differs from pluralism in viewing state power as strongly constrained by the ideological and structural characteristics of capitalist society. *See also* **structuralist approach**.

relative deprivation Relative deprivation and absolute deprivation are often contrasted. Absolute deprivation refers to the inability to sustain oneself physically and materially. Some right-wing groups suggest that this is how Canada should define and measure poverty. Rather, Canada uses a form of relative deprivation; deprivation is not judged against some absolute standard of sustainability but of deprivation in relation to others around you. You may have sufficient money to meet your needs and even meet them adequately, but feel relatively deprived.

release on own recognizance The pre-trail release of an accused from custody on the promise to appear at a future court hearing. There is no bail involved in such releases. *See also* **bail**.

reliability Identifies one of the standards (another being validity) against which the tools used to measure concepts are judged. Reliability refers to consistency of results over time. If a bathroom scale is used to measure the concept of weight, one must ask: Is this tool (the bathroom scale) reliable? Does it provide consistent results? To check this, get back on the scale a second time to see if it produces the same results. Notice that the bathroom scale may be reliable and yet be inaccurate. Are I.Q. tests a reliable measure of "intelligence"? Are official suicide statistics reliable measures of the "suicide" rate? Are questions about which political party a person would vote for a reliable measure of "political preference"? Since in many of these examples it is difficult to assume, like weight, that the results would remain the same over time, it may be more correct to think of reliability as indicating consistency of results among users of the tool or measurement. *See also* **validity**.

religiosity The degree to which one believes in and is involved in religion. For example, attending church; volunteering for the church; giving donations to the church; and believing in the values, morals, and mythology of the religion.

religious right Found more frequently in the United States than in Canada (where its influence is chiefly located in the Conservative party), refers to groups or individuals who combine the economic conservatism of classical liberalism (beliefs in free market economies, small government, and autonomy of the individual) with the socially conservative views of many fundamentalist religions (e.g., against abortion, intolerant of homosexuality, non-supportive of single mothers, propose censorship of children's reading material, recommend reducing rights of criminal offenders, etc.). Since these groups support an economic doctrine which is gaining wide acceptance, they are able to move into positions of power and influence, and their social views are giving shape to many aspects of life. *See also* **neo-conservatism.**

remand To return an offender to custody or to place an accused in custody while certain investigations are made or until the date of trial. Typically, time served in remand may be counted towards any term of custody imposed by the court on a 2-for-1 basis, due to the harshness of remand incarceration and the lack of programs and services. Reference: *R. v. Wust* [2000] 1 S.C.R. 455.

republic This has come to mean a society where there is no hereditary or appointed monarch or emperor as head of state. Originally it referred to a system of political rule where citizens, through representative institutions, participated in government and exercised political power. This meaning derives from the original Latin *res publica*, which means *things public*, those things that are connected to ruling the public realm. In its narrower meaning, the term distinguishes Canada, Britain, Norway, Sweden, Denmark, the Netherlands, Thailand, and other countries formally headed by monarchs from France, Italy, Germany, the United States, and many others where the head of state is a president either directly elected or appointed by an elected assembly.

reserve army of labour In Marxian analysis, that segment of the labour force which is held in reserve, to be called into the work force when need arises. If there were no reserve labour, it might be difficult for new businesses to open or for temporary or emergency projects to be undertaken in the economy. In addition, labour shortage would create upward pressure on wages and increase union power. This reserve labour, of course, needs to be doing something during the period it is held in reserve, so it may be on welfare or working in the household. The term has been useful for understanding women's relationship to the workforce. Women were pulled into the workforce during World War II, and then pushed out when the men returned. During the economic boom of the 1960–70s, women entered the workforce in large numbers, and there is fear that they will be the first fired during recession (although this appears not to have happened in the 1990s recession.) Women, young people, and the elderly may all be thought of as reserve labour, since they have traditionally stayed out of the labour force.

reserves Land set aside, or reserved, for a designated group. In Canada, as the Anglo-Europeans colonized the land and occupied territories previously inhabited by native peoples, they designated lands for native groups. Although reserved for native bands, the lands remained the property of the Crown. In Canada, there are 576 native bands recognized by the government and 2281 reserves (often called reservations) as well as some Crown land settlements set aside for these peoples. These figures reveal a distinct Canadian pattern of creating reserves—many small reserves were created and typically distributed among the larger non-native population. All of the reserve lands in Canada only add up to one-half of the Navajo reserve in Arizona.

residential schools Widely established across Canada during the 19th and 20th centuries, particularly in the north, these schools were established to bring basic education to native and Inuit children. In effect, as well as in intent, these schools served to isolate the young from their own people and became an instrument of attempted cultural assimilation of aboriginal peoples into white European culture. Forced attendance in these schools, which were largely church run, broke the cultural continuity of aboriginal communities and led to the loss of traditional knowledge, skills, and languages. Today, they are seen as an example of colonial attitudes toward native peoples, and it has become apparent that they caused great harm by inflicting psychological and physical isolation and abuse upon generations of aboriginal children. Many native groups have struggled to have churches acknowledge the harm done and to institute healing programs and have pressured the federal government to acknowledge its role in this process. In addition, local programs of healing have been developed, and native communities and the broader society have had to come to terms with the legacy of residential schools.

resocialization Rather profound change or transformation of personality arising from being placed within a situation or environment no longer conducive to maintaining a previous identity. Some choose this kind of transformation by entering a monastery or nunnery, while others have it forced on them by being sentenced to penitentiary. The new identity is a product of these environments and comes from interacting with others and performing the roles required in these settings. *See also* **institution, total**.

restitution Usually a condition attached to a probation order requiring the offender to pay back the victim or the community in some way. This payback may involve financial compensation or it may involve community service of some form.

restorative justice Beginning from the assumptions that the fabric of personal and social life has been damaged by a crime, restorative justice argues that the criminal justice system should be about mediation and conflict resolution in order to restore the emotional well-being and feelings of security of the victim and to repair the damaged social relationships within the community. Reference: Church Council on Justice and Corrections. (1996). *Satisfying Justice.* Ottawa: Church Council on Justice and Corrections.

restraining order Under section 810 of the Criminal Code, a justice of the peace or a judge can receive information from a citizen who fears for her or his person or property, and, if warranted, issue a restraint on the person feared even if he or she has no criminal history or record. Conditions such as abstaining from possessing firearms, avoiding contact with young persons, and in general to keep the peace and be of good behaviour may be imposed. This section of the Criminal Code has withstood a Charter challenge. *See also* **peace bond**.

restructuring Usually refers to the re-organization and rationalization of administration and production in both public and private sectors. In the public sector, it has been encouraged by growing deficits; in the private sector, cost cutting and reorganization has been encouraged by high interest rates, recession, and lower corporate profit margins.

retribution Deriving from the notions of retribute (to give back or return) or to receive in recompense and the Christian sense of deserved, adequate, or fit, the term is now used exclusively to refer to punishment. Retribution is punishment deserved because of an offence and that fits the severity of the offence. Punishment is justified because it makes the offender give up money, personal freedom, or comfort that is equivalent to the harm or loss done to others. Retribution must be distinguished from revenge and retaliation.

retributive justice *See* **distributive justice.**

reverse discrimination Discrimination against a privileged group in order to correct previous discrimination against a disadvantaged group. The accusation of *reverse discrimination* is often directed against those favouring equity programs or affirmative action programs. *See also* **affirmative action.**

reverse onus Normally, the onus is on the Crown to prove the guilt of a person charged with a criminal offence. In some circumstances, however, the onus shifts to the offender to prove his innocence. When this occurs, it is often argued to be in violation of the citizen's right to be innocent until proven guilty. The Supreme Court ruled on one situation of this nature in *R. v. Oakes* when it struck down a section of the Narcotics Control Act, which presumed the guilt of the accused since it required the accused to prove that he did not possess a narcotic for the purpose of trafficking. Reverse onus happens more frequently in bail hearings (also called show cause hearings), where the onus shifts to the accused to justify why he or she should be released. A reverse onus applies in bail hearings to people who have been charged with some of the following: a) an indictable offence while on release for another indictable offence; b) an indictable offence by persons who are not normally residents of Canada; c) failure to comply with a condition of release; d) participating in a criminal organization; e) very serious charges such as murder and treason. Reference: *R. v. Oakes* (1986), 24 C.C.C. (3rd) 321 (S.C.C.).

Riel, Louis Métis leader executed for treason on November 16, 1885 in Regina. Riel played a pivotal role in the development of Métis and First Nations politics and was actively involved in the Northwest Rebellion as well as the Red River Rebellion. His execution continues to haunt the political corridors of Canada and leads to periodic requests for an apology or even a finding of wrongful conviction. Reference: Stanley, George F.G. (1963). *Louis Riel.* Toronto: Ryerson Press.

right to counsel The right of an accused to have a lawyer in any criminal case. This right, however, is not always accompanied by the financial means to hire a lawyer. Financial assistance is not yet deemed a right. *See also* **legal aid.**

rights, civil Those rights designed to protect citizens of a nation from abuse by their governments. These rights typically derive from citizenship.

rights, human Those rights that are deemed to be inherent to all human and thus not derived from constitutions, courts, or laws. They may, however, be codified in treaties, such as the United Nations Universal Declaration of Human Rights. *See also* **Universal Declaration of Human Rights.** Reference: Ignatieff, Michael. (2000). *The Rights Revolution.* Toronto: Anansi.

rites of passage The ritual or ceremonial acknowledgment of a person's passage from one stage of life to the next; for example, a graduation ceremony or retirement party. Many cultures provide a ritualized acknowledgment of the passage to adulthood, but sociologists note that this has all but disappeared from modern societies.

ritual An action performed because of its symbolic significance and its ability to evoke the emotions of those engaged in the performance. These actions are usually clearly specified by the group, and there are additional rules about who can perform the ritual, and when the ritual should be performed. Ritual may be important in maintaining the values of a group or in strengthening group ties. Examples of ritual include communion, aspects of the marriage ceremony, or singing the national anthem before sports events.

robbery The unlawful taking, or attempt at taking, property that is in the immediate possession of another. Not to be confused with theft, where the person takes something not in the immediate possession of another.

Rodriguez, Sue Sue Rodriguez was afflicted with a serious disability that was eventually going to take her life. Wanting to maintain control over her life, but because of her disability, unable to take action herself, she wished the courts to allow someone to assist her in taking her life without facing criminal charges. In a decision of September 29, 1993, the court did not accept these arguments. On February 12, 1994, with assistance, Rodriguez took her own life. Member of Parliament Svend Robinson admitted to being present along with an unnamed doctor, but police did not further investigate the event.

Roe v. Wade *See* **abortion**.

role A position, or status, within a social structure that is shaped by relatively precise behavioural expectations (norms). A role has been described as the active component of status. The individual, placed within a status in a social structure, performs a role in a way shaped by normative expectations. Individuals have varying ideas about normative standards and their own unique values, so role behaviour is not standardized; however radical departure from expected role behaviour will usually result in social sanctions.

role convergence An aspect of one explanation for the rising crime rate among women: their roles have converged with (become similar to) those of men.

role distancing The act of presenting your "self" as being removed or at a distance from the role you are being required to play. For example, by keeping your eyes open when asked to pray or say grace, you communicate to the group that you are making no commitment to the role. A concept from dramaturgical sociology. *See also* **presentation of self**.

role playing Where an individual plays at or pretends to occupy the role of another. This concept is useful for understanding the socialization of children and in particular that stage during which they play at being mothers, fathers, doctors, nurses, or truck drivers. It is during this playing that they master the ability to engage in reflexive role taking and thus to develop their own sense of self. *See also* **role taking, reflexive**.

role strain Captures the stress or tension that may arise from the performance of a role.

role taking, reflexive Where an individual looks at his or her own role performance from the perspective of another person. In taking the viewpoint of another, the individual is able to see him or herself as an object, as if from the outside. When we ask: "Am I talking too much?" or "Am I being responsible?" we are engaging in reflexive role taking: we are using outside standards—the point of view of another—to look at ourselves.

role theory, gender The theory that women's lesser involvement in crime can be attributed to their socialization into traditional roles within the family and in society.

Romilly, Samuel Romilly (1757–1818) was a product of the Enlightenment and a reformer of the criminal law. His viewed helped shape the work of Cesare Beccaria. *See also* **Beccaria, Cesare**.

routine-activity theory A theory developed in the 1970s to explain variations in victimization rates among categories of persons, areas, or over time. Dependent on the notions of lifestyle and opportunity, this theory argues that it is the lifestyles (i.e., routine activities) of young males which explains their high rate of victimization compared to seniors, or that it is the changes in routine activities accompanying the increase in small households and two-income families which has increased the opportunity for property crimes. Reference: Cohen, Lawrence, and Marcus Felson. (1979). "Social Change and Crime Rate Trends: A Routine Activities Approach." *American Sociological Review* 44: 588–608.

royal assent A bill passed by a legislature does not become law (a statute) until it has been approved by the Governor General (federal) or Lieutenant Governor (provincial), the royal representatives in Canada. This stage of law-making is largely symbolic in nature.

Royal Canadian Mounted Police (RCMP) The national police force responsible at the federal level. The RCMP also operates under contract to municipalities and provinces to provide basic policing services to many communities. It was formed in 1873 as the Northwest Mounted Police with a mandate to police the Northwest Territories. In 1904, the force became known as the Royal Northwest Mounted Police, and in 1920 as the Royal Canadian Mounted Police.

Royal Commission on Aboriginal Peoples A Commission of inquiry established by the Conservative government in 1991 as a strategy to obtain First Nations' support for constitutional change after the Meech Lake Accord was defeated in 1990 by Elijah Harper, an aboriginal member of the Manitoba legislature. The Commission reported in 1996, having examined a wide range of matters affecting aboriginal peoples. The report has the potential to help Canadians redefine the relationship between First Nations peoples and the government, although few of its recommendations have been implemented. Reference: Royal Commission on Aboriginal Peoples. (1993). *Aboriginal Peoples and the Justice System.* Ottawa: Minister of Supply and Services.

Royal Commission on the Non-Medical Use of Drugs *See* **LeDain commission.**

Royal Commission on the Status of Women *See* **Status of Women report.**

Royal Newfoundland Constabulary Created in 1874 and sounding like a provincial police force, this is really just the police force for three or four urban centres.

Royal Proclamation of 1763 This proclamation, signed by King George, provides the basis of native land rights in North America. Signed at the conclusion of the Seven Years' War at which time the French signed over much of North America to the British, the document proclaims British rule over the territory. The contents of this proclamation are significant. It acknowledges pre-existing ownership of land by native peoples; it stated that Indian land could only be bought or treatied for by the British government; it established a procedure for obtaining land; and it used the term "Nations or Tribes of Indians." These provisions provide a powerful legal foundation for current disputes over land rights. The Royal Proclamation has an entirely different significance for the Québeçois since it was intended to make the colony of Canada with a British mould: British civil and criminal law was imposed on the Québeçois and Catholics were virtually prohibited from holding public office.

rule of law One of the cornerstones of democratic society, meaning that everyone is subject to the law. It is not just the rule that everyone is covered by the Criminal Code and must be charged and convicted if appropriate. It also means that no one in the society, the prime minister, Cabinet, senior civil servants, judges, or police has power except as it is derived from law. Authority can only come from law, namely the Constitution, a statute, legal regulations, common law or municipal bylaw. There is a rule of law rather than rule by individuals.

rule of thumb It is often claimed that in the "bad old days," men had the acknowledged right to beat their wives with a stick as long as it was no thicker than their thumb. However, there is no evidence that such a rule or understanding ever existed. In common usage, a "rule of thumb" is a term for an approximation and refers to the fact that the top knuckle of a thumb is typically about one inch in width.

Rusche, G., and O. Kirchheimer In their 1939 publication, *Punishment and Social Structure,* these authors examined the changing forms and ideologies of punishment over history, arguing that changes in the mode of production create new changes in punishment and its accompanying ideology to support new class interests.

Rwandan genocide In 1994, elements of the Hutu majority in Rwanda encouraged the massacre of the Tutsi minority group. Approximately one million Rwandans lost their lives. United Nations and Canadian peacekeepers under the leadership of Romeo Dallaire were in Rwanda at the time of massacre and attempted to get greater intervention by the United Nations, but were required to stand by and watch the massacre when no action was taken to intervene in the rising tensions. Reference: Dallaire, Romeo. (2003). *Shake Hands With the Devil.* Toronto: Random House Canada.

S

sacred-profane Émile Durkheim (1858–1917) claimed that all religions divide objects or phenomena into the sacred and the profane. Sacred objects are those that are extraordinary and are treated as if set apart from the routine course of events in daily life. The profane are those objects or phenomena seen as ordinary and constituting the reality of everyday living. Durkheim believed that the celebration of religious beliefs and sacred ritual united the community, integrating individuals, and that it enhanced the sharing of collective sentiments and solidarity in profane areas of social life. The secularization and rationalization of western societies has reduced the realm of the sacred.

SADD Founded in 1981 in Massachusetts as Student Against Driving Drunk (sic), this group is known as Student Against Destructive Decisions. *See also* **Mothers Against Drunk Driving (MADD).**

sample When it is difficult to conduct a census of an entire population, a researcher will work with a portion of that population, a sample, which is thought to be representative of the population in question. Researchers typically try to ensure that a sample has been drawn in a random fashion. This ensures that the distribution of population characteristics corresponds to the assumptions of probability theory, allowing inferences to be drawn about the population. Many times non-random samples are used, however.

sampling Refers to the process or method of drawing a sample from a population. This process can be based on random selection such that each member of the population has an equal probability of being selected (e.g., putting all the names into a hat). Many statistical tests assume a process of random selection. However, the method may not be based on random selection. One might, for example, select for convenience the first 100 people you meet or all the students in an introductory criminology class.

sampling error Any sample is only one of many samples which could have been drawn from a population. Consequently, a researcher may not get the same results with each sample (e.g., the mean or average might vary). As the sample gets larger, this variation is less drastic, and the sampling error is smaller. Social scientists have ways of calculating the sampling error; you can see this in the news many times when a reporter says: "a survey of this size is accurate within 3.5 percent, 19 times out of 20." For example, the 3.5 percent is the sampling error; 95 times of 100 times the mean would fall within +/– the mean or average reported.

sampling frame The actual physical representation of a population, a voters' list or a student class list, for example, from which a sample is actually drawn. A population is a somewhat abstract concept, while the sampling frame is the real listing of members of that population such that you can imagine them being placed into a hat for purposes of random sampling.

sanction A positive or negative response by an individual or group to behaviour and designed to encourage or discourage that behaviour. Positive sanction would include rewards, compliments, applause, or smiles, while negative sanctions would include punishments, frowns, avoidance, or gossip. Sanctions can be informal (coming from friends and neighbours) or formal (coming from authorized institutions like the police, the government, and the school), and must be seen as forms of social control.

saturation charging The practice of the police and crown prosecutor to charge an offender with many offences. Often used as a strategy to ensure that at least one offence will "stick" or to allow the prosecutor some negotiating room when it comes to plea bargaining.

scientific management A method of work organization where management implements a specialized division of labour and sets out detailed instructions for the performance of work. Associated with the innovative methods introduced by Frederick Taylor (1856–1915) to separate workers from their knowledge of the work process, to divide labour so as to pay only for the specific skill required to perform a narrow function, and to establish management as the controller of work and the work process. *See also* **industrial relations**; **Taylorism.**

scientific method The methods and techniques of investigation and analysis used in the sciences to develop theories and design experiments. Usually scientific methods attempt to discover the causes of things and the relationships between variables. The key assumption of scientific method is that a claim or theory can be tested by discoverable and measurable evidence. Scientific experiment and research has led to the development of many laws: mechanics, electrical energy, light, transfer of heat, relativity, etc. The idea of scientific method has been influential in sociology, but scientific methods cannot be applied to many of the topics that interest sociologists, nor can they be strictly applied where they do have relevance. Generally, scientific method involves the steps of gathering of data, by observation and research; formulation of hypotheses; testing by experiment; replication of tests to ensure consistent results; and avoidance of personal bias and pre-judgment. A theory or hypothesis must be stated in a testable form to have scientific status: it must be clear enough that it can be disproven. Early sociologists like Auguste Comte (1798–1857) assumed that sociology would develop into a science of society equivalent to the natural sciences of physics and chemistry, and this view continued to be influential in the sociology of Émile Durkheim (1858–1917). Modern sociologists tend to reject the idea that sociology can be scientific, but they do employ aspects of scientific method in trying to arrive at a rigorous and systematic understanding of aspects of society. *See also* **sociology of knowledge**.

Scotland Yard The headquarters for the London Metropolitan Police force, originally established in September 1829. The name Scotland Yard comes from the original location on Great Scotland Yard.

Scott, Frank (Francis) While some may know Frank Scott (1899–1985) as a poet, he was also Canada's pre-eminent constitutional lawyer from 1940 through the 1960s. He argued important cases before the Supreme Court, assisted the newly elected CCF government of Saskatchewan to write a Bill of Rights, and influenced the thinking of Pierre Trudeau, which resulted in the current Charter of Rights and Freedoms. Scott also represented the voice of English Canada on the Royal Commission on Bilingualism and Biculturalism. *See also* **padlock laws**. Reference: Djwa, Sandra. (1987). *A Life of F.R. Scott: The Politics of the Imagination.* Toronto: McClelland and Stewart.

search and seizure The entering of private property to search for evidence relevant to a particular case and the seizing of such evidence. This police power is tightly governed by rules. A warrant is required in the following circumstances: there is to be a secret recording of conversation; video surveillance; perimeter searches of residential premises; search of automobiles; and installation of tracking devices. A search without a warrant is normally illegal, but there are some exceptions.

second-degree murder *See* **murder, second-degree**.

second reading *See* **first reading**.

secondary deviance As used by Edwin Lemert, secondary deviance refers to deviant behaviour that flows from a stigmatized sense of self; the deviance is thought to be consistent with the character of the self. A person's self can be stigmatized or tainted by public labelling. Secondary deviance is contrasted to primary deviance, which may be behaviourally identical to secondary deviance, but is incorporated into a "normal" sense of self. One may, for example, get drunk several times because one sees oneself as enjoying a party. However, if one notices that friends are hiding their liquor during visits to their house, one may come to see oneself as a "drunk," and then continue to get drunk because one *is* a drunk. The first acts are primary deviance and the second act is secondary deviance. Reference: Lemert, Edwin. (1951). *Social Pathology.* New York: McGraw-Hill.

secondary group *See* **group, secondary**.

secondary labour market Refers to those occupations that tend to be located in the most competitive areas of the economy and are more labour intensive. These occupations tend to pay lower wages, have insecure employment, be less likely to be unionized, and provide less opportunity for advancement. Typical industries are restaurant and hotel services, cashiers, and retail sales. This labour market has been dominated by women and minorities, while the other market (the primary labour market) has been dominated by white males. This term was originally part of what was referred to as *dual labour market theory.* The term *segmented labour market* is now used, but studies continue to find a significant dualism to the labour market, and this continues to be useful for understanding women's occupational location and their low wages relative to men. *See also* **primary labour market**.

secondary sexual characteristics Characteristics that are sex related but are not directly connected with the physiology of reproduction (the sex organs). For example, statistically, men tend to be heavier with more muscle mass and physical strength than women, although there are some women heavier, more muscular and stronger than some men. *See also* **sexual dimorphism**.

sect Usually contrasted with churches or denominations, sects are thought to be small and inward-looking religious or spiritual groups that reject the values of the wider society. Examples would be the Jehovah's Witnesses, Salvation Army, and Christian Science. These groups typically begin with a charismatic leader who articulates a strong rejection of the compromises made with the secular world by other religions. Over time, as leadership is routinized and members experience some upward mobility, there tends to be more acceptance of worldly matters and secular values.

secularization The process of organizing society or aspects of social life around non-religious values or principles. The term is linked closely to Max Weber's concept of a growing "disenchantment of the world" as the sphere of the magical, sacred, and religious retreats in cultural significance before the driving force of rationalization of culture and social institutions powered by emergent capitalism. *See also* **rationalization**.

self-control One of the aims of all socialization is to place a "police person" inside each of us, rather than relying on external controls. Many experience "self-control" when a voice inside says: What will mother think? Will this harm my chances of being accepted as a police recruit? This is effective self-control.

self-government In the Canadian context, this term has clearest reference to the aspirations of First Nations peoples. While the term is as yet without a clear definition, as used by the federal government it means something like self-determination. The Indian Act replaced traditional Indian governments with band councils that acted as agents of the federal government. These councils only exercise those powers granted by the Indian Act. Whatever form self-government takes, it would involve legislative changes to give First Nations peoples the tools to be much more self-determining. For some First Nations peoples, the idea of self-government is an acknowledgment of nationhood. For these groups, their status as self-determining nations was never given up through colonization or treaties, so to have self-government recognized is seen as an acknowledgment of this earlier, and continuing, nationhood. As currently envisaged by federal and provincial governments, self-government is not equivalent to territorial sovereignty, although it implies extensive legal autonomy within the general framework of the federal government's overriding power to make provisions for "peace, order and good government."

self-report study A method for measuring crime involving the distribution of a detailed questionnaire to a sample of people, asking them whether they have committed a crime in a particular period of time. This has been a good method for criminologists to determine the social characteristics of "offenders."

Senate *See* **parliament**.

sentence The disposition of a case upon conviction in a criminal proceeding. Reference: Roberts, J.V., and D.P. Cole. (1999). *Making Sense of Sentencing.* Toronto: University of Toronto Press.

sentencing circle An adaptation of an aboriginal tradition to the problem of sentencing an offender in a fashion that empowers the community itself to resolve the conflict in their midst. Although there are variations, the judge, defendant, lawyers, victim, and community members sit in a circle in an informal environment and discuss the convicted person and the harm done to the victim and to the community. In this broad forum and through examination of a broad array of facts, the circle attempts to decide what is to be done. The circle has been given some direction by the judge and limits may be set. The judge will typically impose the sentence arrived at by the circle. Also known as *circle sentencing.* Reference: Green, R.G. (1998). *Justice in Aboriginal Communities: Sentencing Alternatives.* Saskatoon: Purich Publishing.

separation of powers A constitutional structure of government where legal authority is divided between various institutions. In the United States, the Constitution divides federal authority between the president, Congress, and the Supreme Court, all of which have delimited powers and responsibilities. This concept of government differs from the idea of parliamentary supremacy, which confers complete authority to Parliament and grants it unconstrained legal powers. Canada exhibits a blend of the idea of parliamentary supremacy and the idea of separation of powers, since the written part of the Canadian constitution explicitly divides federal and provincial powers and establishes a framework of constitutional law by which Parliament is restrained in its actions.

sequential analysis As used by ethnomethodologists, this is the same as conversational analysis. Social scientists, for example, have analyzed police interrogations to discover the common-sense methods the police use to obtain a confession. Reference: Have, Paul Ten. (1998). *Doing Conversation Analysis.* London: Sage.

sequestered jury A jury that is isolated from access to the public during the court proceedings or more commonly through the process of their deliberation. A method used to insure that the jury is not tainted by outside biases, false evidence, or inadmissible evidence.

serf An unfree status associated with agrarian economies dominated by feudal social relationships. Serfs were labourers bound to the land and to service to a landlord, but differing from slaves in that they possessed security of the person, the right to personal property, and customary rights to use land and other resources. Serfdom has occurred in many world societies including England, France, Russia, China, and Japan. While serfdom was first extinguished in England in the 16th century, it persisted in Russia until the general emancipation ordered by Tsar Alexander 11 in 1861. A modified form of serfdom, based on indentured or bonded labour, is still widespread in world societies. *See also* **feudalism**.

serial murder Multiple murders which are separated by time and yet committed by the same individual. Murders may be separated by a day or two or several years. *See also* **Pickton, Robert William**; **Olson, Clifford**. Reference: Leyton, E. (1986). *Hunting Humans: The Rise of the Modern Multiple Murder*. Toronto: McClelland and Stewart.

seriousness rule The national governments of Canada and the United States use this rule in deciding how to count occurrences in a multiple crime situation: only the most serious crime is counted.

service economy Usually contrasted with a goods producing economy and refers to an economy based largely on the provision of service rather than manufactured goods. These services may include medical service, accounting, social work, teaching, design, consultancy, short order cook, waiting tables, and driving a taxi. The shift to a service economy is sociologically interesting because it appears to be associated with different labour market demands, differing educational requirements, and differing wage structures. *See also* **goods producing economy**.

sex The biological classification of individuals as males and females. Sociologists would note, however, that even though this is a classification based on biological differences, it is a socially constructed classification. *See also* **gender roles**.

sex typing Refers to stereotypes of the sexes and the consequent actions of characterizing men and women on the basis of these stereotypes. For example, women are mediators and men are competitive; boys prefer trucks, while girls prefer dolls. *See also* **stereotype**.

sexism Actions or attitudes that discriminate against people based solely on their gender. Sexism is linked to power in that those with power are typically treated with favour and those without power are typically discriminated against. Sexism is also related to stereotypes since the discriminatory actions or attitudes are frequently based on false beliefs or overgeneralizations about gender and on seeing gender as relevant when it is not. *See also* **stereotype**.

sexual assault A broader classification of sexual offence than "rape." Rape occured only when sexual penetration was involved, but this new definition of a sexual assault is broader. It is an assault that has as its consequence a violation of the sexual integrity of the victim. There are now three levels of sexual assault that replace earlier offences of rape and indecent assault.

sexual dimorphism Differences between males and females in size and appearance. Sexual dimorphism in humans is greater than in some animals and less than in many. Evolutionary psychologists and biologists are intrigued to understand the function of sexual dimorphism.

sexual division of labour The allocation of a work task, either in the private household or in the public economy, on the basis of the sex of the person. Women may cook the meals and men wash the dishes, or women may perform caring roles such as nursing or social work in the public economy, while men perform the tasks of driving trucks, fighting fires, or manufacturing goods. Most societies have had some division of labour by sex. The sexual division of labour is related to stereotyping. Although this expression seems to have survived criticism from social scientists, it is actually incorrect: the division of labour between the sexes is chiefly *gendered*: it is based on cultural practices rather than any inherent suitability of either sex to perform specific roles.

shaken baby syndrome A form of child abuse first recognized in 1972 when it was realized that some brain damage in babies and young infants is caused by a caregiver shaking the baby violently enough to cause brain injury. During severe shaking of an infant, brain damage can occur.

shaming One way that small and intimate societies deal with deviant or unacceptable behaviour. A sense of humiliation is created through disgracing or discrediting the offender. This approach to social control maintains a connection between the offenders and the society, allowing the person to remain part of the community rather than creating a marginal status. Reference: Braithwaite, J. (1989). *Crime, Shame, and Reintegration*. Cambridge: Cambridge University Press.

Sharpe decision A complex and controversial set of court decisions regarding child pornography. Mr. Sharpe was charged with two counts of possession of pornography and two counts of possession of child pornography for the purpose of distribution or sale. Sharpe was acquitted on the charges of possession of child pornography, and this was upheld on appeal. However, on appeal to the Supreme Court of Canada, the court upheld the law and created two exceptions: the right to protect private works of the imagination or photographic depictions of one's self, and the creation of sexually explicit depictions of children for their own pleasure. The Court ordered that Sharpe be retried and be provided the opportunity to argue that his works met one of these exceptions. Sharpe was successful in making this argument. In 2004, the government drafted a bill to address some of the concerns raised by this case and removed any reference to the notion of "artistic merit." The arts community then raised concerns that they would be the ones charged under the amended law. They raised what they called the *Lolita test*—if the great novel by Vladimir Nabukov would not be permitted under a law, then the law is faulty. Reference: *R. v. Sharpe*, [2001] 1 S.C.R. 45.

Shaw, Clifford R., and Henry D. McKay Shaw (1895–1957) and McKay were associated with the Chicago school and its focus on the effects of urbanization on social organization and rates of crime and deviance. Their early research in the 1940s was centred on analyzing whether crime rates in particular regions of Chicago were associated with the characteristics of the citizens who lived there or were related to the situational environment, or "ecology," of their area. By tracking urban migration patterns, as successive waves of urban migrants and immigrants arrived, it was possible to demonstrate that it was areas of the city, rather than particular population groups, that were consistently correlated to crime rates. This result was explained by the long-established "social disorganization" theory of the Chicago school, which proposed that crime and delinquency were caused by social factors and not by inherent characteristics of individuals and groups. The most important of these social factors is the level of socio-economic stability. Populations subject to rapid transformation of their conditions of life are much more likely to have high crime rates than settled communities. And since social instability affects the lower classes more, they will have higher rates of crime. Reference: Shaw, Clifford R, and Henry D. McKay. (1942). *Juvenile Delinquency and Urban Areas: A Study of Rates of Delinquency in Relation to Differential Characteristics of Local Communities in American Cities.* Chicago: University of Chicago Press [1969].

sheriff That member of the courtroom with the responsibility to supervise a jury, secure the defendant, keep order in the courtroom, and locate witnesses. Also known as the *bailiff.*

Shidane, Arone *See* **Somalia, incident in.**

show cause hearing *See* **reverse onus.**

signifier A term from semiology—the study of signs. For example, the expression "a pig is coming" is the signifier (or the signifier could be a gesture, clothing style, form of architecture, consumer good), while the content of this expression is the signified. The signifier and the signified always exist in some relationship (called signification) and the hearer is always decoding this relationship. For example, in one instance the hearer may "hear" the signifier "pig" and assume that an animal pig is in the area suitable for hunting. Another time, the hearer may "hear" that a policeman is in the area, while at another time the hearer may "hear" that the speaker's supervisor is arriving.

Silent Spring Published in 1962, and written by Rachel Carson, this book was an early call to arms for the environmental movement. Carson portrays the forces that modern society has brought into being which assault nature and human life itself. The title comes from an imaginary community in which "There was a strange silence. The birds, for example—where had they gone? Many people spoke of them, puzzled and disturbed. The feeding stations in the backyards were deserted. The few birds seen anywhere were moribund; they trembled violently and could not fly. It was a spring without voices. On the morning that had once throbbed with the dawn chorus of robins, catbirds, doves, jays, wrens, and scores of other bird voices there was now no sound; only silence over the fields and woods and marsh." When this book appeared and was serialized in magazine form, the chemical industry mounted an expensive campaign to silence Carson. She had done her homework, however, and her facts stood. Reference: Carson, Rachel. (1962). *Silent Spring.* Mariner Books [1994].

Simon Fraser University, criminology at Simon Fraser University in Burnaby, British Columbia, established a criminology program in 1975 under the leadership of Ezzat Fattah. The university now offers a comprehensive interdisciplinary program at the undergraduate and graduate level.

Sinnisiak and Uluksuk In 1917, these two men were charged with the 1913 murder of two priests they had known for some time, and they became the first Inuit tried under Canadian Criminal law. A massive police hunt through the north brought them to custody and to trial in Edmonton in August 1917 on a charge of one of the murders. This trial resulted in acquittal. The Crown was not happy with this outcome, and later that month another trial for the second murder was conducted in Calgary and the two were found guilty. A subsequent death sentence, however, was commuted to life imprisonment; after serving only two years the men were released back into their community. Reference: Moyles, R.G. (1989). *British Law and Arctic Men: The Celebrated 1917 Murder Trials of Sinnisiak and Uluksuk, First Inuit Tried Under White Man's Law.* Burnaby, Northern Justice Society: Simon Fraser University.

situational crime prevention Premised on the belief that most crime is opportunistic rather than being the outcome of those driven to commit a crime no matter what. This form of prevention attempts to reduce the opportunities for crime rather than just relying on the police after the crime has occurred. This approach is also called *effective guardianship.* Reference: Tonry, M., and D. Farrington. (1995). *Building A Safer Society: Strategic Approaches to Crime Prevention.* Chicago: University of Chicago Press.

skinheads Usually describes young people who have shaved their heads. More importantly, they are typically marginalized persons who hold extreme nationalist beliefs and have frequently attacked and killed immigrants who are seen as threatening the racial purity of their new nation.

SLAPP An acronym for the process of using the law to try and silence public criticism of corporate or on occasion political bodies. The initials refer to Strategic Lawsuits Against Public Participation. To sue an outspoken critic by claiming libel forces the critic to stop discussing the matter at issue.

slavery Describes a relationship between people in which one person is not free but is treated as the legally owned property of the other. As such, the slave can be sold or exchanged. Slave relationships have been found in many parts of the world and have sometimes been the central economic relationships of the society. As legal property of their owners, slaves can be forced to produce goods or services whose value remains with the owner.

social bond The degree to which an individual is integrated into "the social." Do they have binding ties to the family, to the school, to the workplace, to the community? While Émile Durkheim (1858–1917) first focused on the importance of the social bond, it has gained wide acceptance in the theory and research of Travis Hirschi. Hirschi argues that as the social bond is weakened the degree of deviant involvement goes up.

social construction of reality An aspect of many micro-interpretive perspectives in sociology, and must be understood as a contrast to positivistic and structural sociology. Rejecting the notion that events or social phenomena have an independent and objective existence, they examine the methods that members of society use to create or construct reality. Émile Durkheim (1858–1917), for example, was a positivist and a structuralist and argued that suicide had an objective existence, independent of himself and others. That is, there was something about the way of death that constituted something as a suicide. An advocate of the social construction of reality perspective would argue that suicide is just a label for a death and is constituted, or created, by the accounts that people like police, family, or coroners give of the death. Our accounting methods then construct reality rather than there being some independent reality which we can describe or explain. This phrase was used in 1966 by Peter Berger and T. Luckmann. *See also* **symbolic interactionism**; **labelling theory**; **phenomenological sociology**; **ethnomethodology**. Reference: Berger, P., and T. Luckmann. (1972). *The Social Construction of Reality*, 2nd ed. London: Penguin.

social contract theory Used metaphorically to suggest that a group of self-interested and rational individuals came together and formed a contract which created society. Each was willing to give up a little bit of freedom to create social rules that would protect self-interest. This theory suggests that individuals were historically prior to societies. It was this view which sociologist Émile Durkheim argued against in the late 19th century with his claim that society must come before the individual since human culture and communication can only arise in society. Reference: Morris, C.W. (1999). *The*

Social Contract Theorists. Lanham, MD: Rowman and Littlefield.

social control theory Attempts to explain why it is that all of us do not commit crime. Or to put this another way: why are most people law-abiding? The answer lies in dimensions of social control, or the many ways in which people are controlled by family, schools, work situations, conscience, etc. Most conventional theories, by contrast, try to explain why individuals commit crime. Reference: Hirschi, Travis. (1969). *Causes of Delinquency*. Berkeley: University of California Press.

social Darwinism A late 19th century social philosophy that unites an interest in social problems (e.g., inequality) with an interpretation of Darwin's work on the origin of species. Advocates argue that the central Darwinian principle of evolution, development and progress, is the survival of the fittest and extinction of the weakest. Applied to social affairs, this implies that those who get ahead in society are the most fit and deserve their position. More importantly, perhaps, this perspective suggests that supporting those who fall behind (by providing welfare, for example) interferes with the principles of evolution and obstructs social progress. Sociologists, of course, believe that social problems like inequality must be understood within a social and cultural context, rather than a context of biological competition. Reference: Hofstadter, Richard. (1992). *Social Darwinism in American Thought*. Boston: Beacon Press.

social democracy A general term for political doctrines that claim an important role for the state and the community in shaping and directing a society's economic and social life. Social democracy differs from socialism because it is committed to preservation of a largely capitalist and free market economy, but shares with it an emphasis on the importance of redistribution of wealth and income, so that citizens may have social and economic conditions that effectively provide for reasonable equality of opportunity. Modern welfare-state liberalism is closely allied to social democratic ideas. *See also* **socialism**.

social disorganization theory The theory that crime and other deviant behaviour is most likely to occur where social institutions are not able to direct and control groups of individuals. It is argued that gangs will arise spontaneously in social contexts that are weakly controlled. Some criminologists think that the concept of social disorganization just reflects middle-class failure to comprehend organization different from their own. Reference: Sutherland, E.H. (1939). *Principles of Criminology* (3rd ed.). Philadelphia: Lippincott.

social formation A term used by critical sociologists with a meaning similar to that of "society." When we talk of Canadian society, however, we tend to think only of one society and imagine it being static. Critical sociologists wish to talk about Canadian society being formed in different ways over time. Each would be a different social formation, although all would be called Canada. Each formation would be characterized by a particular organization of economic and political relationships.

social gospel movement An attempt to use the Gospel, the teachings of Christ, to deal with social problems arising in an expanding industrial nation like Canada. This movement appeared in Canada in the 1880s and was a major force in social and political life through the 1930s. Its central belief was that God was at work in the creation of social change, social justice, and moral reform. This core value can be found in the Social Service Council of Canada (1912), United Church (1925), and the CCF (1932), and played an important part in shaping the nature of sociology in Canada. The movement is particularly associated with the work of J.S. Woodsworth, T.C. Douglas, Grace McInnis, and others. These ideas would now be part of what is referred to as *liberation theology*.

social intervention programs Activities by government, social agencies, and volunteers designed to change and improve the social situation of individuals, groups, and communities; strengthen social bonds; and encourage internalization of social control.

social maps The term *map* is used primarily as a metaphor (although one could actually place data or statistics on a geographic map). Mapping in the first sense means identifying the social characteristics of victims, offenders or inmates, or other groups.

social mobility Upward or downward movement within a stratification system. Liberal theory claims that capitalist societies are open-class and therefore one can expect a high degree of social mobility. According to liberal theory, this movement within a stratification system should result from a person's achievements and should not be based on ascribed characteristics such as sex, race, region of birth, and parent's class position. Social mobility is typically measured by comparing the status positions of adult children to that of their parents (intergenerational mobility), but it can be measured by comparing a person's status position over their own lifetime (intragenerational mobility). Sociologists see social mobility as a useful way to measure equality of opportunity. *See also* **demand mobility**; **equality of opportunity**.

social movement A group of people organized, outside of institutions established for this purpose, so as to bring about political and social change which will satisfy their shared interest or goal. Political parties therefore would not be social movements, although the New Democratic Party often describes itself as part of a social movement. It is more correct to talk about the environmental movement, the gay rights movement, the women's movement, the labour movement, victim's rights movements, prisoner's rights movements, or movements for drug decriminalization. Sociologists are interested in studying the dynamics of such movements and the conditions or forces that make some successful and others less successful.

social relations of production Another way of referring to the class structure. The social relations of production refers to the social relationships that people enter into in the production or delivery of goods and services. From a Marxist perspective, these relationships are inevitably those of owners and non-owners or those who control the work and those who do not control the work. In this way of thinking, social class is founded on the economy of any society, and it is the pattern of class relations that give a society its central character.

social structure The patterned and relatively stable arrangement of roles and statuses found within societies and social institutions. The idea of social structure points out the way in which societies, and institutions within them, exhibit predictable patterns of organization, activity, and social interaction. This relative stability of organization and behaviour provides the quality of predictability that people rely on in every day social interaction. Social structures are inseparable from cultural norms and values that also shape status and social interaction.

socialism A political doctrine that upholds the principle of collectivity, rather than individualism, as the foundation for economic and social life. Socialists favour state and co-operative ownership of economic resources, equality of economic condition, and democratic rule and management of economic and social institutions. *See also* **social democracy**.

socialist feminism A perspective that examines women's social situation as shaped by both patriarchal gender relations and by the class structure of capitalism. It sees gender and class oppression as inseparable, and rather than working for the equality of women within a liberal, democratic, capitalist society, it argues for the equality of women within a society that is not dependent upon the exploitation of one group by another, i.e., a classless society. *See also* **feminism**; **liberal feminism**.

socialization (1) A process of social interaction and communication in which an individual comes to learn and internalize the culture of their society or group. Socialization begins immediately at birth, with the conditioning influences of infant handling, and continues throughout an individual's lifetime. Sociologists recognize the limitless variety of individual experiences of socialization, but have given much attention to general patterns of socialization found in individual societies and groups within them. The sociological use of the term refers to the learning and absorption of culture and not simply to the process of interacting with others. (2) The term is also sometimes used to refer to the collective ownership and management of economic resources (e.g., a nationalized industry) or resource, or to publicly provided and financed services (e.g., "socialized medicine": medicare).

society A human community, usually with a relatively fixed territorial location, sharing a common culture and common activities. There is cultural and institutional interdependence between members of the society, and they are, to some extent, differentiated from other communities and groups. Societies are generally identified as existing at the level of nation states, but there can be regional and cultural communities within nation states that possess much of the cultural distinctiveness and relative self-sufficiency of societies.

sociobiology A perspective on human social behaviour made accessible by the publication in 1975 of E.O. Wilson's *Sociobiology* and Richard Dawkins's 1976 publication of *The Selfish Gene.* This perspective begins with the assumption that humans are above all other animals and therefore the roots of human social behaviour can be found in our evolutionary heritage. Since this way of understanding relies on genetics and biological adaptation, it is not a sociological perspective. The term *sociobiology* has been replaced to a great extent by the term *evolutionary psychology.* Reference: Wilson, E.O. (2000). *Sociobiology: The New Synthesis*, 25th anniversary ed. Cambridge, MA: Harvard University Press.

socio-economic status A term that is often contrasted with that of social class. Socio-economic status, largely an American usage, has developed as a way to operationalize or measure social class on the assumptions that class groupings are not real groups. It is a rather arbitrary category and is developed by combining the position or score of persons on criteria such as income, amount of education, type of occupation held, or neighbourhood of residence. The scores can then be arbitrarily divided so as to create divisions such as upper class, middle class, and lower class. Sociologists are interested in socio-economic status, as they are in class, since it is assumed that this status affects life chances in numerous ways. *See also* **class**.

sociological imagination As used by C.W. Mills (1916–62), this term refers to the ability to imagine and understand the intersection between personal biography and historical social structures. This is indeed the essence of sociology: imagining that every individual's life is given meaning, form, and significance within historically specific cultures and ways of organizing social life. Having a sociological imagination then is identical with being a good sociologist: it is a standard against which to judge sociology. Reference: Mills, C.W. (1959). *The Sociological Imagination.* New York: Oxford University Press.

sociology A social science that examines the structure, organization, and culture of societies and their processes of social change and social interaction. Sociology encompasses a wide range of diverse theories and perspectives. Broadly, it can be separated conceptually into critical or conflict versus functionalist perspectives. The former deals with such topics as inequality, class conflict, gender relations, and political economy, while the latter is focused on the social processes that stabilize and maintain existing societies and support social integration. Sociological perspectives differ also in their areas of focus, with "macro" perspectives being interested in the way society as a whole shapes individual experience and institutional dynamics, while "micro" approaches like symbolic interactionism are centred on the analysis of patterns of social interaction between individuals and within groups. The sociological approach to crime is interested in the social correlates of crime including issues of class, status, gender, levels of community integration, development of ethnic and youth subcultures, etc., and in the way crime is socially constructed both by the exercise of power and in processes of social interaction and interpretation. While criminology was initially included within sociology departments and often treated as the sociological study of deviance rather than specifically of crime, specialist criminology departments gradually emerged since the focus of criminology gradually became centred on the analysis of the causes of crime and means for its reduction and on penal and correctional policy. Criminology therefore became associated with pragmatism, social experimentation, and social work, rather than the more theoretical and conceptual approach of sociology. Reference: Eichler, M. (2001). "Women Pioneers in Canadian Sociology." *Canadian Journal of Sociology* 26(3); Hiller, H. (2001). "The Most Important Books/Articles in Canadian Sociology in the 20th Century." *Canadian Journal of Sociology* 26(3).

sociology of knowledge The study of the social bases of what is known, believed, or valued both by individuals and society. The essential idea is that knowledge itself, how it is defined and constituted, is a cultural product shaped by social context and history. In this view, knowledge cannot be treated as a thing in itself, as an objective, universally true body of facts and theory, but must be understood in the social context in which it originated. The principal ideas of postmodernism are closely linked to this long tradition in philosophy and the social sciences. *See also* **postmodernism**. Reference: Mannheim, Karl. (1952). *Essays on the Sociology of Knowledge.* New York: Oxford University Press.

sodomy Anal sex, prohibited by the Criminal Code of Canada until 1969.

solicitor general A minister in a provincial government responsible for the law and its enforcement. Usually the courts, the police, and provincial prisons fall under the jurisdiction of the solicitor general.

solitary confinement Also known as *administrative segregation.* The isolation of a prison inmate in a small, sparsely furnished cell for causing trouble within the prison. Thus, a form of punishment within the institution. This practice received a great deal of attention in 1975 when prison inmate Jack McCann asked the Supreme Court of Canada to evaluate the solitary confinement practices in British Columbia Penitentiary. McCann had spent a total of 1471 days in solitary confinement, confined for 23.5 hours a day and sleeping on a thin mattress on a concrete floor with a light kept on at all times. The Supreme Court declared his isolation as "cruel and unusual" punishment. However, while British Columbia Penitentiary was soon replaced, the practice continues in all penitentiaries. Reference: Jackson, M. (1983). *Prisoners of Isolation.* Toronto: University of Toronto Press.

Somalia, incident in On March 16, 1993, Shidane Arone, a 16-year old Somali was beaten to death by Canadian soldiers after being captured. In December of the previous year, the United Nations authorized a peace-enforcement mission to Somali in response to mass starvation as a result of civil war. Canadian soldiers from the Airborne Regiment were sent—a troop, however, with a reputation of having a "bad attitude" and lack of respect for authority. The situation in Somalia was more chaotic than anticipated, and US soldiers were soon harassed. Canadian troops were given permission to shoot at thieves under certain circumstances. Canadian troops made many "home movies"; these showed troops engaging in behaviour that did not bring much honour to Canada. The killing of Shidane Arone resulted in a cover up by the Armed Forces and eventually in an inquiry. The person thought to have been most directly involved in the beating of Arone attempted suicide three days after the incident, and the resulting brain damage prevented him from going to trail. It was later thought that the behaviour of the Canadian troops may have been as a result of a reaction to Mefloquine, an anti-malaria drug that is now known to produce a form of "madness" in many users. Reference: Desbarats, Peter. (1997). *Somalia Cover-Up.* Toronto: McClelland and Stewart.

somatotypes Refers to body types and behind this idea lies the belief of early criminologists that there were distinctive body types and these types were associated with personality and temperament. It was believed that the mesomorph with a well-built, muscular body (note the sexist connotation of this) was associated with an aggressive personality, insensitivity to pain, and tendency to act impulsively. Reference: Sheldon, William. (1954). *Atlas of Men: A Guide for Somatyping the Adult Male of all Ages.* New York: Harper and Brothers.

Sons of Freedom *See* **Doukhobors.**

Sophonow, Thomas Wrongfully convicted of the 1981 murder of Barbara Stoppel. The jury in Sophonow's first trial could not reach agreement, so he was tried twice more; each time the conviction was overturned by a court of appeal. The Supreme Court of Canada prevented a fourth trial, and, in 2002, the police apologized to Sophonow, and an inquiry recommended a large compensation package for the three and a half years Sophonow spent in prison and the almost 20 years of harassment. Reference: Honourable P. Corey. (2001). *The Inquiry Regarding Thomas Sophonow.* Winnipeg: Minister of Justice.

soul As used by Michel Foucault (1926–84), it refers to what psychologists mean by the psyche, the self, subjectivity, or human consciousness. Foucault argues, for example, that the development of the penitentiary in the early 19th century resulted in a shift from punishing the body to punishing the soul.

sovereignty The authority possessed by the governing individual or institution of a society. Sovereign authority is distinct in that it is unrestricted by legal regulation since the sovereign authority is itself the source of all law. The idea of state sovereignty appears to have developed first in Europe, in the late middle ages, where it emerged once a division was made between the sacred authority of the church and the secular authority of the state. So long as state power was subject to religious institutions—like the Catholic church—state sovereignty could not emerge. In Britain, state sovereignty is possessed by the Crown in Parliament: law passed by Parliament and consented to by the Crown has unchallengeable legal authority. In Canada, the locus of sovereignty is more ambiguous since the written parts of Canada's constitution, the Constitution Act, 1867, and the Constitution Act, 1982, prescribe a federal–provincial division of powers and special procedures for constitutional amendment that limit the authority of the Crown and Parliament. Major changes to Canada's constitution require the unanimous consent of Parliament and the 10 provincial legislatures thus suggesting that political sovereignty in Canada is shared by the Crown in Parliament and the Crown and legislatures of Canada's 10 provinces.

spanking The Criminal Code of Canada protects parents and guardians of young children from prosecution when they use physical force to discipline their children. There is a social movement aimed at removing this protection and treating spanking as child abuse or as assault.

Sparrow case A legal case advancing the aboriginal rights of native peoples in Canada. Ronald Sparrow, a Musqueam, was charged with violating federal regulations while fishing in an area not covered by existing treaties. A 1986 Court of Appeal ruled that section 35(1) of the Canadian Constitution meant that an aboriginal right to fish for food continued to exist in non-treaty areas of the province. Reference: *R. v. Sparrow* [1990] 1 S.C.R. 1075.

speciesism The attitude that it is naturally right and appropriate to give priority to human interests and demands over those of all other living creatures. It has led to endangerment and extinction of many animal species and to extensive environmental damage and depletion.

specific deterrence As used in criminal justice, refers to crime prevention achieved through instilling fear in the specific individual being punished such that they refrain from future violation of the law. Also referred to as individual deterrence. *See also* **general deterrence**.

specific land claims Claims to land made by native groups covered by treaties but where the terms of treaties have not been met or land has been removed over the years without consent. *See also* **Calder case**; **comprehensive land claims**.

speedballing The practice of mixing cocaine and heroin.

spirit of capitalism According to Max Weber (1864–1920), the spirit of capitalism is rationalization—being methodical and calculating in the pursuit of profit. Weber argues that this drive to organize work to most efficiently achieve the goals of profit or business success had its origins in Protestantism. *See also* **Protestant ethic**.

sponsored immigrant Under the Immigration Act, any Canadian or permanent resident is able to sponsor a range of close relatives as immigrants to Canada. Family class members must only meet the criteria of good health and character. The other two classes of immigrants are refugees and independents (including entrepreneurs).

spuriousness The incorrect inference of a causal relationship between two variables where the relationship is in reality only accidental. Researchers attempt to identify or eliminate spuriousness by the use of random assignment in an experimental design or through the use of control (extraneous) variables in the manipulation of data during analysis. *See also* **causality**; **control variable**.

Squamish Five In the early 1980s, five young Canadians grew restless with the progress of the "revolution" and, attempting to put some backbone into social activists of the time, engaged in a series of "direct actions." These actions included the dynamiting of hydro transmission lines in British Columbia on May 31, 1982; bombing of a Litton Industries plant in Ontario, which injured 10 people and killed one man; and firebombing of three Red Hot Video stores in Vancouver. The five were eventually charged and all received lengthy prison sentences, the leader received life imprisonment. Reference: Hansen, Anne. (2001). *Direct Action: Memoirs of an Urban Guerilla*. Toronto: Between the Lines.

Stalinism Refers to the period from 1926 to 1953 when Joseph Stalin was leader of the Soviet Communist Party and all-powerful dictator of the Soviet Union. Stalinism claimed absolute domination of the communist party over all aspects of Soviet life, politics, and culture and justified mass murder and policies of mass terror in an attempt to establish communism. The communist party itself was repeatedly purged and leading members executed, exiled, or imprisoned. It is estimated that as many as 20 million people may have died in famines as a result of Stalin's policies of forced agricultural collectivization, as well as many hundreds of thousands more in political purges, displacements of populations, and the rigours of the vast system of prison camps established by Stalin's secret police.

stalking Anti-stalking laws have been passed in several jurisdictions—in Canada, the offence is known as *criminal harassment* (passed in August 1993)—to prevent harassment or intimidation even when there has been no physical harm done to the victim.

standard of proof There are two quite distinct standards of proof, one applying to civil cases and the other to criminal cases. In a criminal case, the standard of proof is called "proof beyond a reasonable doubt." The judge or jury does not have to be absolutely certain of the guilt of the defendant, but there must be no reasonable doubt about guilt or innocence. In a civil case, the standard is called "preponderance of the evidence," in which more than half of the evidence must support one side or the other.

standpoint feminism *See* **feminism, standpoint**.

staple As used by Harold Innis (1894–1952), a natural resource exported to a more advanced economy. According to Innis, the character of these resources and their export have given shape to the development of Canadian society. Staples such as beaver pelts, cod, wheat, and forest products have each shaped settlement patterns, transportation routes, and the structure of power.

staples trap Refers to economic or social forces which trap a nation or region within the export of a particular staple. The particular settlement patterns, characteristics of the labour force, methods of capital accumulation, or transportation routes make it difficult for British Columbia, for example, to move away from a major reliance on forest products even after the richest and most accessible forest resources have been consumed. *See also* **staple**.

star chamber Seldom used, but a term referring to an unfair judicial proceeding. A meeting place of medieval English kings which developed into a form of court, abolished in 1641 because of its abuse by monarchs, and named after the stars painted on the ceiling.

stare decisis A key principle of the common law tradition in English Canada. Translated from the Latin, the phrase means "to stand by decided matters," and embodies a set of rules concerning which court rulings are binding on other courts. In general, the decisions of a higher court are binding on those of a lower court.

state As defined by Max Weber (1864–1920), the institution that claims the exclusive right to the legitimate exercise of force in a given territory, through the use of police to enforce laws or the army to maintain civil stability. Institutions of the state include government and agencies like the army, police, judiciary, crown corporations, welfare bureaucracies, and regulatory bodies. While there have been stateless societies, most complex societies have state systems of formal government and administrative bureaucracies.

state capitalism A term proposed by critical sociologists and social theorists to describe the political and economic structure of Soviet-style communist systems. The core idea is that state ownership of the means of production, as in Russia and other previously communist regimes, did not lead to any emancipation of the workers but merely substituted bureaucratic domination by the state and state officials for that of owners of capital. *See also* **communism**.

statistical school Associated with early social scientists like Adolphe Quetelet (1795–1874) and Andre-Michel Guerry (1802–66), who began to explore the structure of emerging European societies with the assistance of statistical methods. While their early use of statistics is important, they also developed a structural explanation of crime and other social problems. Although this work was to become important later, it was overshadowed by the importance given to the more individualistic theories of Lombroso. Reference: Beirne, Piers. (1996). "The Invention of Positivist Criminology: An Introduction to Quetelet's Social Mechanics of Crime." In Brian C. MacLean, *Crime and Society: Readings in Critical Criminology*. Toronto: Copp Clark.

statistically significant When researchers study within groups or between group differences, they need a technique to determine if this difference would have occurred by chance. Various statistical techniques can determine this, and if it is unlikely the differences could have occurred by chance, it is called a statistically significant difference. Usually a .05 level of significance is used (there are 5 chances of 100 trials that this difference would occur by chance), but other levels can be used.

statistics Refers to a collection of tests or techniques that are applied to the data, or observations, which social scientists have gathered. There are two categories of statistics: descriptive and inferential. Descriptive statistics are used to describe characteristics of the sample or population the researcher is working with; for example, one can calculate a mean, standard deviation, etc. Inferential statistics are used for drawing inferences about a population based on the observations of a sample. For example, reports of opinion polls routinely note that "a sample of this size is accurate to within x percent 19 times out of 20." This is the inference to be drawn about the population from which the sample was drawn.

status A position in a social structure regulated by norms and usually ranked according to power and prestige. Status differs from class in that it is a measure of a person's social standing or social honour in a community. Individuals who share the same social class may have very divergent status. For example, people's status is affected by ethnic origin, gender, and age, as well as their level of recognition in the community. While status is statistically related to class, it is common for individuals to have inconsistent class and status locations. Most sociologists use both the concepts of class and status to describe the systems of social stratification (the way individuals are ranked in various hierarchies of income, wealth, authority, and power) found in societies.

status, achieved A position in a social structure that has been attained by the individual as a result of the individual's abilities, work, and personal involvements. While occupational statuses are generally achieved, often in a competitive process, one can also achieve more personal statuses; for example, "married" is an achieved status. *See also* **status, ascribed**.

status, ascribed A status that is automatically transmitted to an individual at birth or at a particular time in the life cycle. An individual is accorded this status through inheritance or as a result of such characteristics as sex, ethnicity, or physical features.

Status Indian A native person who is registered under the Indian Act as an Indian, and a non-status Indian is one whose ancestors were never registered or who lost status for various reasons. Women and their children lost status, for example, when they married a non-native man or a native man who did not have status. Under Bill C-31 (1985), these people have been able to regain their status. Court decision are beginning to make the distinction between status and non-status Indians less significant.

status offence A delinquency or crime that can only be committed by people occupying a particular status. The Juvenile Delinquents Act (replaced in 1984), for example, created criminal offences of school truancy, incorrigibility, sexual immorality, and violations of liquor laws. Only young people could be charged with or found to be in a state of delinquency because of these behaviours. It was found that approximately 20 percent of young girls coming to youth court did so because of their sexual behaviour, while few boys were brought to court on these grounds. *See also* **double standard**.

Status of Women report A Royal Commission Report tabled in the Canadian House of Commons in 1970. The Commission of Inquiry had been created in 1967 and, chaired by Florence Bird, held public hearings into the status of women in society and made numerous recommendations to government. The report is built on the premises of liberal theory and measures women's status against the values of equality, individualism, and freedom.

statutes Laws enacted by a sovereign law-making body such as a provincial legislature or the House of Commons.

statutory rape Sexual intercourse with an underage person with or without consent.

statutory release A form of release from prison prior to the expiration of the full sentence. Upon completion of two-thirds of a prison sentence an inmate is eligible for statutory release and if granted must serve the remainder of the sentence on parole. Statutory release can be denied if there is good reason to believe the inmate is likely to commit an offence causing death or serious bodily harm or if the offender's office was listed in schedule 1.

steam bath raids A Toronto story erupting on February 5, 1981, when 150 police simultaneously raided four Toronto gay bathhouses, arresting 286 clients and 20 staff. By next day there were 3000 protestors at a late night rally and on February 20, 4000 people attended another protest demonstration. On March 12, Toronto City Council established a committee to investigate relations between police and gay people, and when this reported on November 3, 1981, police were pressured to educate their members about community relations with gay people. Although many individuals were tried and sentenced, this event marks a step in increasing official recognition of the rights of gay people to free association to practise their lifestyle.

stereotype This term derives from the printing process and refers to a plate made by taking a cast or mould of a surface. A stereotype then is anything that lacks individual marks or identifiers, and instead appears as though made from a cast. In sociology, the stereotype (the plate or cast) is always a social construction, which may have some basis in reality, but is a gross generalization (e.g., women like romance novels). To stereotype is to apply these casts, or gross generalizations, to people or situations rather than seeing the individual variation. *See also* **sexism.**

stigma As used by Erving Goffman (1922–82), a differentness about an individual which is given a negative evaluation by others and thus distorts and discredits the public identity of the person. For example, physical disabilities, facial disfigurement, stuttering, a prison record, being obese, or not being able to read may become stigmatized attributes. The stigma may lead to the adoption of a self-identity that incorporates the negative social evaluation. Reference: Goffman, Erving. (1962) *Stigma.* New York: Prentice Hall.

stigmata Physical signs of some special moral position. While having Christian origins, Lombroso used the term to refer to physical signs of the state of atavism (a morally and biologically inferior person). The stigmata of criminality for Lombroso were things like the shape of ears, length of fingers, and the slope of the forehead.

Stonewall riot On a weekend in June 1969, the New York police, continuing a policy of harassment of homosexuals, visited the Stonewall Inn, charging that liquor was being sold without a permit. As the homosexual clientele were being taken to the police wagon, a spontaneous show of resistance emerged, and the police were forced to retreat and call for reinforcements. This resistance is now given substantial symbolic value and is seen as the birth of the modern gay rights movement.

strain A concept central to a functionalist approach or to systems theory, both of which assume that society is like an organism or mechanical system. This system is sustained by harmony and integration. However, if something begins to go wrong, this is a sign of a fault in the system, or of strain. The system has to find ways to adapt to this strain or correct it or it will lead to the transformation of the system. Robert Merton's (1910–2003) theory of crime (anomie) in an example of strain theory. He claims that there is often a strain between the culturally defined goals we all strive for and the legitimate means provided for us to achieve those goals. *See also* **anomie.**

stratification A social division of individuals into various hierarchies of wealth, status, and power. There is disagreement about how to describe stratification systems—some sociologists favour the concept of class and others discuss status differentiations.

structural explanation An explanation for crime (such as homicide) that focuses on social structure (usually this refers to inequality, poverty, or power differentials). For example, the patriarchal structure of the family might help explain the abuse of women and children within the family. Sociologist Rhonda Lenton argues that the racial structure of the US and the depth of its poverty (and the weakness of its welfare state) compared to Canada, might help explain the difference in homicide rates. Reference: Lenton, R. (1989). "Homicide in Canada and the U.S.A.: A Critique of the Hagan Thesis." *Canadian Journal of Sociology* 14: 163–77.

structural functionalism A perspective used to analyze societies and their component features that focuses on their mutual integration and interconnection. Functionalism analyses the way that social processes and institutional arrangements contribute to the effective maintenance and stability of society. The fundamental perspective is in opposition to major social change. *See also* **Durkheim**; **macro-perspective.**

structuralism (French) Refers to French social theorists such as Claude Levi-Strauss (1908–) and Jean Piaget (1896–1980) who claim that in the most ordinary of events there is a hidden structure or pattern (often called deep structure, a term taken from linguistics), which is not immediately apparent, but can be discerned by careful analysis. For example, what can be learned from the names given to pets; from food categories; from the way a child compares volume in two containers? For the early structuralists, the hidden structures in these practices reveal the structure of the human mind. This being so, there should be some uniformity in the pattern found in these practices around the world.

structuralist approach An approach to understanding the role of the state within a conflict or Marxist perspective. The state is seen as captured by the structure of capitalism, and, while having a degree of autonomy or freedom from the dominant class of society, finds it must act so as to reproduce the economic and social structures of capitalism. This approach typically sees the state doing this through attending to three functions: capital accumulation, legitimation, and coercion. *See also* **capital accu-**

mulation; coercion; instrumentalist Marxism; legitimation; relative autonomy.

structuration A term used by British sociologist Anthony Giddens in order to capture elements of macro and micro-sociology, structure and agency, determinism and free will. By structuration Giddens means that human actors recreate through their interactions (and this makes social change possible) the very social structures which constrain their actions. It involves the reproduction on a daily basis of the structures and institutions of society.

subcultural transmission Part of a wider theory which argues that behaviour is learned through socialization into the norms and values of the society. This is taken further to argue that some groups have values which are supportive of illegal behaviour. Those exposed to this subculture are more likely to exhibit deviant or criminal behaviour.

subculture A culture-within-a-culture; the somewhat distinct norms, values, and behaviour of particular groups located within society. The concept of subculture implies some degree of group self-sufficiency such that individuals may interact, find employment, recreation, and friends and mates within the group.

subjectivism In traditional positivistic and macro-structural sociology, the subjectivity of the researcher and of the subjects is seen as something to be avoided. The preferred stance for the researcher is objectivity, making the assumption that the observation of the world can occur in a neutral fashion without being influenced by theory or cultural or personal assumptions. The subjectivity of the subjects being studied is to be avoided, since it is assumed that peoples' lives are shaped by structural and cultural forces of which the subject may be unaware. More recent sociology (*see also* **interpretive theory**; **ethnomethodology**) is open to acknowledging the subjectivity of both researcher and subjects. One might study, for example, the ways in which the coroner interprets notes, slash marks, family environments, or medical histories, in an effort to arrive at an interpretation of a death. The coroner's subjectivity then is a valid area for investigation. Similarly, one might be interested in how the scientist too is also involved in arriving at an interpretation and examining how this is shaped by the subjective assumptions made. Subjectivism then is an approach to doing science which acknowledges and makes room for subjectivity. *See also* **macro-perspective**; **objectivity**.

subpoena A court order requiring an individual to appear in court to give testimony.

substantive law That portion of the Criminal Code that specifies which acts constitute crimes and what the punishments shall be. Substantive law is often contrasted to procedural law, which lays out the rules which agents of the state must follow in investigating and convicting offenders.

sufficient condition In a causal relationship, a sufficient condition (or variable) is any variable which is sufficient to bring about the effect in question. For example, a growing unemployment rate might be sufficient to cause an increase in the crime rate. Obviously many other factors (variables) could also cause the increase. Typically there are many conditions sufficient to cause an increase, or a decrease, in crime. *See also* **necessary condition**.

suffrage The right to vote in political matters; the franchise. Suffragists were early members of the women's movement who protested in order to win women the vote. The beginnings of the suffrage movement in Canada can be dated to the founding of the Toronto Women's Literary Society in 1877. The Canadian Woman Suffrage Association grew from this organization under the leadership of Dr. Emily Stowe. Women achieved the federal vote in 1918. Provincial voting rights for women were achieved between 1918 and 1940, first in Manitoba and last in Quebec. Reference: Howard, Irene. (1992). *The Struggle for Social Justice in British Columbia: Helena Gutteridge, the Unknown Reformer*. Vancouver: University of British Columbia Press.

summary offence Generally speaking, a less serious offence (than an indictable offence) and one receiving six months or less in prison or a fine of up to $2000. Summary offences also impose certain restrictions on the police regarding arrest and upon courts. These crimes are tried by lower courts. Some offences, however, are hybrids and can thus be defined as summary or indictable *See also* **indictable offence**; **hybrid offence**.

summons A judicial order requiring an accused person to appear in court to deal with the alleged offence(s).

superego A concept developed by psychoanalyst Sigmund Freud (1856–1939) that describes one of three components of the individual personality or self. The personality consists of the id, the innate impulses and drives; the ego, the unique and individual self; and the superego, the internalized social norms or conscience. Much Freudian analytical theory is based on articulating the development of these aspects of self and their relationship.

superstructure A term from Marxist social analysis central to the materialist concept of history and social development. Marx argues that the fundamental base of any society, which permeates and shapes all its other legal, political, and intellectual characteristics, is the social relations of production: the social and technological way that production is organized and carried out. These relations of production provide the social foundation on which develops the superstructure of legal and political relations and human intellectual ideas and consciousness.

Supreme Court of Canada The Supreme Court of Canada, established in 1875, has been Canada's highest court since 1949 when appeals to Britain's Judicial Committee of the Privy Council were abolished. It is the final appeal court in all areas of law. The court has nine judges, three of whom must be judges or lawyers from the civil-law bar of Quebec. With the adoption of the Charter of Rights and Freedoms in the Constitution Act, 1982, the role of the court was greatly expanded as it now adjudicates the validity of laws in the light of these new constitutional guarantees. It is empowered to strike down laws which conflict with the Charter. For examples of the Supreme Court's judgments see the following judgments: **Burlingham case**; **Calder case**; **Delgamuuk**; **Mack case**; **Malott case**; **Morgentaler, Henry**; **Sharpe decision**; **Sparrow case**; **Therens case**; **Van der Peet decision**; **Wust case**. Reference: Bushnell, Ian. (1992). *The Captive Court: A Study of the Supreme Court of Canada*. Montreal-Kingston: McGill-Queen's University Press.

surplus The excess of production over the human and material resources used up in the process of production. In simple societies, there was often little if any surplus since the production from hunting and gathering was entirely used up in subsistence. With the development of animal herding and settled agriculture, production exceeds immediate subsistence needs and social inequality and class division becomes possible when particular individuals or groups are able to take control of this surplus.

surplus value In Marxist theory, this is the value created by individual labour which is left over, or remains in the product or services produced, after the employer has paid the costs of hiring the worker. It is this value which the worker produces but does not receive that allows the capitalist owner to expand their capital. *See also* **labour theory of value**.

Sutherland, Edwin (1883–1950) Leading scholar in the sociology of deviance and famous for his theory of differential association published in 1934 and elaborated in 1939. The theory relates the propensity for crime among certain groups to problems of social disorganization and the effects that socialization into deviant lifestyles has on behaviour and normative orientations. If an individual associates with others within a deviant subculture, then he or she is more likely to engage in crime.

Sydney tar ponds Sydney Steel Corporation of Sydney, Nova Scotia, began to manufacture steel in the 1900s and for 80 years deposited waste in "tar ponds" in areas surrounding the plant and very close to downtown Sydney. These ponds included a great many hazardous wastes from the manufacturing process. These "tar ponds" are perhaps the greatest environmental hazard in Canada, and while efforts to clean up the mess began in the 1980s, little has been accomplished. People in the area now have high levels of cancer-causing agents in their bodies, and many are demanding that governments move them to safe sites.

symbolic communications All communication with others is symbolic and involves the use of language, sound, bodily gesture, and expression.

symbolic interactionism A sociological perspective that stresses the way societies are created through the interactions of individuals. Unlike both the consensus (structural functionalist) and conflict perspectives, it does not stress the idea of a social system possessing structure and regularity, but focuses on the way that individuals, through their interpretations of social situations and behavioural negotiation with others, give meaning to social interaction. George H. Mead (1863–1931), a founder of symbolic interactionism, saw interaction as creating and recreating the patterns and structures that bring society to life, but more recently there has been a tendency to argue that society has no objective reality aside from individual interaction. This latter view has been criticized for ignoring the role of culture and social structure in giving shape, direction and meaning to social interaction. *See also* **micro-perspective**. Reference: Blumer, Herbert. (1969). *Symbolic Interactionism.* Englewood Cliffs: Prentice-Hall.

syndicalism A political doctrine advocating worker's ownership and control of the productive resources of a society. Syndicalism emerged in France in the late 19th century and was influential in much of Europe. Syndicalism (*syndicat* is a Latin-French term for *union*) was founded on the idea that organizations of workers within any particular industry or service provided the organizational basis for the direction and administration of the means of production on collective and co-operative principles. Syndicalists envisaged a revolutionary, but largely non-violent, overthrow of private property and the workers seizing ownership and control. The resulting power structure would be highly decentralized with each industry and service being owned and directed by the workers involved within it. Syndicalism envisaged social revolution being achieved by the complete unification of workers within each sector of the economy, and thus they opposed the craft-specific structure of traditional labour unions and advocated industrial unionism that would bring all workers within each industry into a one collective organization. *See also* **craft unions**.

Szabo, Denis (1929–) Often called "the founder of Canadian criminology," he was born in Budapest and came to Canada in 1958 after the Soviet invasion of Hungary and was appointed Professor of Criminology at the University of Montreal. In 1969, he became director of the International Centre for Comparative Criminology and, in 1984, became Chairman of the Board of Directors ICCC. His work has been mostly written in French, and although it has received international recognition, including the prestigious Edwin E. Sutherland Award from the American Society of Criminology in 1968, this has limited his influence on Canadian criminology outside Quebec. He is author and co-author of a large number of books and scholarly articles. Works available in translation include: Szabo, Denis. (1977). *Criminology in the World.* Montreal: International Centre for Comparative Criminology, University of Montreal; Szabo, Denis and Alice Parizeau. (1977). The *Canadian Criminal Justice System.* Lexington, Massachusetts: Lexington Books.

T

Taber, Alberta In 1999, a 14-year-old student entered his school in Taber, dressed in a black trench coat and carrying a sawed-off rifle, and opened fire on students. One student was killed and a second seriously injured. It was discovered that the young shooter had been mercilessly bullied in school, and for the public, this made bullying a social problem. Cases like this have many interests for criminologists. The most obvious is why these events happen, but less obvious is the question of why these events almost always happen in a small town, the place the public believes is the safest place to raise children. *See also* **Columbine high school**. Reference: Newman, Katherine. (2004). *Rampage: The Social Roots of School Shootings.* New York: Basic Books.

taboo A Polynesian word, first encountered by a European during the voyages of Captain Cook, meaning literally "marked off." It refers to those special articles or symbols within a culture that are given a distinct status as sacred, metaphysical, or dangerous. Incest, for example, is a taboo most are familiar with.

Tarde, Gabriel (1843–1904) French sociologist and criminologist who rejected racial and biological theories of criminality and developed a theory of imitation. The theory proposed that individuals learn behaviour in interaction with others by a process of imitation. Where an individual associates with others who engage in criminal behaviour and has direct contact with deviance, then his or her own deviance becomes more likely. An individual is also more likely to imitate deviant behaviours that are shown by people with superior situational status. Reference: Tarde, Gabriel. (1903). *The Laws of Imitation.* Trans. New York: Henry, Holt and Co.

target suitablity A target refers to a person or a property which an offender may approach to commit a crime. Some targets are more suitable than others. If a home is unlit, shrubs block a view of the front door, there is no neighbourhood watch sticker, the door has an old-fashioned and ineffective lock, then this may be a target that an offender would view as suitable.

Taylorism The work management principles followed by Frederick Taylor (1856–1915) designed to transfer control of the work process to management and to achieve the greatest rate of productivity from workers through dividing labour and having work performed in a manner detailed by management. *See also* **industrial relations**; **scientific management**. Reference: Taylor, F. (1919). *Shop Management*. New York: Harper.

team policing A form of community policing that focused on establishing a long-term team of police officers to police a neighbourhood and to work with social agencies in the community.

temporary absence A form of conditional release from prison that allows inmates to attend programs in the community or to participate in employment for a specified period of time. Temporary absences may be escorted or unescorted.

terrorism Actions taken with the intent of instilling fear in civilians in order to achieve political ends. The designation of an act as "terrorism" is, however, more difficult than the definition suggests, since one person's terrorist may be another's freedom fighter. After the events of September 11, 2001, anti-terrorism legislation was passed in Canada and in many other countries. *See also* **Anti-Terrorism Act**.

textual analysis An analysis of written or spoken texts as a way to understand social life. While this form of analysis has become more common with post-modern sociology, it is derived largely from French structuralists such as Claude Levi-Strauss, Michel Foucault, and Jean Piaget who studied human thought, myths, story telling, and texts. Foucault, for example, argues that the way we see and understand the world, which is represented in written or spoken texts, is central to understanding a particular time period or society and the way power is organized.

Thatcher, Colin Son of Ross Thatcher, premier of the province of Saskatchewan in 1964. Colin entered politics himself, becoming a Cabinet minister in the government of Grant Devine. On May 17, 1981, JoAnn Thatcher, Colin's estranged wife, was murdered. Colin Thatcher was convicted of paying a man $50 000 to kill his wife and sentenced to life in prison. In 2004, Thatcher was successful in using the "faint hope" clause and obtained the right to apply for parole. His application was, however, subsequently rejected by the parole board. Reference: Siggins, Maggie. (2001). *A Canadian Tragedy: The Story of Colin Thatcher*. Toronto: McClelland and Stewart.

theory All sciences use theory as a tool to explain. It is useful to think of theory as a conceptual model of some aspect of life. We may have a theory of mate selection, or the emergence of capitalist societies, or of criminal behaviour, or of the content of dreams. In each case, the theory consists of a set of concepts and their nominal definition, assertions about the relationships between these concepts, assumptions, and knowledge claims. Carl Jung's theory of the self, for examples, begins by asserting the key concepts—introversion and extroversion, and the relationship between these two components—one is dominant and the other subordinate. It assumes that the dominant characteristic will be displayed in behaviour and the subordinate one in our dreams or unconscious. The content of dreams can be explained by bringing Jung's model to the inquiry. In the classic model of how science is conducted, the scientist begins with a theory, deduces a hypothesis about the real world from the theory, and then engages in the necessary research to determine if the hypothesis is true or false. In this way science is always about theory testing. *See also* **hypothetico-deductive model of science**.

Therens case In *R. v. Therens* (1985), the Supreme Court of Canada broadened the definition of detention when it ruled that if one is requested to provide a breath sample, there is sufficient psychological pressure to imply that a detention has occurred. Reference: *R. v. Therens* (1985), 18 C.C.C. (3rd) 481 (S.C.C.).

third reading *See* **first reading**.

third world This way of categorizing societies has lost much of its meaning with the break-up of the Soviet Union and the decline of communism as an economic system. First-world countries once referred to the developed, capitalist societies, while second-world identified the developed socialist societies. Third-world countries were those large political communities in the initial stages of development, while fourth-world societies are those that are traditional communities marginalized from economic development and political power. The concept of "fourth world" has been applied to the aboriginal communities of North America.

thug A corruption of an Hindi word (*thagi*) referring to a cult of assassin priests who murdered unwary travellers on Indian roads. The British had been concerned about three moral offences in India, which they attempted to eradicate: *sati*, female infanticide, and *thagi*. *Thagi* was probably a product of overactive imaginations on the part of the British, although there were probably ordinary highway robberies. Nevertheless, a few thousand Indians were arrested for this offence, and about 1400 were executed or transported in the early 19th century. The term now refers to a violent criminal or more generally to a bully.

ticket of leave The name given to parole from its introduction in 1899 until 1958 when it was replaced with the Parole Act.

token economy A behaviour therapy procedure based on operant learning principles; individuals are rewarded (reinforced) for positive or appropriate behaviour and are disciplined (punished) for negative or inappropriate behaviour.

Topping, C.W. Professor of sociology at the University of British Columbia from 1929 to 1953. Before he retired, Topping was able to negotiate funding from the provincial government to establish an undergraduate and a graduate program in criminology at the university, the first such program in Canada. This program was clearly tied to the belief that the new philosophy of rehabilitation was going to require an educated and professional workforce. Malcolm Matheson became the first person to receive a graduate degree from the program (1958) and rose to become the Deputy Director of Corrections for the Province.

tort An area of law concerned with intentional violations of the private rights of individuals or neglect of legally recognized duties of care to others. In these cases, the public interest is not directly harmed. This is an aspect of civil law and is usually contrasted with criminal law (where the public or society is considered to be the injured party), although sociologists note that the distinction between the two is somewhat arbitrary and shifting.

torture The inflicting of severe pain on a person as punishment or as a means of interrogation or intimidation. Cesare Beccaria was responsible for eliminating torture from the criminal justice system, but it is still widespread around the world as a means of intimidation or interrogation and used by secret police or soldiers. Courts, however, have had a great deal of trouble in deciding just how much pain has to be imposed for torture to be established. Reference: Conroy, John. (2000). *Unspeakable Acts, Ordinary People: The Dynamics of Torture*. New York: Alfred Knopf.

Tory A member of the Tory political party. A term originating in 17th century Britain and referring to that party, supported largely by aristocratic interests, which defended royal prerogatives and divine inheritance of the throne and was resistant to democratic ideals and the growing political and economic power of the middle class. In modern Canada, the term is used to refer to the Conservative Party. *See also* **conservatism**.

total institution *See* **institution, total**.

trade unions, state coercion and Several historical examples can be found of the state using the police as instruments of class control. Two important examples of conflict are provided here. (1) A landmark strike of General Motors workers in Oshawa, Ontario, March 2, 1937, marks the birth of industrial unionism in Canada. American union members, under the leadership of John Lewis, had broken away from the American Federation of Labor over its refusal to consider organizing unions along industrial lines rather than around crafts or trades. As mass production grew (the famous "line" of the automobile plants) the idea of craft unions made little sense to workers. The breakaway unions created the CIO, the Committee for Industrial Organization, in 1935, and made tentative visits into Canada. This new union came to represent the 4000 Oshawa workers. The union was accused of being a front for communism and its victory was declared to be a threat to the productivity of the province. The Liberal premier of the province became directly involved in fighting against the union and in negotiations. Government links to big business were more than apparent. The victory of the union was a symbolic victory for the CIO and began the creation of unions as we know them today. The Liberals won the next election on an anti-labour campaign, but their shift to the right created a space for the newly emerging CCF party and, more importantly, pushed the working class away from the Liberals. This legacy was to last for much of the remainder of the century. (2) On September 12, 1945, workers at the Ford plant in Windsor went on strike, perhaps the most important event in Canadian working class history. Among other demands, the workers wanted the plant to become a union shop and for there to be automatic union dues check off by the employer. The strike came to a less than spectacular end, but the union did agree to have an arbitrator examine their issues. Ivan Rand was selected for this, and his report indicates that he was open to the evolution of worker rights. His final recommendations turned down the union shop proposal, but did offer a dues check off procedure. This procedure (now called the Rand formula) is still present in most unionized workplaces. The agreement means that workers do not have to be members of the union to work in a shop (they can withdraw from the union if they wish); however, they must pay union dues if they are to benefit from the negotiations carried out by the union. The CCF had taken an unpopular position during this strike (requesting that the government take over the running of the plant) and this damaged their links to the labour movement. This fracture was not healed until the creation of the NDP in July 1961. *See also* **Winnipeg general strike; Regina riots**.

tranquillizers Drugs with the capacity to reduce emotional feelings and levels of anxiety.

transnational corporations Corporations whose sales and production are carried out in many different nations. As a result of their multinational reach, these corporations are often thought to be beyond the political control of any individual nation state.

transportation This sentence was introduced in England in 1615 with transportation to the West Indies and the American colonies chiefly for capital offences and as a substitute for the death penalty. In 1718, terms of transportation were established at 14 years for capital offences and 7 years for a range of non-capital offences. After the American revolution of 1776, transportation to that destination ceased, and in 1787, the new destination of Australia was established. The first voyage left England in May 1787 with 717 prisoners of whom 48 died during the voyage. Their destination was Sydney Cove and their arrival on January 28, 1788 marked the foundation of the colony of New South Wales. A second contingent left in 1789 and 278 prisoners died during this voyage. Transportation virtually ended in 1853, although there were some isolated cases until 1868. In all, from 1787 to 1867 a total of 158 702 prisoners from England and Ireland and 1321 from other parts of the empire were transported to Australia.

transsexual An individual who has physically or psychologically crossed the boundary between the sexes and thus becomes the other sex. These people may or may not engage in cross-dressing. While movement may be in either direction, more transsexuals are men who have become women. Western cultures have been criticized frequently for being extremely dualistic in gender or sexual identities, making little room, or no room, for a third or fourth gender. Hinduism by contrast has an elaborate repertoire of sexual transformations, bisexuality, and sexual expression. The term *transgender* is now preferred since it clearly suggests that sexual categories are themselves social constructions.

treaties An agreement or contract between two or more sovereign nations creating obligations and responsibilities for both parties. The British and French colonizers of what is now called Canada and the Canadian government itself have negotiated many treaties with the native nations who occupied the land. These treaties are now protected by the Canadian Constitution. *See also* **numbered treaties**.

treaty Indian A native person or descendant of a native person who signed a treaty. The registration list under the Indian Act was drawn up to include those band members who signed treaties, so all treaty Indians are also status Indians (unless they have lost their status). Treaties were signed with bands in parts of British Columbia, Ontario, and the Northeast Territories, and most of Alberta, Saskatchewan, and Manitoba. *See also* **numbered treaties; status Indian**.

triads These Chinese groups came into existence in the 17th century as resistance fighters against the Manchu invaders. They eventually developed into crime groups and now have a foothold in many parts of the world. Reference: Durbo, James. (1993). *Dragons of Crime: Asian Mobs in Canada.* Toronto: McClelland and Stewart.

trial by jury A method of determining guilt or innocence developed after 1215. The English had a jury in place, consisting of 12 knights, for adjudicating real estate taxes. This method was transferred to the criminal law, and after some time they became the decider of facts.

trial by ordeal The way by which guilt and innocence was determined prior to the practice being prohibited by the Fourth Lateran Council of the Catholic Church in 1215. The method involved subjecting the accused to some ordeal (for example, holding a very hot metal rod). If God intervened and saved the accused, he or she was deemed innocent. However, if he or she failed the ordeal (the hand was burned), he or she was deemed guilty.

tribalism The use of this term must be understood against the assumption that citizens of the modern world would develop significant identification only with large groupings which included a plurality of social categories. For example, the identity of "Canadian" would include many ethnic groups, sexual preferences, social interests, and religious groupings. Tribalism is used to describe those situations where broad social identification has broken down so that people identify themselves exclusively with a narrower category. For example, people may organize their lives around ethnic identification or sexual preference or religious belief. This retribalization of the society is thought to lead to fragmentation and divisiveness as people identify with an in-group, making a shared sense of citizenship among larger groupings more and more fragile. *See also* **identity politics**.

Truscott, Steven Steven Truscott, 14 years old, was convicted in adult court in 1959 of the murder of 12-year-old Lynn Harper. Controversy over the quality of the evidence and the legal process dogged the case for many years. Canadian law allowed for the execution of Truscott, but his sentence was commuted by Minister of Justice Davey Fulton. By the end of the century, evidence is revealed that there was a much more likely suspect, but by this time, Truscott is living in the community, and not yet prepared to push for wrongful conviction. Reference: Sher, Julian. (2001). *Until You Are Dead: Steven Truscott's Long Ride into History.* Toronto: Alfred Knopf.

truth in sentencing One demand of a growing body of criticism about the criminal justice system. It is believed that when a judge delivers a sentence that this should be the sentence the offender actually receives. The sentence must not be reduced by the parole board or by "good time" policies. This philosophy is most strongly stated when it is claimed that "life should mean life."

type 1 error In inferential reasoning or statistics, rejecting a hypothesis when it is true and should be accepted. The probability of making such a mistake is indicated by the level of significance used, so the probability of this error can be controlled by altering the level of significance. Types 1 and 2 errors are linked, however, so that reducing one increases the other. Researcher will try to achieve some balance between the two types or alter the balance to meet the needs of a specific situation.

type 2 error In inferential reasoning or statistics, accepting a hypothesis when it is false and should be rejected. Also known as a *false positive.*

typification Alfred Schutz (1899–1959), a phenomenologist, suggests that in all of our encounters with others, with the exception of "we-relationships" (the most intimate of relationships), we experience and understand the other in terms of ideal types. We form a construct of a typical way of acting and assume typical underlying motivations or personality. For example, we make prior assumptions about the personalities and behaviour of a doctor, priest, or judge. Ethnomethodologists have studied the use of this process of typification as a tool for understanding how people such as coroners, prosecutors, police officers, and others achieve a sense of concreteness and predictability in their work. Coroners, for example, may operate with a sense of a typical suicide, prosecutors with a sense of a "normal" crime of child abuse, police officers with a sense of the "normal" or typical resident of a particular neighbourhood. *See also* **ideal type**. Reference: Emerson, R.M. (1969). *Judging Delinquents: Context and Social Process in Juvenile Court.* Chicago: Aldine.

typology A set of two or more ideal types used for categorizing behaviours, events, societies, groups, etc. For example, Émile Durkheim (1858–1917) developed four types of suicide: anomic, egoistic, altruistic, and fatalistic. Ferdinand Tonnies (1855–1936) identified two types of society: *gemeinschaft* and *gesellschaft. See also* **ideal type**.

U

ultra vires From the Latin, meaning to act beyond the scope of powers. Government powers in Canada are distributed between the federal and provincial governments; each government then must act within its own power. If provinces pass criminal law, for example, this would be ruled *ultra vires* since criminal law is an exclusive federal power.

underclass A term similar in use to Marx's concept of lumpenproletariat. A group that is not in a regular economic or social relationship with the rest of the community. Refers to the chronically unemployed, those who live on the proceeds of petty crime, panhandlers, or bag ladies. American sociologists use this term since a large underclass is thought to pose a threat to the stability of society, because they are not adequately connected to the institutional and cultural regulation that is experienced by most social members.

underground economy *See* **informal economy**.

Uniform Crime Reporting Since 1961, Canada has had a Uniform Crime Reporting System developed by Statistics Canada and the Canadian Association of Chiefs of Police. This system is designed to provide a measure of reliability for crime statistics through providing police agencies with a standardized set of procedures for collecting and reporting crime information.

United Empire Loyalists Those residents of the United States who remained loyal to the British Crown during the American War of Independence and fled to Canada. Approximately 40 000 émigrés arrived in Canada; most settled in Nova Scotia, although some 7000 relocated in Quebec to provide the first substantial British population in the province. The attitudes and political philosophy of these new settlers are seen as significant for understanding the subsequent development of Canada. *See also* **Constitutional Act, 1791**. Reference: Stewart, Walter. (1985). *True Blue: The Loyalist Legend.* Don Mills: Collins Pub.

United Nations *See* **Universal Declaration of Human Rights**.

units of analysis Most social research looks for patterns when comparing "things" one to another. The things that researchers are comparing or examining are referred to as the units of analysis, or the units to be analyzed. The most frequent unit of analysis is the individual, suggesting that researchers look for patterns among a collection (perhaps a sample) of individuals. Research can also be conducted in which a pattern is sought among a collection of groups; the group would be the unit of analysis. For example, like Durkheim, one might try to determine what social factors are linked to the variation in suicide rates among nations or regions. One can also look for patterns among things like newspaper stories, advertisements, a category of social interaction, social events, or speech utterances. In this case, the unit of analysis would be what Earl Babbie has called *social artifacts.*

Universal Declaration of Human Rights Following World War II and the horrific experiences of that struggle, many nations set to creating the United Nations. The original Charter of the United Nations contained a general statement on human rights. The need for a more detailed and substantial statement on human rights was seen and a commission was established to create such a document. This commission wrote the Universal Declaration on Human Rights (drafted largely by a Canadian John Peters Humphrey), which was adopted by the General Assembly of the United Nation on December 10, 1948. This document was described as humanity's response to the death camps of the Nazis, the countless refugees, and the tortured prisoners-of-war. In 1966, the United Nations adopted two further documents on human rights: the Covenant on Civil and Political Rights and the Covenant on Economic, Social and Cultural Rights. These covenants contain many of the rights asserted in the Universal Declaration, but they differ in that they are legally binding on those nations signing the covenants. The first of these covenants declares that everyone has the right to life; freedom of thought; equal treatment in the courts; freedom of assembly; and no one shall be subject to torture, slavery, or forced labour. The second declares that everyone has the right to the enjoyment of just and favourable work conditions; to form trade unions; an adequate standard of living; education; and to take part in cultural life; and enjoy the progress of science. In 1989, a third covenant was added, the Convention of the Rights of the Child. These four documents together comprise what is called the International Bill of Rights.

universality A philosophy concerning the provision of the benefits of the welfare state which declares that all citizens have access regardless of their need. For example, all citizens receive the same access to health care in Canada, regardless of their income. The underlying principle is that less powerful citizens can be more easily deprived of benefits, or benefits can be more easily reduced, if they are not received by most people in the population. In recent years, the principle of universality has been seriously eroded in Canada. The baby bonus, once given to mothers of all children, has been replaced with a child tax credit, which gives income to mothers on the basis of their household income. *See also* **means test**.

University of British Columbia, criminology at *See* **Topping, C.W.**

University of Toronto, criminology at *See* **Centre of Criminology.**

Upper Canada Established upon the division of the province of Quebec in 1791 as a result of the Constitutional Act, this territory was to eventually become the province of Ontario. British colonization of this territory was encouraged. *See also* **Lower Canada**; **Constitutional Act, 1791**.

urbanism Similar to the notion of modernity, this term refers to the form of social organization and values typically found in large urban settings. The central values are those of individualism and impersonality and the major characteristics of social organization are a developed division of labour, high rates of geographic and social mobility, and predominance of impersonality in social interactions despite the acute social interdependence. *See also* **mass society**.

utilitarianism (1) The theory that individuals are best able to define their needs, desires, and goals, and where they have freedom to make choices the result will be the greatest possible satisfaction for the greatest number. This is an individualistic perspective because it claims that individuals making free choices necessarily leads to a society where satisfaction and happiness are maximized. The theory overlooks the potential for one individual's choice to constrain or remove the choices of others. (2) As a justification for punishment utilitarianism asserts the utility of the act of punishment or the punishment of a particular offender. The utility of punishment refers to any future benefit for the society (or the greatest number), which can be derived from the act. Justifications in terms of deterrence (individual or general), rehabilitation, incapacitation, and crime prevention are all aspects of utilitarianism. Utilitarian justifications are contrasted with retribution. *See also* **retribution**.

uxoricide The killing of one's wife.

V

vagrancy (1) William Chambliss examined the historical origins of the first vagrancy law in 1349, a response to land owners who were having difficulty finding workers because of the black death and the fact that many owners had sold serfs their freedom in order to raise funds for military campaigns. Men were not permitted to refuse work and churches not permitted to give support to those refusing work. This example is frequently used in the sociology of law to show how rule makers respond to the needs of the economically powerful. (2) Canada had vagrancy rules in the Criminal Code. Vagrancy "C" referred to "being a common prostitute or nightwalker found in a public place who does not, when requested, give a good account of herself." The Royal Commission on the Status of Women (1970) objected to this law, claiming it discriminated against women. This section was replaced with a soliciting law in 1972. Reference: Chambliss, William. (1964). "A Sociological Analysis of the Law of Vagrancy." *Social Problems* 12: 67–77.

validity One of two criteria (the other being reliability) by which researchers judge their results or measurement tools. A valid result is one that accurately measures what it claims to be measuring. Using shoe size as a measurement of intelligence is not a valid measure of intelligence. It lacks face validity since it is not obvious that it is measuring what it claims to measure. One test of validity might be the extent to which your measurements allow you to make predictions about future behaviour. If your measurement of intelligence does not predict how people perform on exams, then perhaps it is not a valid measurement of intelligence. *See also* **external validity**; **internal validity**; **reliability**.

values Relatively general cultural prescriptions of what is right, moral, and desirable. Values provide the broad foundations for specific normative regulation of social interaction. *See also* **norm**.

Van der Peet decision A 1996 decision by the Supreme Court of Canada clarifying aboriginal rights. The case came to the court because a lower court had convicted Van der Peet, of the Stolo peoples of British Columbia, of violating a section of the B.C. Fishery Regulations for selling fish caught under a food fish licence. Van der Peet was arguing that aboriginal rights (section 35 of the Charter of Rights and Freedoms) gave native people the right to sell their fish food, since this was an aspect of traditional life. The Supreme Court did not overturn the Van der Peet conviction, but did clarify the test that must be met to establish aboriginal rights. Briefly, the aboriginal defendant must demonstrate that the practice in question was an aspect of native life prior to European contact. Reference: *R. v. Van der Peet* [1996] 2 S.C.R. 507.

vandalism Willful and ignorant destruction of property or of works of art or architecture. It originates with the name given by early Roman writers to loose groupings of Teutonic tribes who came into early conflict with the Roman army and the Roman Empire. After military defeat by other warring tribes, they retreated to Spain in 409 and subsequently sailed to Africa where in 439 they attacked and took control of the great city of Carthage. In 455, the Vandals then sailed for the coast of Italy and conquered the City of Rome where they systematically gathered and carried off all movable wealth, but it is not clear that there was the mindless destruction that they later became labelled with. In about 536, after a series of military defeats, the Vandals disappeared as a distinct people.

variables A term central to quantitative sociology and to macro-structural sociology. The term refers to that which varies, rather than being constant. In particular, its reference is to structural features that vary (things like gender, age, race, social class) and have an influence on behaviour or attitudinal variables (discrimination or attitudes about abortion). Researchers work out ways to measure these variables (often by asking questions) and determine their importance in understanding human behaviour. Those variables thought to be causal variables are called independent variables and those thought to be effects are called dependent variables. A variable has two or more values; the variable of sex, for example, has the values of female and male. *See also* **dependent variable**; **independent variable**.

venire The group of citizens called for jury duty from which an actual jury is selected.

verstehen Associated with the writing of Max Weber (1864–1920), *verstehen* is now seen as a concept and a method central to a rejection of positivistic social science (although Weber appeared to think that the two could be united). *Verstehen* refers to understanding the meaning of action from the actor's point of view. It is entering into the shoes of the other, and adopting this research stance requires treating the actor as a subject, rather than an object of your observations. It also implies that unlike objects in the natural world human actors are not simply the product of the pulls and pushes of external forces. Individuals are seen to create the world by organizing their own understanding of it and giving it meaning. To do research on actors without taking into account the meanings they attribute to their actions or environment is to treat them like objects. *See also* **ethnographic research**; **positivism**.

vertical mosaic A term introduced by John Porter (1921–79) to describe Canadian society. The term *mosaic* is used to capture the multiethnic and multiracial character of the society and the term *vertical* implies that these ethnic and racial groups are arranged into a hierarchy. A similar term would be ethnic stratification. Reference: Porter, John. (1965). *The Vertical Mosaic.* Toronto: University of Toronto Press.

vice squad A division within many police departments dealing with "moral" offences such as gambling, prostitution, drugs. It is within this division that many police constables find themselves giving in to corruption.

victim impact statement Introduced in 1988 under Section 735 of the Criminal Code of Canada, victims were given the right to record a statement detailing the injuries suffered, loses incurred, and the overall emotional effect of their victimization. This was to be introduced to the court after the conviction of the offender and prior to sentencing. A 1996 Statute directed that victim impact statements be considered in sentencing.

victimization survey A survey of a random sample of the population in which people are asked to recall and describe their own experience of being a victim of crime. These surveys are a valuable tool for criminologists as they provide a measure of unreported crime (sometimes called the *dark figure of crime*). The first such Canadian survey was conducted in 1981. A survey on victimization has been included in the General Social Survey since 1988. Reference: Skogan, W. (2000). "Criminal Victimization in Canada, 1999." *Juristat* 20(10).

victimless crime The conventional conception of crime implies that there is a victim of the criminal behaviour who experiences harm. There are, however, criminal behaviours like illegal gambling, drug use, and selling sex, where the victim does not experience harm and is indeed a willing participant. Many argue that crimes of this nature are victimless and should not be regulated by criminal law.

vigilante A person or group of persons who engage in law enforcement and the dispensation of justice without authority, often in the face of what they perceive to be inadequate law enforcement or administration of justice.

violent predators This group of offenders is particularly found among sexual offenders, a group who appear to be hunters or predators and violently sexually assault citizens. This group tends to be thought of as *psychopaths*, but not all psychopaths are violent offenders.

voir dire From the French, "to say the truth." Also referred to as a trial within a trial. Can refer to the process by which potential jury members are questioned by the prosecution and the defence. Can also refer to the examination of the admissibility of evidence during a trial, in the absence of the jury.

Vold, George (1896–1967) Professor of sociology at the University of Minnesota and later at Stanford Law School and contributor to the development of conflict perspectives within criminology. Instead of viewing crime as an individual's violation of law, Vold seeks to locate it in the dynamics of competing group interests. In social life, individuals inevitably affiliate with groups that will promote their needs, interests, and desires, and these diverse groups engage in interaction and competition with each other over control of power, economic resources and social status. The groups that are most successful in mobilizing the necessary support and authority are able to pass laws that constrain the opportunities and limit the goals of other groups, thus exerting pressure on them to violate the law. His most important book was *Theoretical Criminology* originally written in 1958. Reference: Vold, George, Snipes, Jeffrey B., and J. Thomas Bernard. (2002). *Theoretical Criminology.* New York: Oxford University Press.

Volstead Act Passed by the United States Congress on October 28, 1919, this legislation prohibited the manufacture and sale of alcohol in the United States. Since a ready market existed for this prohibited good, organized crime in America gained a ready foothold. Many Canadians also became rich during the subsequent prohibition era, making fortunes from illegal cross-border traffic in liquor; however, rather than pursuing organized crime, they became successful businessmen. Canadians were not allowed to ship liquor to the US legally, but they could ship to Cuba and other countries from which the liquor could be smuggled into the US. Not surprisingly, American boats were found to make four or five trips to Cuba in one day.

W

Waco siege On April 19, 1993, after a 51-day siege of the home of the Branch Dravidian religious group in Waco, Texas, the FBI begin to spray gas into the compound in the hope of driving the last remaining members of the "cult" from the building. Before long the buildings are on fire, and in the end 74 people are dead. The siege began when the Bureau of Alcohol, Tobacco and Firearms tried to execute warrants on David Koresh, the leader of the Branch Dravidians, and to search the compound. Four agents were killed in gunfire as well as six Branch Dravidians. This tragedy is now steeped in mystery and charges of government murder and cover-up.

Wade v. Roe *See* **abortion**.

waffle group Established within the New Democratic Party in 1969, this group led by Mel Watkins and James Laxer attempted to move the NDP further to the left by espousing clearly socialist and nationalist ideals. The leadership of the party believed that these ideas were unappealing to the public and would challenge the political legitimacy and electability of the NDP. The group was eventually expelled from the party. *See* **Co-operative Commonwealth Federation**.

waiver Usually applied to any rights an accused may have, suggesting that the accused can give up or put aside any specific right. The accused may, for example, waive the right to contact a lawyer.

Walnut Street Jail This jail located in Philadelphia was transformed in 1790 to a form of penitentiary. Following the teachings of William Penn and in particular his forbiddance of corporal punishment, the Quakers introduced the idea of single cells and silence along with the notion that prisoners could be rehabilitated by struggling with God through silence and isolation. Walnut Street Jail was small and soon became overcrowded, ending the experiment. However, the experiment provided for a new model of penitentiary, which became known as the Pennsylvania system, and given concrete representation in the massive Eastern Penitentiary built in 1829.

war crimes During World War II, Allied nations were determined to prosecute German war criminals and defined "war crimes" as plotting aggressive warfare and committing atrocities against any civilian population. This definition was used in the trials of war criminals, which began in 1945. In recent years, there have been suggestions that Canada (for its involvement in the fire bombing of German civilians) and the United States (for the dropping of atomic bombs on largely civilian-inhabited cities) as well as other nations were also guilty of committing atrocities against civilians, but these nations were never brought to trial. In the 1990s, the United Nations again initiated tribunals to prosecute war criminals in the former Yugoslavia and in Rwanda. It is estimated that there are 4000 war criminals living in Canada, many of them having entered from Nazi Germany. In 1985, Canada established a commission (under Mr. Justice Deschenes) to examine the problems of war criminals in Canada. Reference: Mr. Justice Deshenes. (1986). *Commission of Inquiry on War Criminals.* Ottawa: Minister of Supply and Services; Littman, Sol. (1988). *The Rauca Case: War Criminals on Trial.* Toronto: Paper Jacks.

War Measures Act A 1914 statute giving emergency powers to Cabinet, allowing it to govern by decree (without the usual approvals of democratic institutions) in times of war, invasion, or real or apprehended insurrection. It was this power the federal government invoked in 1970 to deal with the FLQ crisis, which the government called a state of "apprehended insurrection." The Act had been used in early years to intern members of the communist party, Japanese-Canadians, Jehovah's Witnesses and Italian-Canadians. In 1988, this statute was replaced with the Emergency Act.

warrant A writ (a type of permit) is issued by a officer of the court, directing a law enforcement officer to perform certain actions and thus given protection from legal proceedings if conducted properly. For example, a warrant is needed to search a house and to tape telephone conversations.

warrant of the Governor General When a person is found to be unfit to stand trial for reasons of insanity, the person may be confined indefinitely under this warrant (or certificate) until Cabinet decides otherwise.

Warren, Roger On September 18, 1992, nine men, hired as replacement workers during a strike-lockout in the "Giant" gold mine in Yellowknife, were travelling to their work site many stories below ground when a bomb exploded under their transportation, killing everyone. After much investigation, Roger Warren, a locked-out worker at the mine, was charged and later convicted. Although he confessed and provided the police with evidence that perhaps only the guilty person would know, Warren later claimed his confession was untrue and that he was innocent of the crime.

watch style of policing A less professional style of policing that focuses on resolving situations informally if possible. This leads to greater discretion among constables and less reporting. Communities with this style of policing have a lower official crime rate as a result.

Watergate affair When the offices of the Democratic Party of the United States were burgled (the offices were in the Watergate apartment complex), public confidence in elected officials took a decidedly negative turn. The investigation into this break-and-enter of June 17, 1972, revealed the involvement of White House staff and the knowledge of President Nixon. It was also learned that the president had kept secret tapes of White House conversations containing evidence of corrupt financial affairs and efforts to evade the truth about illegal (and thus secret) bombings of Cambodia. President Nixon was forced to resign from office under threat of impeachment.

welfare state A term that became widely used in the 1940s to refer to the development of state-initiated programs that provide citizens with minimum income, old age pensions, unemployment, health insurance, and universal access to a range of social services. In Canada, the development of the welfare state gained momentum after 1940 when Unemployment Insurance was introduced. In the next few years, programs to fund hospitals, old age pensions, old age security, and unemployment relief were established. The development of the welfare state represents a softening of classical liberalism that defined the role of the state very narrowly. It is not surprising that as classical liberalism returns (often called *neo-conservatism*) there is an attack on the welfare state. *See also* **liberalism**.

Westray mine disaster On May 9, 1992, the Westray mine in Pictou County, Nova Scotia exploded, killing 26 miners. The federal government was involved in financing the mine in spite of cautions about safety contained in engineering reports. Once in operation, workers feared for their safety and provincial safety inspectors identified numerous safety infractions that were never corrected. Although an inquiry was held and regulatory and criminal charges laid against the owner and four managers, little was accomplished. This event is frequently used by criminologists to illustrate the problems of prosecuting corporations in criminal court. Reference: Comish, Shaun. (1993). *The Westray Tragedy: A Miner's Story*.

Whig A member of the Whig political party. A term originating in the 17th century in Britain and referring to that party, supported largely by the new commercial interests, which defended the power of Parliament against royal prerogatives and thus encouraged the democratic revolution in Britain. The term was transplanted to the American colonies and referred to the supporters of independence from Britain. An American Whig political party was formed and it remained a major party until the 1850s, when it was succeeded by the Republican party. The term has had little currency in Canada, although the Whig ideal of popular parliamentary government was a strong force in 19th century Canadian politics. *See* **liberalism**.

white collar Originally used as a contrast to blue-collar workers and captured the distinction between non-manual and manual labour or workers. With the rise of the service economy and the shrinkage of manual labour, the term has become less useful.

white-collar crime As originally used by Edwin Sutherland (1883–1950) in 1945, referred to the illegal activities of businesses and corporations committed to furthering the goals of the business. These acts were not regulated by criminal law, but by regulatory laws of various kinds. These acts included false advertising, anti-trust violations, environmental pollution, or dumping product on the market below cost. Criminologists now call this corporate crime or organizational crime and reserve the term white-collar crime for those illegal acts committed by people in positions of trust (usually in white-collar jobs) for personal gain. For example, making personal long-distance calls on an employer's account. Reference: Sutherland, Edwin. (1983). *White-Collar Crime: The Uncut Version*. New Haven: Yale University Press.

white slavery A term from the late 19th century to depict and perhaps explain prostitution. It was believed that sex-trade workers were forced into prostitution by men. While this was true in a small number of cases, most young women entered into prostitution at this time because of their economic marginalization, resulting from changes to the factory system. The term is still used to refer to sex-trade workers in developing nations.

widening the net A sociological thesis claiming that as alternative methods of punishment are introduced to the criminal justice system, they simply expand the numbers of people brought under the control of the state. This is thought to happen because the new measure does not usually replace an old measure, but provides a means for bringing people previously ignored into the criminal justice system.

wild boy of Aveyron *See* **feral child**.

Wilson, Bertha First woman appointed to the Supreme Court of Canada. She served from 1982 to 1991.

Winnipeg general strike This strike lasted from May 15 to June 25, 1919, and resulted from post-war inflation, the influence of the new and revolutionary industrial unionism, and the example of the successful Russia revolution of 1917. When negotiations broke down with a wide range of Winnipeg employers over rights to collective bargaining, better wages, and improved working hours on May 15, almost 30 000 workers struck within hours. Workers were joined by a wide range of public service employees, including the police, municipal employees, firefighters, postal workers, and utility workers. Employers responded with the organization of a "Committee of 1000" and were assisted by the federal government, which threatened to fire all federal employees who participated, arrested strike leaders, and changed the immigration acts to allow for deportation of strike leaders. On June 21, Royal North-West Mounted Police charged a strikers demonstration, killing one demonstrator and injuring at least 30 more. Federal troops then occupied the city, and on June 25, the strikers had to come to terms with defeat and called the strike off. Reference: Bercuson, David. (1990). *Confrontation at Winnipeg*. Montreal-Kingston: McGill-Queen's University Press.

wire tap evidence The Supreme Court of Canada has ruled that the police cannot use electronic surveillance at their sole discretion. Rather, a balance must be achieved between the rights of the individual and the needs of the state to enforce the law. In maintaining this balance, the police must seek judicial authorization for a wire tap, and they must have reasonable grounds for believing that such an invasion of privacy will yield evidence of an offence.

Wolfenden report A 1959 British report of the Departmental Committee on Homosexual Offenses and Prostitution (chaired by Sir John Wolfenden). Its major recommendation was that sexual activity between consenting adults should no longer be a criminal offence. This report had influence in many western nations, and in 1969, after Pierre Trudeau became minister of justice, Canada repealed sections of the Criminal Code that had made homosexual activity a criminal offence.

Wolfgang, Marvin, E. (1924–98) Professor of criminology at the University of Pennsylvania and associated with subculture of violence theory. This theory sought to explain the high rate of violent crime among American Blacks as the product of a uniquely violent subculture in which widely diffused violent values supported and encouraged violent behaviour and gave status to those who engaged in it. This theory has had many critics and it has defied empirical validation. Reference: Wolfgang, Marvin E., and F. Ferracuti. (1967). *The Subculture of Violence: Towards an Integrated Theory in Criminology*. London: Tavistock Publications.

Women's Legal Education and Action Fund (LEAF) Formed in April 1985 to pursue litigation under the equal rights provisions of the Charter of Rights and Freedoms in order to change aspects of Canadian society and to improve women's position in society.

women's liberation thesis The theory, within criminology, that women's involvement in crime will come to more closely resemble men's as gendered differences between women and men are diminished by women's greater social participation and equality. Although sounding plausible, there is little empirical evidence to support this theory. Reference: Adler, Freda. (1975). *Sisters in Crime*. New York: McGraw Hill.

women's movement A broad term for a range of social and political organizations and activities like research, writing, and criticism that have the main goal of advancing the status of women in society and overcoming cultural marginalization of women's perspectives and experience in society.

working class This term has been found more frequently in Britain, and while having an imprecise meaning, generally includes skilled and unskilled manual workers (perhaps synonymous with blue-collar workers) and sometimes lower levels of white-collar workers. Is similar in meaning to lower class, unless it is used in a more Marxian sense to refer to those who work for a living; i.e., the proletariat.

world systems theory Derived from the work of Karl Marx and made into a developed set of ideas by Immanuel Wallerstein. He shows that capitalism is not just an economic system bounded by national borders highlighting class inequality. Rather, capitalism must also be seen as involving relationships among nations and these relationships too are based on inequality. Those nations that developed capitalistic economies early then went on to dominate other nations through colonization or simply through linking the economies of the nations in ways that favoured the more dominant nation and placed the others into a condition of dependency on the dominant nation. This state of dependency tended to hamper the development of the other economies. *See also* **dependent development**; **metropolis-hinterland theory**. Reference: Wallerstein, Immanuel. (1974). *The Modern World System*. New York: Academic Press [1980].

World Trade Center, New York The centre of the financial district of New York, occupying approximately 10 square blocks and providing employment for 50 000 workers, the World Trade Center was totally destroyed on September 11, 2001, when terrorists crashed two hijacked passenger airplanes into the structure. During the same attack on America, a hijacked airplane was crashed into the Pentagon, and a fourth plane crashed into a field, presumably it was destined for the White House. Approximately 3500 people were killed in the two attacks, and the world thrown into uncertainty. The World Trade Center had also been the site of a terrorist attack in 1993 when a powerful car bomb exploded in a delivery area. *See also* **bin Laden, Osama**. Reference: National Commission on Terrorist Attacks Upon the United States. (2004). *The 9/11 Commission Report*. Washington: Government Printing Office.

writ of certiorari An order to a superior court (e.g., an appeal court) that the record of a lower court be brought forward for review.

writ of habeas corpus A legal procedure requiring judicial determination of the legality of holding a person in custody.

Wust case *See* **remand**.

X

xenophobia An individual's irrational and obsessive hatred of people perceived as different and foreign. Related to the concepts of racism and ethnocentrism. All of these can be overcome by the study of the social sciences and coming to appreciate the ideas of culture and social structure as tools for understanding ourselves and others.

XYY A biological theory of criminal behaviour based on the study of chromosomes. In 1965, Patricia Jacobs reported that men in prison were more likely to have an extra Y chromosome (XYY) than men outside of prison (XY). Dubbed "supermales," these offenders were thought to be taller and more aggressive than the average male. This theory had a short life, however, and more recently attention has shifted to the study of genes.

Y

Young Offenders Act (YOA) Passed in 1984 to replace the Juvenile Delinquents Act. The YOA took years of negotiation to work its way through the legislative process and produced a controversial act designed to deal with the criminal behaviour of those aged 10 through 17. Over the years, the YOA was made more punitive and the rights of the community given priority over the best interests of the child. In addition, the Act was criticized for a number of reasons, among them the fact that it had a very unclear philosophy, produced one of the highest incarceration rates in the western world, resulted in wide sentencing disparities, there was little reintegration of inmates back to the community, and it had little recognition of victim's rights. In 2003, the YOA was replaced by the Youth Criminal Justice Act (passed in May 2001 and implemented in 2003). *See also* **Youth Criminal Justice Act**; **Juvenile Delinquents Act**. Reference: (July 1994). "The Young Offenders Act: Ten Years After Implementation." *Canadian Journal of Criminology* (special issue) 36(3).

Youth Criminal Justice Act Implemented in April 2003 to replace the Young Offenders Act. This relatively new Act has a very clear statement of philosophy and establishes clear reasons for the use of incarceration. In addition, the Act allows for both police cautions and Crown cautions (both of which terminate prosecution) and allows for extra-judicial measures (forms of diversion), allows the youth court to impose adult sentences, thus eliminating the process of transferring a youth to adult court. Further, it imposes a period of mandatory supervision on offenders when released from custody amounting to one-half of the period of custody, allows for the publishing of young offender's names if given an adult sentence, and introduces a role for victims.

Z

zero tolerance A philosophical approach to violence and drug use that gained popularity in schools and other institutions during the 1990s. As the name implies, institutions were to adopt a policy of no tolerance for specified behaviour. This would suggest, for example, that those engaging in violence in the school property would be expelled from school. The removal of discretion from authorities would ensure a consistent practice and eliminate inequality in its application. While the policy sounds good in its simplicity, research has shown that the policy has escalated the number of young people excluded from school and demonstrated a pronounced racial bias in its enforcement.